MW00395822

Honoring the History of the

Brandeis Library

Honoring the History of the BRANDEIS LIBRARY

An Insight into Brandeis' Special Collections

EDITED BY SARAH M. SHOEMAKER

BRANDEIS

UNIVERSITY

PRESS

Waltham, Massachusetts

Brandeis University Press
© 2021 by Brandeis University
All rights reserved
Manufactured in the United States of America
Designed by Richard Hendel
Typeset in HTF Didot and Bulmer by Tseng Information Systems, Inc.

All images courtesy of the Robert D. Farber
University Archives & Special Collections Department,
Brandeis University

For permission to reproduce any of the material in this book,
contact Brandeis University Press, 415 South Street, Waltham MA 02453,
or visit brandeisuniversitypress.com

Library of Congress Cataloging-in-Publication Data

Names: Shoemaker, Sarah M., editor.

Title: Honoring the history of the Brandeis Library : an insight into
Brandeis' Special Collections / edited by Sarah M. Shoemaker.

Description: Waltham, Massachusetts : Brandeis University Press, [2021]
Summary: "Honoring the History of the Brandeis Library is an
illuminating look at Brandeis's unique and invaluable rare text
collection. It features items including rare books, artistic works,
photographs, manuscript collections, Judaica materials, historically
significant archival collections, and more"—Provided by publisher.

Identifiers: LCCN 2021011321 | ISBN 9781684580507 (cloth)

Subjects: LCSH: Brandeis University. Library. Robert D. Farber University
Archives and Special Collections. | Rare books—Massachusetts—Waltham—
Bibliography. | Manuscripts—Massachusetts—Waltham. | LCGFT: Essays.

Classification: LCC Z733.B8225 H66 2021 | DDC 026/.09097444—dc23

LC record available at https://lccn.loc.gov/2021011321

5 4 3 2 1

IN HONOR OF MADALYN FRIEDBERG

Madalyn Friedberg is the quintessential Brandeis citizen. Madalyn found a home at Brandeis, first as the long-time treasurer for the Central Westchester Chapter of the Brandeis National Committee, and most recently as the committee's national president—a role in which she made extraordinary achievements.

This significance of this book extends beyond its beautiful and unique contents. This book is a symbol of what makes Brandeis special. It will create a Brandeis connection whenever and wherever it is opened.

Whom better to dedicate this book to than a person who has been doing precisely that in her many roles at Brandeis University?

Thank you, Madalyn!

BETH BERNSTEIN
Brandeis National Committee

CONTENTS

FOREWORD

When Brandeis opened its doors seventy-three years ago, it was a bold and audacious undertaking, a sign of optimism in the aftermath of the Second World War. Since 1948, the Brandeis National Committee (BNC), formerly known as the Brandeis University National Women's Committee, has never wavered in its commitment to Brandeis.

The history of the BNC has brought together over 100,000 foster alumni who have devoted their personal talents and financial resources to the growth of the Brandeis Library. Stocking the empty library of a brand-new university was an unprecedented challenge, but over seven decades the BNC not only filled the shelves of the university but built those shelves, funded construction of the Brandeis library, purchased books and materials, and continue to support the university in many other areas including scholarships and scientific research.

The Brandeis National Committee is bringing the library into the future by supporting the Special Collections and Archives through the Honoring Our History Campaign to digitize unique collections highlighting social justice.

To honor the fiftieth anniversary of BNC in 1998, former national president Belle Dorfman Jurkowitz '55 wrote *Strictly by the Book*, documenting the first fifty years of the organization and its amazing accomplishments. As Belle noted, the past is prologue to the future. We think about our history while we answer the needs of tomorrow. We hope that our BNC volunteers—who believe in education as a solution to the problems of an ever-changing society—will strive to maintain the excellence that has become synonymous with Brandeis University.

BETH BERNSTEIN MA'90
Brandeis National Committee
Executive Director

PREFACE

I first met Sarah Shoemaker six years ago when I joined Brandeis University's library team. She quickly became a valued colleague and trusted friend, and she has proven herself to be an invaluable resource at Brandeis for her excellent work with faculty, students, and institutional advancement. Sarah serves as the associate university librarian for archives and special collections at Brandeis. Over the years, she has led a very small team of archivists and librarians in developing a noteworthy collection, exploiting it for teaching and learning, and highlighting rare and unique material to audiences composed of international scholars, donors, Brandeis National Committee members, and friends of Brandeis University.

The collection in this book highlights a very small selection of the collection we have here at Brandeis. Often when I ask Sarah a question, she will give me an initial response and follow up with: "But we can talk about it more if you want." Initially, I did not understand this caution. Why couldn't I immediately get the most used item in the collection? Why couldn't I immediately learn what items pertain to the history of science? Why couldn't I immediately find out what we hold that relates to humor and first amendment rights? When I took on the position of the Brandeis National Committee University Librarian, I finally realized what her cautious responses signified. With over ten thousand rare books, artifacts that show the best and worst of humanity, archives of some of the most important scholars of the twentieth century, and a collection that, without removing it from the boxes, would stretch more than two dozen miles from one end to the other, there's a lot to choose from. I began to understand that her cautious replies acknowledge what we have in the archives and special collections without limiting the amazing possibility of things yet to be discovered. And I learned that Sarah's caution usually indicates that I must think of a query as a curatorial question that takes this intricacy into account.

This book contains sixty highlights from the Robert D. Farber University Archives and Special Collections, part of a collection acquired over 70 years that represents more than 1,500 years of history. These collections are diverse, ranging from accounts of historic events to those of the current struggles for social justice, and they are important and relevant to our lives not only as a history of the past but also for how they are connected to our future. There are materials describing the false accusation and murder of Leo Frank, where we can see first-hand how judgments based on race and ethnicity led to denunciations and death. There are the Buffalo Bill Dime Novels, which offer snapshots of popular culture from the mid- to late-nineteenth century, which capture the day-to-day lives of a past generation, and which also show that humanity has not come very far to the present day. There are items as different as nineteenth-century Burmese manuscripts written on palm leaves, Shakespeare's first folio, and Marcel Proust's musings on the grim realities of the business of publishing.

This compilation shows just a fraction of the history of knowledge available in the Brandeis Library, and I can think of no editor more thoughtful and more expert than Sarah to bring these highlights to you. Some may entertain you, some may frighten you, some may reveal truths you do not want to see, and some may embarrass you with the self-knowledge that they reveal. Libraries are repositories of knowledge. They bring together different truths without judgment and provide relevant context for us to learn and make informed opinions. Libraries do this now with datasets and journal articles delivered to our laptops, but they also do this by reminding us of the rich past, allowing us to learn both from our successes and from our mistakes.

I am proud of the work done by the staff in Archives and Special Collections, who have carefully stewarded these collections and provided important context to the materials presented. Congratulations to Sarah Shoemaker for bringing this extraordinary book together in such an elegant and insightful way.

MATTHEW SHEEHY
Brandeis National Committee University Librarian
Brandeis University
August 2020

Honoring the History of the
Brandeis Library

INTRODUCTION

The Brandeis Library's Special Collections comprise a rich and varied set of rare books and unique manuscripts that spans several centuries—yet as a collection they have a comparatively short history. The foundations of Special Collections, like the foundations of Brandeis University itself in 1948, were built by people who believed in the mission of Brandeis and wanted to see the new enterprise succeed and flourish. The collection was built on love of the book, and love of the university.

The Brandeis Library now holds thousands of rare books and tens of thousands of linear feet of manuscript collections—the manuscript boxes laid end-to-end would stretch further than the length of the Boston Marathon. The rare book collection includes incunabula (books printed before 1501) as well as a large number of first and critical editions, fine press publications, and early printings on subjects including American and European Christianity, classical studies, early exploration, English and American history and literature, Hebraic and Judaic studies, the history of science, Shakespeare, and Leonardo da Vinci. The Special Collections department's manuscripts and visual/photographic collections, which date primarily from the thirteenth through the twenty-first centuries, are also broad in their topical and geographical scopes; they include archival collections that document American and European political leaders and social reformers; the Holocaust, antisemitism, and Jewish resistance to persecution; conflicts in the United States and abroad; Jewish-American and émigré writers, composers, and performing artists; left- and right-wing movements in the United States and Europe; and Jewish feminism, among other subjects.

These collections fuel the work of students, faculty, scholars, and researchers at Brandeis and beyond, from first-year students' explorations to doctoral research and faculty publications, from individual creative endeavors to multi-institutional digital projects. Where the value of libraries of yore was measured by the number of rare and priceless gems kept in the vaults, now the value of a library—including a Special Collections library—can be also seen in how it furthers the projects of its community, how it makes those prized jewels available in productive ways to feed scholarship across disciplines and around the world.

In a 1972 publication, the members of the Society of Bibliophiles at Brandeis University opined: "What a library is to a university, so the bibliophilic section of the library is to its whole. The metaphor might be extended to say the relationship is also like that of the head to the body or the Sabbath to the rest of the week. To a people of the book (Am ha-Sefer) the creation and nourishment of a great library becomes a prime obligation. In addition to the usual sources and references, it is recognized that a special body of inspirational material—rare books, manuscripts, letters, engravings and memoranda—the essence of the creative spirit must be succored in this part to establish the very essence of greatness in the whole." It is precisely this creative spirit that Brandeis Special Collections aims to spark and sustain among the many users of its materials worldwide, within the vibrant work of the Brandeis Library.

Two groups and many individual donors are to thank for the rich collection of materials that now call Brandeis home. The Brandeis National Women's Committee, now the Brandeis National Committee, was created in 1948 to establish and maintain a library for the newly formed university. The group began with eight founders, supporting a library originally housed in a converted horse stable. Now, as the Brandeis National Committee, it is the largest "friends of the library" group in the world, with more than 20,000 members around the country, who have raised more than $140 million for the university. This year, the Brandeis National Committee has designated the digitization of selected Special Collections materials related to social justice as a focus of their work. This essential support will make many rare and unique materials available in a way they have never been before, providing a window from the connected world to the reading room in Waltham.

The aforementioned Brandeis Bibliophiles, a group of book collectors and book lovers whose official charter and charge began in 1961 and lasted until the 1980s, acquired many wonderful pieces and collections for the university's collections. Individual donors among them also bestowed some of the collection's high spots, including three Shakespeare folios, rare first editions of English and American literature, an extensive collection of Spanish Civil War posters, collections of rare books on the history of science, and much more, numbering tens of thousands of items. These collectors were devoted to creating a foundation for the future, "on behalf of generations yet unborn." As their publication proclaimed in 1981: "In the long and noble tradition of bibliophilia some collectors have assembled noteworthy materials primarily to gratify their own interests while others have employed their knowledge and expertise to contribute to the future advancement of learning."

The remarkable collections at Brandeis and those who work with them in the name of the advancement of learning have inspired many others to donate many fine and unique materials—books, manuscript collections, posters, diaries, photographs, letters, publications, sound recordings, and much more—to the university. The collections in turn have inspired researchers from around the world in their intellectual work.

The descriptions in this book were originally part of the Special Collections Spotlight project, which was born in 2007 as an online monthly showcase displaying various collections, pieces within collections, individual books, book collections, artifacts, and other elements of Special Collections that caught each author's interest. The descriptive essays, each accompanied by several images, were written by faculty members, graduate students, interns, librarians, archivists, and researchers. The chosen collections — usually selected by the authors — spanned centuries and continents as well as a wide range of subject matter. As researchers and casual explorers alike around the world have turned increasingly to online sources of information, the online essays have been significant in drawing attention to Special Collections at Brandeis as well as to the Brandeis Library itself, where researchers can turn for more in-depth information and hands-on study.

Selections are presented here in roughly chronological order. This is to show the span and range of the collection and allow each piece to lead to the next by the passage of time rather than by subject, since one person's exploration of Spanish Civil War propaganda is another person's study of twentieth-century public art. Archival research does not always depend on looking only where a clear answer is expected to be found; it can also be fruitful to look in adjacent neighborhoods and hope for happy introductions and chance meetings between subjects.

The items in Brandeis Library's Special Collections are indeed treasures — treasures not to be guarded against human view, but to be cherished, preserved, used. They are here not to be admired from afar, but to be engaged with, learned from, appreciated up close. From Thomas Aquinas to Sophie Tucker, from medieval theology to modern Jewish feminism, from Diderot to Lenny Bruce, these ideas and figures and thoughts and messages remain alive through the ways they are employed as the basis of new thoughts. Special Collections of the Brandeis Library takes rightful pride in its rare and unique collections. We hope that this book will provide a window through which readers can enjoy them fruitfully as well.

SARAH SHOEMAKER
Summer 2020

spūs quidā gyā ppā abs ulla sug-
gestione et ?m ōim h° malorū capud
est dyā⁰ ī quā illū imitat ?m id
Sap 2 īuidia dyā mors ītroiuit
ī orbem terrarū imitat aut illū q
sūt exparte illiq ¶ Ad terciū dō q
sua pcta queunt ī suasione a deo
licz ab inuicē differat ?m qūpone ad
dīsa cōmutabilia bona

Ad octauū sic pcedit' uidet' q angelus n
sit caput malorū uniuq ē
corpus n sūt duo capita sed dyā ē
caput intrinsecus malorū n go angelus
ē com caput ¶ 2° angelus ē mbrū
dyā sed caput distinguit a mebris
go angelus n ē capud malorū ¶ 3°
caput hr īfluencia ī mebra sz angelus
nullaz hr īfluencia ī malos homines
q eū pcesserūt go angelus n ē caput
malorū ¶ Sz ō ē q dr Job 14 sr
īllud ī tragedie quasi de naturalibus dr
glō dom malorū [illegible]
adam ī quorū capud existit [illegible]
queritur ¶ 1° dō q sic pupdom est
ī corpore [illegible] ī ueniūt sz ordo
[illegible] et uirtus īfluendi q̄ [illegible] go adoc
cūc [illegible] n dr ēē angelus capud malorum
q̄ eiq [illegible] precessit sic [illegible] potz
dyā sic ēē n dr ēē malorū capud
[illegible] uirtute īfluendi [illegible] aliqs
[illegible] ad malū sit [illegible]
ī ducendo [illegible] q [illegible] fuerit
[illegible] sūt ī malicia īducti n eiq
malicia sūt imitati Vn ?m hoc n
poterit dici capud ōim malorū sed
aliq [illegible] relinquit go q dicat capt
ōim malorū [illegible] malicie pfone Vn
[illegible] thes 2 ondens sc [illegible] sit deq
dr glō [illegible] plenitudo dīni-
[illegible] plenitudo ōis
malicie n [illegible] eiq sit
assumpta a dyā⁰ ī unitate psone
sic [illegible] aftio dei p q dyā⁰

malicia sua eminenciq ei īfluit suggē-
do q ōibus aliis et ?m hoc ōis
alii mali q̄ precesserūt sūt q̄ quidam
figura antichristi ?m id ē thes 2 mistiū
iā opat' iniquitatis ¶ Ad pm̄ go dō q
dyā⁰ et antichristus nō sūt duo capita s
unū q̄ antichristus dr ēē capud ī quā
plenissime inuenit' ī eo ipsa malicia
dyā Vn sr id 2 thes 2 ondens se
tamq̄ sit deus dr glō ī ipso erit
capud ōim malorū sz dyā q ē
rex sup ōis filios supbie n aut dr
ī eo ēē pvisione [illegible] n' pmtiusca
[illegible] q̄ sola trinitas mēte illabit'
ut dr [illegible] dogmatibus sed
pmaliāe [illegible] ¶ Ad 2m dō q sic capud
xpi ē deus et tn̄ ipse ē capud ecce
ut [illegible] ē ita antichristus ē mebrū
dyā et tn̄ ipse ē capud malorum
¶ Ad 3m dō q antichristus nō dr capud
ōim malorū [illegible] similitudine īfluencie
s [illegible] similitudine [illegible] pfonis in eo
eni dyā q̄ malicia sua ducet
ad capud [illegible] modū quo dr abs adapt'
[illegible] pm dre [illegible] pferit

Deinde considerandū ē de scientia xpi
Et qua duo consideranda [illegible]
sūt [illegible]
2° [illegible] Circa pmū
queruntur q̄ [illegible] aliq scias
ptr dīnaz ¶ 2° utrū hūit scias q̄ hnt
bn ut [illegible] ¶ 3° utrū hūit scias
īditā ut īfusā ¶ 4° utrū hūit aliq̄
scientia acqsita

Ad pm sic pcedit' uidet q ī xpō n fuit
aliq̄ scia ptr dīnā ad [illegible] noticia
ē scia ut pea aliq̄ cognoscat' [illegible]
xpus p sciam dīnā cognoscebat ōia
[illegible] go fuisset q ī eo eēt q̄da
alia scia ¶ [illegible] lux minor pmaiorez
obfuscat̄ [illegible] ōia scia creata copat' ad
sciam dei increata sic lux minor ad maiorē

Thomas Aquinas's *Summa theologica*

"Endeavoring to avoid these and other like faults, we shall try, by God's help, to set forth whatever is included in this sacred doctrine as briefly and clearly as the matter itself may allow." With these words, Thomas Aquinas concluded his brief introduction to his *Summa theologica* (written between 1265 and 1274), which remains one of the most important documents in the history of Christianity. In the text, Aquinas applied Aristotelian philosophy to Catholic theology, outlining a philosophical framework in support of Catholic belief.

The collection holds the third part, or *Tertia pars*, of the *Summa*. This section of Aquinas's text treats the subjects of the incarnation and life of Christ, explicating the Catholic mystery of the union of the divine and the human before turning to a philosophical defense of the sacraments. This mid-fifteenth-century manuscript of the *Summa* comprises 157 leaves written in a single hand, and remained for several centuries in the library of a Carthusian monastery in Bavaria.

Aquinas (1225–1274) was a Dominican friar and theologian who created the *Summa* to aid beginning theology students. His text is highly structured, a masterwork of the scholastic method. It is divided into questions, each of which is discussed through a series of objections to that question, followed by an answer to the question and answers to each objection. As it dealt with the whole of Catholic theology, this approach provided a philosophical, logical basis for Catholic belief, and represented a monumental shift in Catholic theology. Aquinas, of course, did not exist in a vacuum—the general structure of his philosophy was Aristotelian. While much of the classical tradition had been largely lost in the West, it had been preserved in the Islamic world. Aristotelian thought in particular played an important role in the intellectual life of Muslim society. There it had become a subject of study for numerous scholars, some of whom are cited in the *Summa* (most notably the Andalusian polymath Averroes, referred to as "the commentator" by Aquinas). Because of the novel intellectual exchanges between the Christian and Muslim worlds that occurred as part of the Reconquista of Spain, Aquinas was able to take advantage of newly accessible Aristotelian literature and commentary.

Compared with other theologians or philosophers, Aquinas's continued importance more than seven centuries after his death is extraordinary. Indeed, his popularity created a new school of philosophical inquiry that came to be known as Thomism. In 1910, Pope Pius X underlined the continued relevance of Aquinas to the Catholic Church: "St. Thomas perfected and augmented still further by the almost angelic quality of his intellect all this superb patrimony of wisdom

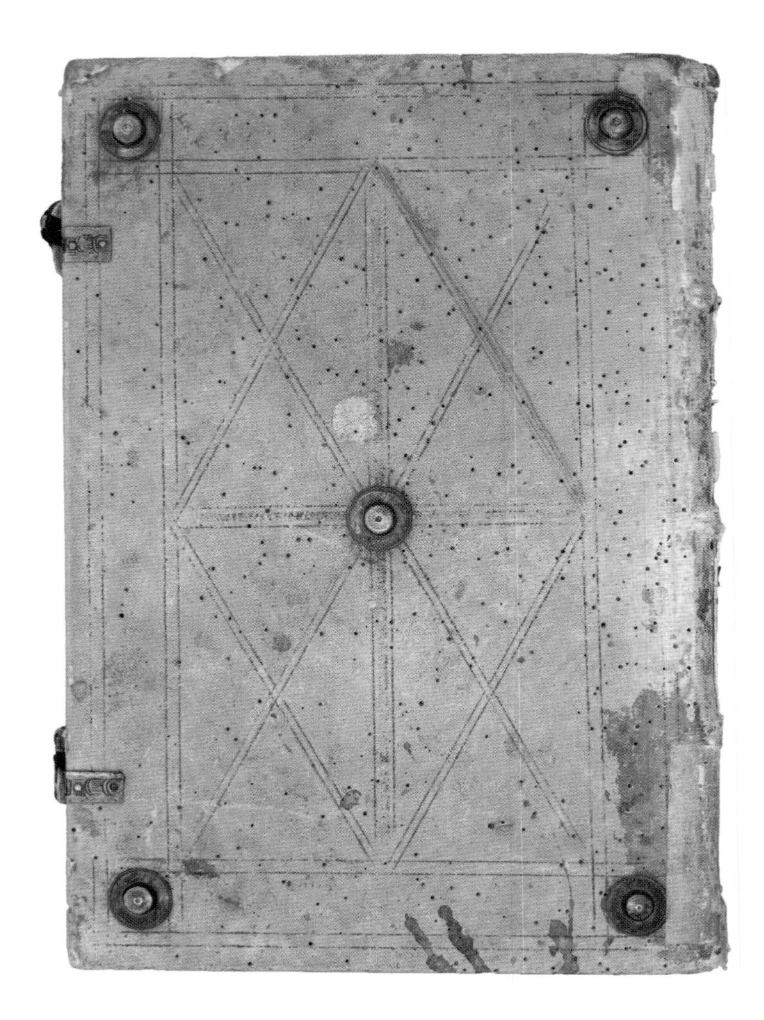

which he inherited from his predecessors and applied it to prepare, illustrate and protect sacred doctrine in the minds of men."

The *Summa* thus remains a keystone of both Christian theology and Western philosophy. In the words of Jean-Pierre Torrell, a leading Thomist scholar, "the 'luck' of the *Summa* was that it was a textbook . . . its durability can be explained by the generations of professors and students who read and reread it, pored over it, commented on it, and made it relevant, keeping it alive."

Through his *Summa*, Aquinas reconceptualized Christian theology in Europe by connecting Christianity and classical thought. In the Western tradition, he outlined the notion of a "just war" and advanced novel arguments about the meaning and purpose of human life—all intertwined with and based in his Catholicism.

Description by Sean Beebe, PH.D. 2020

DONATED TO BRANDEIS BY PETER H. BRANDT

A Few Illuminated Medieval Manuscripts at Brandeis

Spanning more than a hundred years and several countries, the illuminated medieval manuscripts at Brandeis share similar artistic patterns that were widespread during the Middle Ages. Notable examples include an early-fourteenth-century French breviary fragment; two books of hours, one the Italian Office of the Virgin from the fifteenth century, and one a fifteenth-century text created in France; and a 1485 copy of *De pictura* (On painting), written by Leon Battista Alberti between 1420 and 1430.

Illumination in the selected texts can be divided into three categories: colored initials, ornately designed initials, and miniature paintings. Colored initials appear in all of the manuscripts, with red and blue the two colors most frequently used. The illuminated letters in medieval manuscripts vary in size—some are the same as the surrounding black text, whereas others occupy an entire page. Size variation indicates hierarchical variation—the larger the letter, the more important the moment in the text.

In the pages from Alberti's *De pictura*, an initial I and an initial O depict colored letters that are only a little larger than one or two lines of the regular text, with decorations inside the letters. These differences in size and color help to divide the page into recognizable segments and thereby increase the legibility of a page that has no lowercase letters or punctuation.

Swirling linear designs, called "penwork flourishing," encompass some capital letters in the fifteenth-century Italian Book of Hours. Designs such as these can fully surround the page or decorate only a portion. An example from *De pictura*, portraying a large seven-line O, also features the color green. Because the letter is larger and more elaborately decorated than the capitals in the Italian Book of Hours, viewers can assume that it marks an important moment within the text. This type of letter is called a puzzle initial because of the blank space between the red and the blue hues, thereby creating a puzzle-like appearance.

The fifteenth-century Italian Book of Hours also contains an example of a heavily illuminated initial letter D. The borders are drawn in a different style; the letter spans seven lines of text and features swirling designs. The flowers on this initial are easier to recognize as flowers, with the leaves displaying subtle shading, increasing the verisimilitude.

The most ornately illuminated initials in this group are inhabited initials, which depict human or animal figures inside the letter. Although only a few inches high,

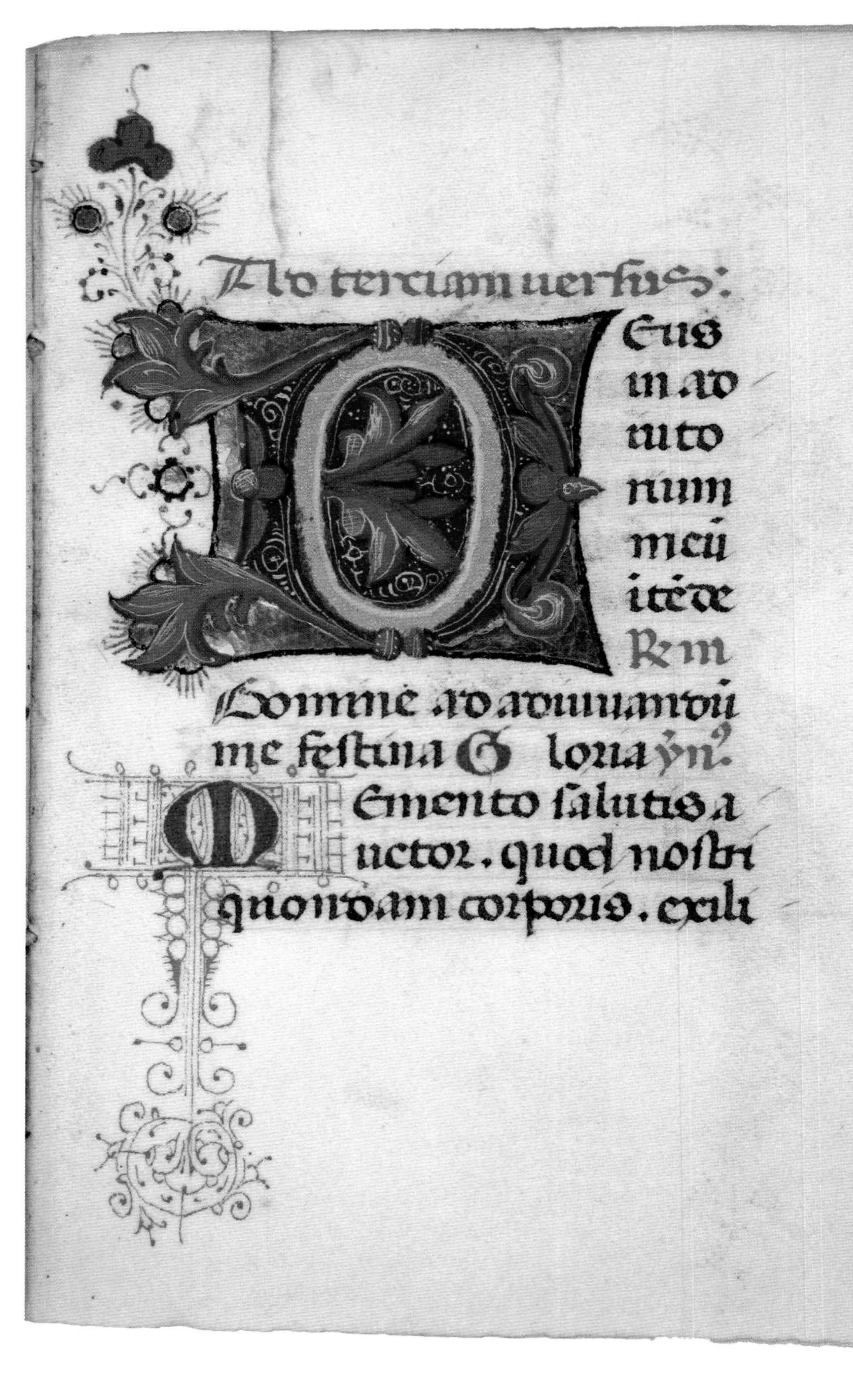

Ad terciam uersus:

Deus in adiutorium meum intende. R. Domine ad adiuuandum me festina. Gloria. Ymnus.

Memento salutis auctor. quod nostri quondam corporis. exili

one example from the fifteenth-century Italian Book of Hours shows the Virgin Mary holding the baby Jesus inside a letter D. A border of swirling lines, flowers and fruit surrounds the miniature painting.

Perhaps even more developed is a fifteenth-century French Book of Hours, which contains ten pages of miniature paintings that do not fit inside letters but appear on their own, above the text. A Book of Hours frequently includes more illumination than other texts because pictures helped readers recognize where one prayer ended and another began, particularly important because medieval manuscripts did not divide texts into chapters. Often the paintings do not directly parallel the narrative of the text, and instead show moments in the life of Christ.

Although they are only a few inches tall, these texts display amazing detail. The level of artistry bespeaks the importance of books in medieval culture. They were highly prized and expensive, written and illustrated by hand and with great care.

Description by Leah Lefkowitz, B.A. 2011

FIFTEENTH-CENTURY FRENCH BOOK OF HOURS, GIFT OF PHILIP D. SANG; FIFTEENTH-CENTURY ITALIAN BOOK OF HOURS, HISTORY OF ORIGINAL ACQUISITION UNKNOWN, POSSIBLY THE GIFT OF PHILIP D. SANG; LEON BATTISTA ALBERTI, *DE PICTURA*, 1485, GIFT OF BERN DIBNER

The First Bookplate

From the early days of printing, bookplates have provided a unique resource for scholars, enabling them to trace the history of particular volumes as well as map the transmission of texts. The history of the ownership of a book—its provenance—often provides information as to who may have been reading what books and even the means for the intellectual reconstruction of famous libraries, held by both individuals and institutions.

Brandeis has the distinction of holding an example of the earliest known bookplate, which originated in the collection of Brother Hildebrand (Hilpbrand) Brandenburg of Biberach. Scholars date the bookplate to the 1470s, and it must have been completed by 1480, when Brother Hildebrand, a Carthusian monk, donated his collection, including the bookplates, to his monastery in Buxheim, Germany, an important and influential center of learning in the Carthusian order and home to a renowned library.

The convention of pasting a bookplate, also known as an *ex libris* (from the library of), into the volumes in a personal library began in Germany in the late fifteenth century and only gradually spread to France, Italy, England, and the rest of Europe. Even after the advent of printing and the beginning of mass production of books in the latter part of the fifteenth century, the possession of large libraries remained the privilege of the elite. Thus bookplates, which signified the ownership of volumes or functioned as gift plates to record the giver of a large donation, tended to be heavily armorial in nature, constructed around the family crests of their noble owners.

With a famous plate such as that of Hildebrand, it is possible to trace the history of the volume nearly from the time of its composition. The Brandeis copy is found in a manuscript of Part III of the *Summa theologica* of Thomas Aquinas, one of the most important texts of the medieval period. This large folio volume contains 157 paper leaves with the text written in two columns in a single cursive Gothic hand.

The manuscript was composed around 1460, and thus Hildebrand was likely its original owner. In each volume Hildebrand pasted a bookplate or gift plate that indicates him as the donor. It depicts an angel bearing a shield with the Brandenburg crest. These plates are wood-block prints that he then colored by hand, and in many texts they are accompanied by a short inscription by Hildebrand identifying the contents of the volume.

The manuscript spent much of its life in the hands of the Carthusians, for

Incipit tercia pars prime sancti thome ordinis fratrum predicatorum

The first Book-plate

the monastery at Buxheim held the volume until the sale of its collection in 1883, more than 400 years after Hildebrand's original donation. This small and austere order is often recognized as being the most rigorous in the Roman Catholic tradition.

The use and importance of bookplates is not confined to the early years of printing but continues to the present day, as new designs grace institutional and personal collections. Tracing a book through the centuries gives some idea of its continued importance—as a valuable piece of scholarship, as an important religious text, as an historical artifact, as a work of art, and finally, as a resource for students and scholars, particularly in the Brandeis community, who represent the next chapter in the long history of this manuscript.

Description by Adam Rutledge, PH.D. 2017

Nuremberg Chronicle (Liber Chronicarum)

With its religious, secular, and mythical themes, Hartmann Schedel's *Nuremberg Chronicle* is considered the first German world history, a recompilation of ancient records and medieval accounts. Composed in the city of Nuremberg (hence the name), the text illustrates to the modern reader the strengths and limitations of early modern history, Renaissance learning, and a fifteenth-century understanding of the world. Two rare editions reside at Brandeis: the original Latin first edition, printed during the first part of 1493, and the vernacular edition published in German several months later.

The most impressive aspect of the *Chronicle* is its exquisite printing and finely detailed woodcuts, which took over two years to complete. The volume was revolutionary for its incorporation of text with related images, virtually unheard-of prior to the sixteenth century. Designed and illustrated by Michael Wohlgemut and Wilhelm Pleydenwurff, the book contains over 1,800 images made from more than 600 individual woodcuts—more than any other previously printed volume. A teenage Albrecht Dürer, the famed Renaissance painter, apprenticed under Wohlgemut during the initial phases of the illustration of the *Chronicle*, leading to strong indications that some of the designs can be attributed directly to his hand, or at least to his influence.

The collection of woodcuts prominently features European cityscapes, biblical scenes, and royal and papal portraits, as well as depictions of legendary narratives and figures. For instance, a portrait of Merlin, the sorcerer of Arthurian fame, can be found displayed among those of true historical figures, such as Attila the Hun or the crown heads of Europe.

The *Nuremberg Chronicle* was first published by Anton Koberger, Europe's largest printer, in Latin for an elite and religious readership, with a subsequent German edition released in December for the literate upper-middle class. The German version, translated by Nuremberg's treasury writer, George Alt, is slightly shorter and omits some esoteric detail found in its Latin counterpart. Another small difference is seen in the typeface employed by Koberger. The German edition features Schwabacher type, derived from a semi-Gothic form, while the Latin edition utilizes the Italian Rotunda style common to similar texts of the era. While some 800 Latin editions and 408 German editions were printed, it was the later, smaller-run vernacular translation that enjoyed a higher degree of

NVREN

Nurmberg

success after publication. Today, only 300 German and 400 Latin editions exist throughout the world.

Perhaps the most controversial and incendiary aspect of the book, defaced in numerous copies but intact in both Brandeis volumes, is an image of Pope Joan. The *Nuremberg Chronicle* perpetuated a legend that was supported by men such as Martin Luther, and promulgated by later authors, claiming that a woman disguised as a man was elected as pope of the Catholic Church in the ninth century, only to be exposed when she gave birth to a child during a service. The image of Joan, depicted with her newborn child, can be found discreetly displayed among the portraits of actual Catholic popes. According to scholar Craig Rustici, author of *The Afterlife of Pope Joan*, the *Chronicle* "breaks with conventional narratives, in which the beginning of Joan's motherhood marks the end of her pontificate, to portray her as simultaneously pope and mother." It is through such imagery that Schedel's work most clearly presents the blending of fact and lore as history.

The Brandeis editions provide access to a scarce historical text still vibrant in its original bold black ink, virtually unaltered since leaving a Nuremberg printer over six centuries ago. The *Chronicle* offers an overview not only of Renaissance knowledge but also of art, culture, and the development of printing.

Description by Craig Bruce Smith, M.A. *2009,* PH.D. *2014*

LATIN EDITION OF 1493 GIVEN BY THE BIBLIOPHILES OF BRANDEIS UNIVERSITY; GERMAN EDITION OF 1493 GIFT OF LEWIS K. AND ELIZABETH LAND

Walter F. and Alice Gorham Collection of Early Music Imprints

The development of music printing at the onset of the sixteenth century changed the European musical world. Before Ottaviano Petrucci's first printed collection in 1501, written music was available only to those who had the time or the money to copy it by hand. With the advent of printed music, new works could be disseminated quickly and across great distances.

An even greater boost to the publication of music came with the development of type that contained both the note and a complete set of staff lines. Petrucci's beautiful publications depended on a laborious process in which the staff lines, notes, and text were each laid down with separate impressions. The new type enabled a single-impression process, making affordable music available to many more. The interrupted lines and blocky presentation were a small price to pay for greater availability. The educated classes could now emulate the nobility, purchasing the latest compositions and making music in their homes. Composers, freed from their dependence on courtly posts, could now profit directly from their work and also improve their job prospects through enhanced reputations (though patrons were still a necessity).

The second half of the sixteenth century saw a flowering of music publishing; the market for chamber music helped drive the growth of the madrigal and motet as forms well suited to home music-making, for both voices and instruments. So that a group of singers or instrumentalists could easily read the notes, music was commonly published in separate partbooks, one book for each vocal or instrumental line. Since there was no conductor, a full score was unnecessary, and any one of the participants could supply the *tactus*—the pulse that keeps the parts together.

Any one publication, therefore, was made up of several partbooks, each one a thin pamphlet with no more than a paper cover. To protect and preserve them, the buyer could seek out a bindery to make a more permanent cover. It often made sense to bind together several partbooks from different publications into a larger volume, each representing one voice or instrument. This highly practical system had one drawback: since the individual parts were not physically attached to one another, it was inevitable that over time these partbooks would become separated. Today it is rare to find a complete set of sixteenth-century partbooks intact. However, single partbooks do occasionally become available. Brandeis is very fortunate to have several in the collection.

The Walter F. and Alice Gorham Collection of Early Music Imprints, established in 1998, includes eight partbooks, ranging from slim publications to large bound collections. These books contain parts to hundreds of pieces from the second half of the sixteenth century, published by some of the most influential printing houses of Italy and northern Europe. Among the most prolific publishers of the day was Angelo Gardano, who produced almost a thousand publications over the course of his career. The Gardano printing house was founded in Venice in 1538 by Angelo's father, Antonio. Antonio (originally Antoine) had moved from France to Venice in the 1530s. He was a composer in his own right and acquainted with many of the leading musicians working in Italy. One of these was among the most influential composers and teachers of his time, the Netherlandish composer Adrian Willaert, who was born around 1490 and died in Italy in 1562.

Although Willaert's works had appeared in anthologies, it was the monumental *Musica Nova* that exemplified the significance of his work. The book was unusual in its time for containing both sacred and secular music. Duke Alfonso d'Este subsidized the printing of this seminal work in 1559, for which Gardano devised a new format. His previous publications had been oblong, but this one is an upright quarto. He also introduced a newly designed typeface and decorated initials for this publication.

In 1611 the Gardano firm passed to a third generation. Angelo's daughter Diamante and son-in-law Bartolomeo Magni retained the illustrious name. Starting in that year, the printing house brought out six volumes of madrigals by Carlo Gesualdo. Those who know Gesualdo's name today are likely to associate him with two things: chromaticism and murder. The Italian nobleman, who lived from 1561 to 1613, was early viewed as a dilettante but earned the title of musician through his many publications, most notably the six volumes of five-part madrigals. His visibility increased after the assassination of his first wife and her lover, as did his "mad passion" for music; this was further enhanced by his connections with the court of Ferrara after his marriage to Leonora d'Este. As a prince, Gesualdo was not constrained by economics to write music that would widely please, freeing him to push the boundaries of the madrigal with chromatic alterations and rhythmic surprises. The Gorham Collection boasts the only complete set of *altus* partbooks to his madrigals in this country.

Like that of the Gardano family in Venice, the name Gerlach was associated with printing in Nuremberg. When Katherina Berg married Theodor Gerlach in 1565 she was already an experienced printer, as well as a widow twice over. Gerlach, who had probably been employed as a printer by her late husband, continued to run the company until his death in 1575, after which Katherina managed the firm on her own for another seventeen years. Among their many publications were a number of large collected editions of individual composers, among whom Orlando di Lasso figured prominently. Lasso (1532–1594) was a prolific composer widely known and admired in his day. In 1568 he issued the first of many

TENORE

DI GIO: PICCIONI

ORGANISTA DEL DOMO

D'ORVIETO

IL QVARTO LIBRO

De Madrigali à Cinque Voci.

Nouamente Composto & dato in luce.

In Venetia Appresso Angelo Gardano.

M. D. LXXXXVI. D

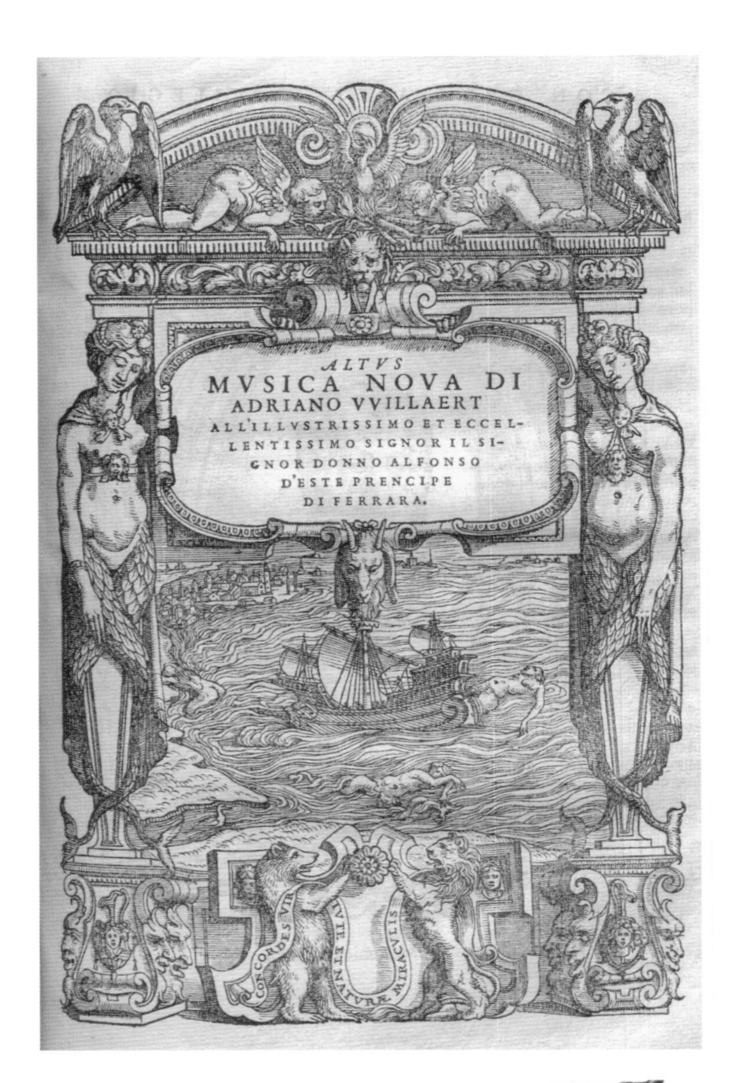
ALTVS
MVSICA NOVA DI
ADRIANO VVILLAERT
ALL'ILLVSTRISSIMO ET ECCEL-
LENTISSIMO SIGNOR IL SI-
GNOR DONNO ALFONSO
D'ESTE PRENCIPE
DI FERRARA.
CONCORDES VIRTVTE ET NATVRÆ MIRACVLIS

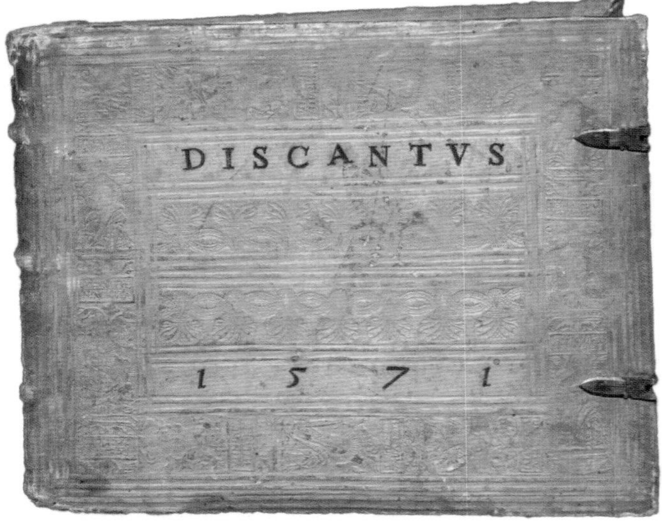
DISCANTVS
1 5 7 1

volumes of motets under the title *Selectissimae cantiones*. Brandeis owns a copy of the *quintus* partbook of this work.

Probably the most compelling source of polyphonic music in the collection is a hefty volume of *superius* partbooks from the mid-1500s, bound in tooled leather and stamped 1571. The first six partbooks in the volume are anthologies of motets published in Antwerp by Hubert Waelrant and Jan de Laet under the title *Sacrarum Cantionum*. Together, they give a vivid snapshot of mid-century Franco-Flemish sacred music.

The partbooks in the Gorham Collection represent a rich source of repertoire in its original notation, ranging from works by some of the most prominent composers of the day to some so obscure that they appear in no other publication.

Description by Sarah Mead, professor of the practice of music and director of the Brandeis Early Music Ensemble

Geneva Bible

LONDON: DEPUTIES OF CHRISTOPHER BARKER,
PRINTER TO THE QUEENES MOST EXCELLENT MAJESTIE, 1589

Issued at a time when the Roman Catholic Church had banned all vernacular translations of the Bible, the English Geneva Bible was published in completed form in 1560. Building on the work of William Tyndale and Myles Coverdale, whose early translation appeared in 1535, the Geneva Bible was the first in English to draw its translation entirely from the original Greek and Hebrew texts rather than from the Latin Vulgate. Its title derives from the fact that the translation was prepared by English reformers living in the Protestant stronghold of Geneva, Switzerland, having fled England during the reign of the Roman Catholic Mary, Queen of Scots. It is also often called the Breeches Bible, owing to its unusual translation of Genesis 3:7, in which Adam and Eve are described as fashioning "breeches" to cover their nakedness. This is the edition of the Bible that Shakespeare read and from which he quotes in his plays. Its influence continues to the present day through its incorporation in the King James translation, which remained the standard English Bible for several centuries.

While the 1560 edition was issued in modern, Roman type, a minority of editions were printed using the older Gothic-style type, including this example from 1589. The pages of the volume are quite dark compared to other books of a similar age, largely as a result of the lower-quality paper used in the printing. The choice was not a mistake, for the intention of the Protestant reformers in preparing this translation was to make the Bible both more accessible and more affordable for lay Christians, although the price would still have been out of reach for the majority of the population.

As part of the Protestant teaching that every Christian had the ability to read and interpret the Bible for himself or herself, another significant innovation in the Geneva Bible is the presence of printed marginal notes, offering aids to the reader for understanding the text. These notes range from translators' explanations for their choice of words to theological exposition, and it is the latter that exhibit this edition's strong anti-Catholic bias. Attacks on the Roman Catholic Church are especially prevalent in the marginal notes to the Book of Revelation, one example of which may be seen in the explanation for Revelation 17:3–4, found in notes *d* and *f* in the margin.

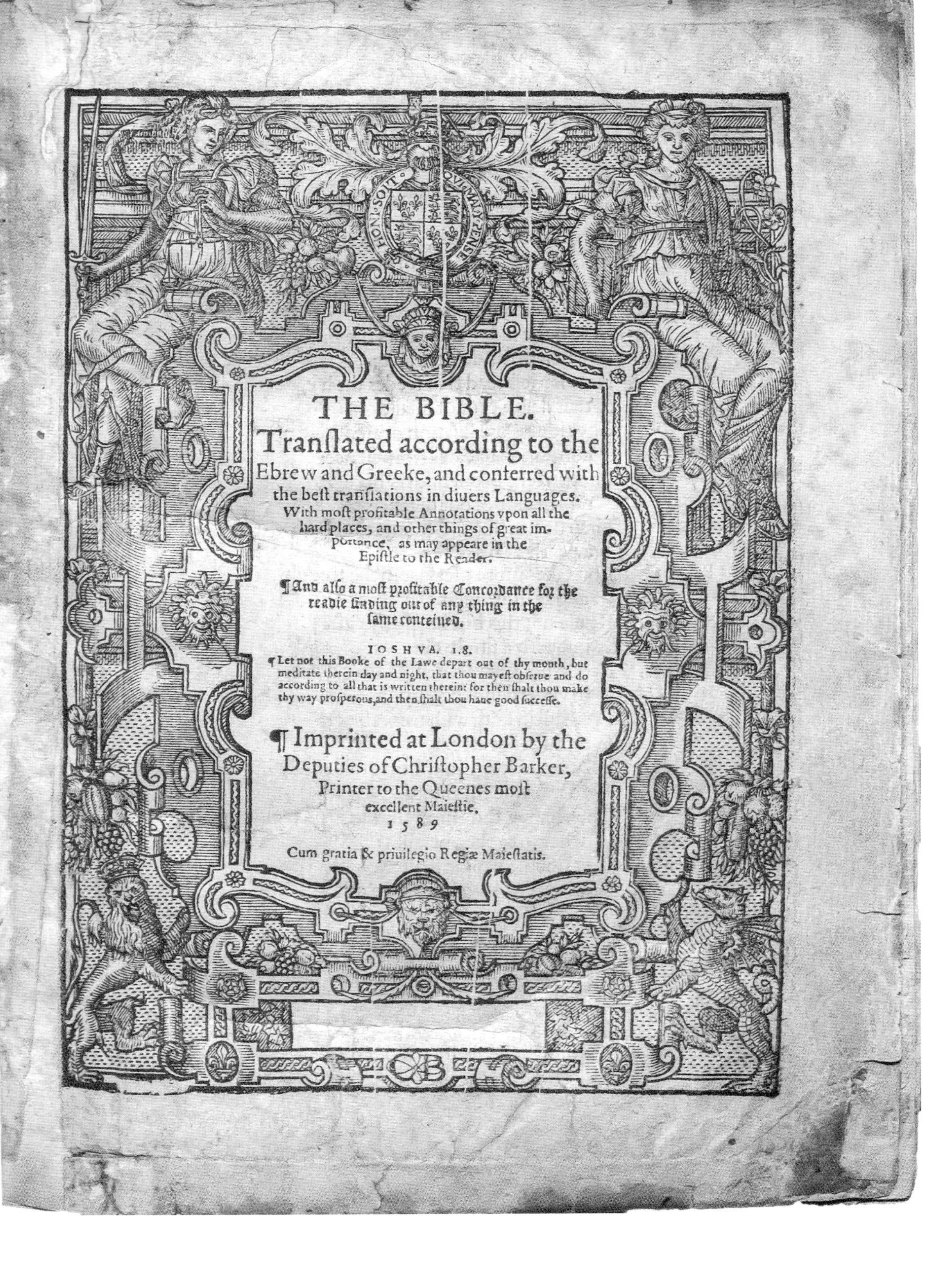

THE BIBLE.

Tranſlated according to the Ebrew and Greeke, and conferred with the beſt tranſlations in diuers Languages.

With moſt profitable Annotations vpon all the hard places, and other things of great importance, as may appeare in the Epiſtle to the Reader.

¶ And alſo a moſt profitable Concordance for the readie finding out of any thing in the ſame contained.

IOSHVA. 1.8.

¶ Let not this Booke of the Lawe depart out of thy mouth, but meditate therein day and night, that thou mayeſt obſerue and do according to all that is written therein: for then ſhalt thou make thy way proſperous, and then ſhalt thou haue good ſucceſſe.

¶ Imprinted at London by the Deputies of Chriſtopher Barker, Printer to the Queenes moſt excellent Maieſtie.
1589

Cum gratia & priuilegio Regiæ Maieſtatis.

CHAP. III.

1 The womã ſeduced by the ſerpent, 6 entiſeth her husband to ſinne, 8 They both flee from God. 14 They three are puniſhed. 15 Christ is promiſed. 19 Man is duſt. 22 Man is caſt out of Paradiſe.

Nowe * the ſerpent was more [a] ſubtill then any beaſt of the fielde, which the Lord God had made: and hee [b] ſayde to the woman, Yea, hath God in deede ſayde, Yee ſhall not eate of euery tree of the garden?

2 And the womã ſaid vnto ỹ ſerpẽt, We eate of the fruite of the trees of the garden,

3 But of the fruite of the tree, which is in the middes of the garden, God hath ſaid, Ye ſhall not eate of it, neither ſhall ye touch it, [c] leaſt ye die.

4 Then * the ſerpent ſaid to the woman, Ye ſhall not [d] ‡ die at all,

5 But God doeth knowe, that when ye ſhal eate thereof, your eyes ſhalbe opened, & ye ſhalbe as gods, [e] knowing good & euill.

6 So the woman (ſeeing that ỹ tree was good for meate, and that it was pleaſant to the eyes, and a tree to be deſired to get knowledge) tooke of the fruite thereof, and did * eate, and gaue alſo to her huſband with her, and he [f] did eate.

7 Then the eyes of them both were opened, and they [g] knew that they were naked, and they ſewed figge tree leaues together, and made themſelues ‡ breeches.

8 ¶ Afterwarde they heard the voyce of the Lord God walking in the garden in the ‖ coole of the day, and the man and his wife [h] hid them ſelues from the preſence of the Lord God among the trees of the garden.

9 But the Lord God called to the man,

Wiſd. 2.24.
a As Satan can change him ſelfe into an Angell of light, ſo did hee abuſe the wiſedome of the ſerpent to deceiue man.
b God ſuffered Satan to make the ſerpent his inſtrument & to ſpeake in him.
c In doubting of Gods threatning, ſhe yelded to Satan.
2. Corin. 11.3.
d This is Satans chiefeſt ſubtiltie, to cauſe vs not to feare Gods threatnings.
‡ *Eb. die the death*
e As though he ſhould ſay, God doeth not forbid you to eate of ỹ fruite, ſaue that he knoweth that if ye ſhould eate thereof, ye ſhould be like to him. *Ecclus. 25.26. 1. tim. 2.14.* f Not ſo much to pleaſe his wife, as mooued by ambition at her perſwaſion. g They begin to feele their miſerie, but they ſought not to God for remedie. ‡ *Ebr. things to girde about them to hide their priuities.* ‖ *Or, winde.* h The ſinnefull conſcience fleeth Gods preſence.

GENEVA BIBLE, REVELATION 17:3–4

So he caried mee away into the wildernesse in the Spirite, and I sawe a woman sit upon a scarlet coloured *(d)* beast, full of names of blasphemie, which had seven heads and ten hornes.

And the *(f)* woman was arayed in purple and skarlet, and guilded with golde, and precious stones, and pearles, and had a cup of golde in her hand; full of abominations, and filthinesse of her fornication.

(d) The beast signifieth the ancient Rome; the woman that sitteth thereon, the newe Rome which is the Papistrie, whose crueltie and bloodshedding is declared by scarlet.

(f) This woman is the Antichrist, that is, the Pope with the whole body of his filthy creatures, as is expounded, Verse 18. whose beauty onely standeth in outward pompe and impudency, and craft like a strumpet.

Description by Adam Rutledge, PH.D. *2017*

Perry Miller Collection on the Colonial Religious Experience in America

Some two hundred rare and first-edition books of significant historical and literary value are part of an extensive collection of seventeenth- and eighteenth-century works of religion, history, and law from the personal library of the late Harvard University professor Perry Miller, who died December 9, 1963.

Born in Chicago in 1905, Miller received his bachelor's degree from the University of Chicago in 1928 before beginning graduate work in American literature at Harvard in 1931. Miller attributed his decision to study seventeenth-century New England Puritanism—despite his professor's warnings that the field had been exhausted—to an "epiphany" he experienced as a young man while hunting adventure on the banks of the Congo River. "It was given to me, equally disconsolate on the edge of a jungle in central Africa," Miller wrote in 1956, "to have thrust upon me the mission of expounding what I took to be the innermost propulsion of the United States." In graduate school, Miller began his search for the "drums of case oil flowing out of the inexhaustible wilderness of America" in the Puritan migration from Europe to North America.

Miller challenged the dominant view of the Puritan life as repressive and reactionary, instead portraying New England's founders as emotional individuals who struggled to balance the overwhelming experience of migration with absolute piety and the belief that the future of mankind depended on the success of their settlement. New England Puritans shared an unwavering sense of mission that informed the establishment and guided the development of Massachusetts Bay Colony. How Puritans grappled with, explained, and justified that mission in light of the extreme challenges and obstacles preventing its success provides the foundation for subsequent American intellectual life.

Miller filled his library with the works of Puritan theologians and seventeenth-century intellectuals who profoundly influenced New England Colonial leaders. Among the holdings is a 1634 edition of John Preston's *The New Covenant, Or The Saints Portion*, originally published in 1630, which Miller considered a "prerequisite to any understanding of thought and theology in seventeenth-century New England."

Miller also purchased a first edition of Samuel Willard's *A Compleat Body of Divinity*, which at the time of its publication in Boston, in 1726, represented the largest volume produced by a Colonial press. The book consists of weekly lectures delivered by Willard from 1688 until his death in 1707, in which he attempted to "clarify and explicate" Puritanism in light of Anglican attacks. Nearly 250 years after its publication, Miller wrote that the book continued to serve as "a landmark in American publishing and a magnificent summation of the Puritan intellect."

Although famous for his contribution to the scholarship on Puritan thought and American intellectual history, Miller also taught American literature, including a class on American Romanticism. The Harvard professor filled his library with several works by important Romantic authors, including James Fenimore Cooper and Washington Irving. The collection includes an original copy of Cooper's two-volume *Sketches of Switzerland*, published in 1836 as the first part of his travel series *Gleanings in Europe*.

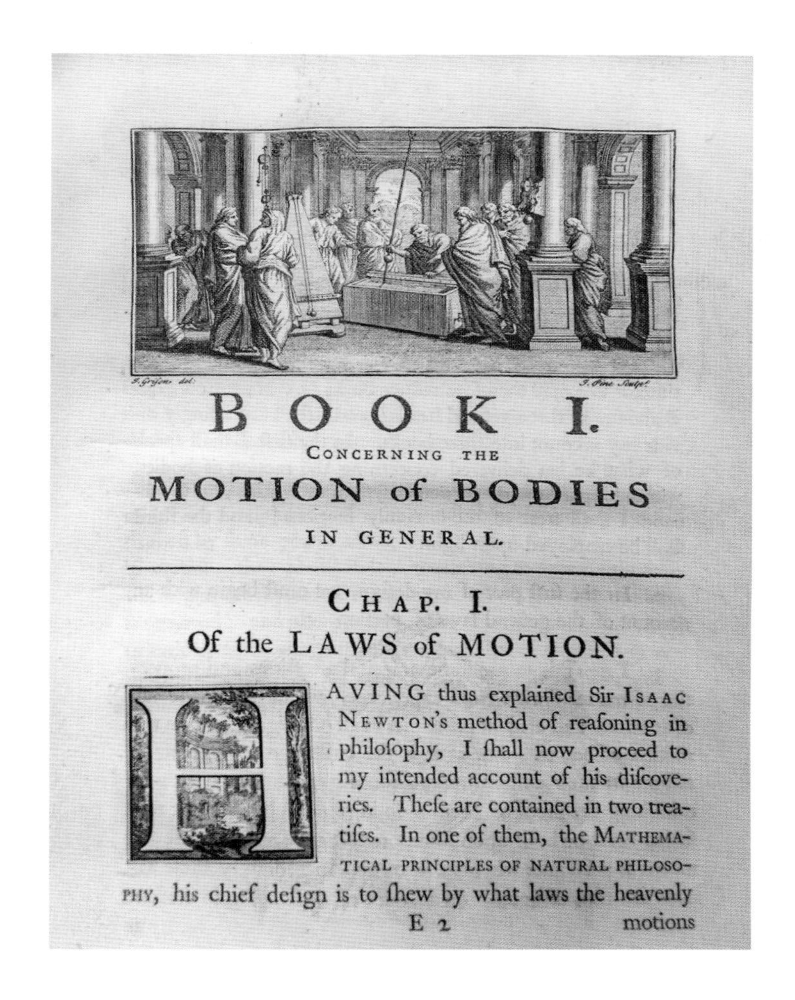

BOOK I.

CONCERNING THE

MOTION of BODIES

IN GENERAL.

CHAP. I.

Of the LAWS of MOTION.

HAVING thus explained Sir ISAAC NEWTON's method of reaſoning in philoſophy, I ſhall now proceed to my intended account of his diſcoveries. Theſe are contained in two treatiſes. In one of them, the MATHEMATICAL PRINCIPLES OF NATURAL PHILOSOPHY, his chief deſign is to ſhew by what laws the heavenly

E 2 motions

The wide range of subjects covered in Miller's library supports the notion that the professor viewed himself as free-thinking. In addition to his collection of books on history and literature, Miller also acquired rare and first editions on science and law, including tracts by Hugo Grotius and Matthew Hale, as well as Henry Pemberton's *A View of Sir Isaac Newton's Philosophy*.

From seventeenth-century Christian theology to nineteenth-century transcendental literature, Miller acquired works that helped transform American intellectual development. These important volumes of religion, history, law, science, and literature reveal the professor's steadfast commitment to uncovering the motor of the American experience.

Description by Alexandra Wagner Lough, PH.D. 2013

BRANDEIS UNIVERSITY ACQUIRED THE COLLECTION IN THE FALL OF 1964 FROM MILLER'S WIDOW, ELIZABETH MILLER

Bern Dibner Collection in the History of Science

Industrialist, philanthropist, and one of the most famous American book collectors of the twentieth century, Bern Dibner was born in 1897 in a village near Kiev, in Ukraine, and immigrated with his family to New York when he was seven. After attending the Hebrew Technical Institute, he matriculated at the Polytechnic Institute of Brooklyn, graduating as valedictorian in 1921 with a degree in electrical engineering. His work soon took him to Cuba, where he was placed in charge of unifying the country's electrical system on a single grid. In the process, he developed an electrical connector to link the previously incompatible transmission lines of the various local Cuban systems, and with this invention Dibner founded Burndy Engineering (an onomatopoetic play on his name, "Bern D."), later known as the Burndy Corporation.

Once the success of his company was assured, Dibner decided to retire from active management and pursue his intellectual and scholarly interests. As an inventor, he was fascinated by Leonardo da Vinci; Leonardo's passion for technology as well as for the arts resonated with his own and catalyzed his interest in studying the history of science. In 1930 Dibner traveled to Europe and enrolled in courses at the University of Zurich, where he studied history, with a focus on Renaissance culture, science, art, and technology.

These studies led to Dibner's fascination with rare books as the physical and intellectual record of human achievement and scientific and technological progress, and he began accumulating materials and housing them in his office at the Burndy Corporation. As the collection continued to expand, in 1941 he decided to found a library "to acquire and maintain the books, manuscripts, laboratory records, photos, drawings, and reports that record the progress of science." Over the following decades, the Burndy Library grew to be the preeminent American collection of materials on the history of science, housing tens of thousands of rare and obscure volumes.

Dibner's interests extended beyond collecting, however, and the Burndy Library imprint may be found on thirty-seven scholarly publications, twenty-one of them authored by Dibner himself. His most famous work remains *The Heralds of Science*, a descriptive catalog of two hundred "epochal books and pamphlets in the physical and biological sciences in the Burndy Library that were instrumental in establishing our age of science." Over the years, Dibner donated portions of his collection to various institutions.

B
C
C
C
H
F
F
E
E
E
A

Dibner's association with Brandeis began very early in the university's history, distinguished by his influence in the development of the special-collections resources. As a member of the Brandeis Bibliophiles, a group of prominent book collectors devoted to supporting the fledgling library system, Dibner contributed several major collections, including nearly 150 extremely rare and valuable texts in the history of science. The collection encompasses incunabula (texts printed before 1501, in the earliest years of printing); three early editions of works of Galileo; and first editions of the publications of Albert Einstein and other twentieth-century luminaries. Together, they provide a remarkable record of scientific progress and human achievement over the past five centuries.

Perhaps the most visually striking artifact is a book with the descriptive title *Della trasportatione dell'obelisco vaticano et delle fabriche di nostro signore papa Sisto V.* Published in 1590, it describes one of the greatest engineering feats of the Renaissance: the moving of an obelisk to St. Peter's Square and its erection before the basilica of St. Peter in the Vatican. A huge folio, the volume includes dozens of full-page plates, many of which combine detailed scientific depictions with allegorical and mythical figures who preside over the engineers' labor.

Description by Adam Rutledge, PH.D. *2017*

McKew Parr Collection

MAGELLAN AND THE AGE OF DISCOVERY

At the time of its donation, the McKew Parr Collection was considered one of America's premier private collections devoted to the era of exploration from the mid-fifteenth through the mid-eighteenth century. Compiled by Connecticut state senator Charles McKew Parr, the nearly seven thousand items were amassed to support his research on the Portuguese explorer Ferdinand Magellan. In 1953 the senator published a biography titled *So Noble a Captain: The Life and Times of Ferdinand Magellan*, renamed *Ferdinand Magellan, Circumnavigator* in the second edition. In 1961 the senator and his wife donated the holdings to Brandeis.

The materials are primarily in Spanish and Portuguese, but there are English, French, Dutch, and Latin texts as well. Parr considered this a working collection, gathered primarily for scholarly interest. Included are almost three hundred volumes published before 1850, most of which are contemporary accounts of the process of exploration and colonization—often firsthand descriptions of Colonial encounters and the administration of European holdings abroad. Of special mention are two seventeenth-century texts.

The first is *Conquista de las Islas Molucas* (1609), written by Bartolomé Leonardo de Argensola, a Spanish historian and poet who took holy orders and was later appointed royal chaplain and historiographer of Aragon. This text was commissioned by the Council of the Indies to commemorate the Spanish recapture of the Moluccan Islands of Ternate and Tidore in 1606. It was well received upon publication and remains an important source on Spanish and Portuguese exploration in the East Indies, the conquest of the Philippines, and the history of the spice trade. Representative of the book's content is an allegory of the Spanish conquest of the Moluccas. The amazon queen "Maluca" is depicted seated astride a crocodile, wearing a feather headdress and holding a sword in her left hand while in her right she raises a horn of plenty filled with the fruits of her lands. Her gaze is upward to a rainbow with the royal crest of Spain shimmering in the light, signifying, with the word *simul*, that the sun never sets on the Spanish empire.

The second text is *El devoto peregrino, y Viage de Tierra Santa*, written in Spanish by Antonio del Castillo and first published in Madrid in 1654. This popular account of a journey to the Holy Land was reissued in many later printings. Antonio del Castillo was a Franciscan friar sent by his superiors to the Holy Land in the first part of the seventeenth century. In this volume, he describes his visits

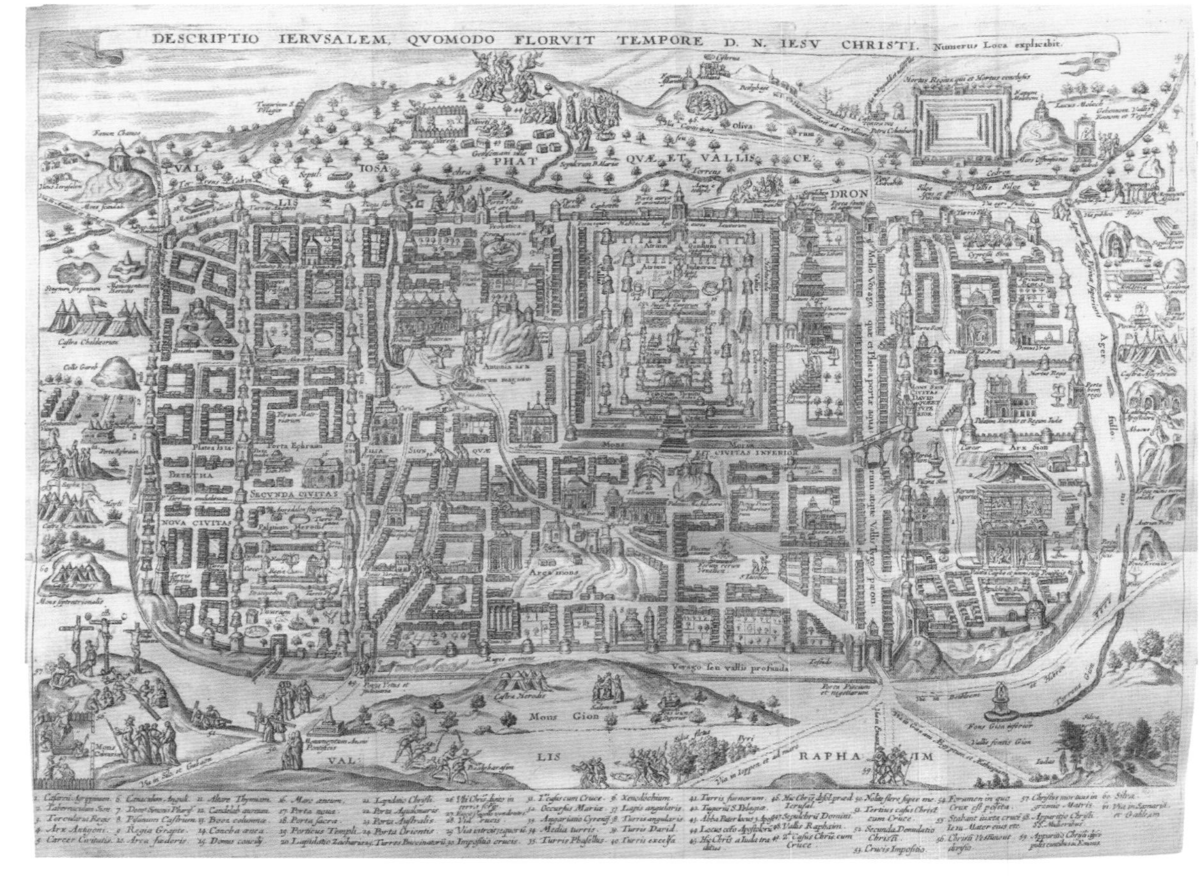
DESCRIPTIO IERVSALEM, QVOMODO FLORVIT TEMPORE D. N. IESV CHRISTI. Numerus Loca explicabit.
VAL
IOSA
PHAT
QVÆ ET VALLIS
CE
DRON
SECVNDA CIVITAS
NOVA CIVITAS
CIVITAS INFERIOR
Antonia arx
Acra mons
Mons Gion
Vorago seu vallis profunda
VAL
LIS
RAPHA
IM

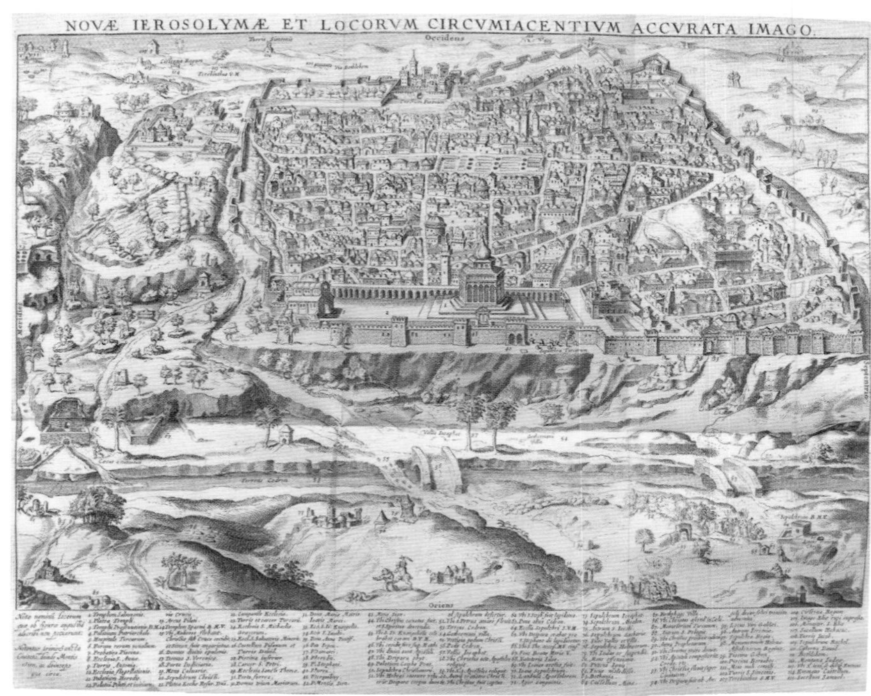
NOVÆ IEROSOLYMÆ ET LOCORVM CIRCVMIACENTIVM ACCVRATA IMAGO.
Occidens
Oriens

to Jerusalem, Nazareth, Jaffa, and the mountains and desert of Judea, with particular emphasis on the holy places he encountered.

Most striking in this volume are the numerous folded plates illustrating various aspects of the friar's travels, particularly two large printed maps of Jerusalem, one representing the city as it might have looked in the first century and the second portraying the city as it looked in the early seventeenth century. Both of these maps are fascinating in their detail, with more than one hundred individual sites singled out for additional description. These include, in the first map, the entire Via Dolorosa, the Way of the Cross, with all fourteen Stations of the Cross illustrated in miniature, culminating in a depiction of the crucifixion and the tomb of Jesus. Shown opposite is Judas, the disciple who betrayed Jesus, hanging from a tree. In addition to such obvious Christian imagery, care was taken to depict the Jewish character of the city. The map features the Palatium Davidis et Regum Iude (the Palace of David and the King of the Jews), and an intricate depiction of the temple, complete with the Holy of Holies (Sanctum Sanctorum), in which the Ark of the Covenant is shown guarded by two cherubim.

The second map depicts the city from the opposite side, looking down upon Jerusalem from the Mount of Olives to the east. A striking difference is the accurate depiction of the Muslim holy sites, the Dome of the Rock and the al-Aqsa Mosque, atop the Temple Mount in the center of the image. As in the first map, numerous locations are singled out for special mention, including the Tomb of Isaiah (Isaiae Sepulchrum).

Description by Adam Rutledge, PH.D. *2017*

Dante's *Divine Comedy*, Censored by the Spanish Inquisition

From a number of rare works by Dante Alighieri at Brandeis, a 1564 edition of *La Divina comedia* (*The Divine Comedy*) from Arévalo, Spain, holds a special place, revealing a centuries-old connection to the Spanish Inquisition in its pages.

Best described as an allegory, Dante's *Divine Comedy* was completed in 1320. With over 14,000 lines in *terza rima*, the work is complex and multilayered. Written in the first person, *The Divine Comedy* tells of the poet's journey through the three realms of the dead—*Inferno* (Hell), *Purgatorio* (Purgatory), and *Paradiso* (Paradise)—with the Roman poet Virgil, and later Dante's courtly love, Beatrice, as his guides. In the poem, Hell is described as an inverted cone, with Lucifer in residence at the bottom. The pilgrimage up from Hell is a climb to the top of the Mountain of Purgatory. Along the way, Dante and Virgil pass warriors, kings and emperors, fellow poets, popes, and citizens of Florence, all amending the sins of their life on earth. On the summit is the Earthly Paradise, where the two poets meet Beatrice, and Virgil departs. Dante is then led through the various spheres of Heaven, and the poem ends with a vision of the deity.

Florentine politics and religion provided an important background for Dante's work, as he reckoned with a number of historical incidents and figures involved in the political struggles between the papacy-inclined Guelphs and the empire-supporting Ghibellines during his lifetime. In 1266, Ghibelline domination in Italy ended, but political alliances and strife endured, as the Guelphs divided into two factions, the Blacks and the Whites. In 1302, the Blacks, under Pope Boniface VIII, expelled the Whites, including Dante. He died in 1321.

This sixteenth-century edition of *The Divine Comedy* is the first of three published by the Sessa family of Venetian printers. The title page features a portrait by Giorgio Vasari of Dante in caricature with an enlarged nose (because of the exaggerated nose, this edition is referred to in Italy as the *Edizioni del gran naso*). Scenes are depicted in beautiful woodcuts. The volume is an innovative hybrid, the work of Roman publisher and editor Francisco Sansovino (1521–1583), and includes the poem encircled by commentaries from Florentine humanist Cristoforo Landino (1424–1498), Lucchese academic Allesandro Vellutello (1473–?), and Sansovino himself, all of them well-known Dante critics of their respective times.

In the pages of the Brandeis volume, traces of the Spanish Inquisition remain. The powerful tribunal court system of the Catholic Church and Spanish Catho-

lic monarchs was established in 1478 by Ferdinand II and Isabella to maintain Catholic orthodoxy and consolidate power in their kingdoms. To curb the spread of heretical ideas in Spain, for a time the church functioned under the influence of the *Index Librorum Prohibitorum* (*Index of Forbidden Books*), an attempt to stop the contamination of the faith and the corruption of beliefs and morals of Roman Catholics through the reading of what was deemed immoral or theologically erroneous text.

Sopra la sua Comedia dell' Inferno, del Purgatorio, & del Paradiso.
Con tauole, argomenti, & allegorie, & riformato, riueduto, & ridotto alla sua uera lettura,
PER FRANCESCO SANSOVINO FIORENTINO.
In Venetia, Appresso Giouambattista, Marchiò Sessa, & fratelli. 1564.

At the outset, inclusion in the *Index* meant complete censure of a text; however, this proved not only impractical but contrary to the goal of maintaining

CANTO VNDECIMO.

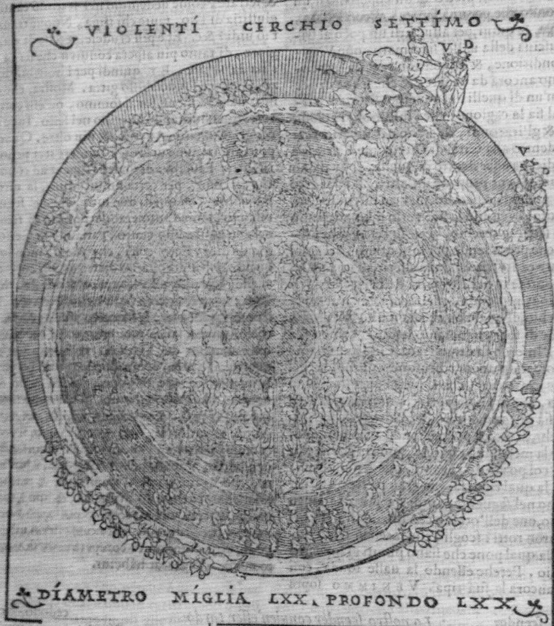

ALLEGORIA.

Land. PEr la ripa che fa gran pietre rotte in cerchio, si mostra che gli heretici uolendo passar piu oltre di quel che si cõuien loro, fanno d'una cosa soda, & intera, che è la uirtù, molti pezzi col disseminar diuerse bugie. Per lo puzzo dimostra gli effetti ch'escono da gli heretici, i quali ammorbano coloro che credono a le loro persuasioni. Per lo racconto da Virgilio a Dante i peccati, che ui si puniscono, si nota che la ragione mostra al senso il male, & la pena del male, acciò che spauentato, si ritragga a buona uia, lasciando i soggetti de' peccati, & attendendosi alla uirtù.

ARGOMENTO.

GIunto Dante su la ripa del settimo cerchio, offeso da una grandissima puzza ~~uenne la sepoltura di Papa Anastasio, che fu heretico~~. Intende da Virg. che ne' cerchi seguenti c'hãno a uedere che son tre, è punito il peccato della uiolẽza, della fraude, & dell'usura. Domanda a Virg. perche cagione ne la Città di Dite non son puniti, i lussuriosi, gl'iracõdi, gl'auari, i prodighi, & i golosi. Gli chiede poi, come l'usura offende Dio. Vanno poi colà doue si discende nel settimo cerchio.

IN su l'estremità d'un'altra ripa;
Che faceua grã pietre rotte in cerchio;
Venimmo sopra piu crudele stipa,
Et quiui per l'horribile soperchio
Del grande puzzo, che l'abisso gitta,
Ci raccostãmo dietro ad un coperchio
D'un grand'auello, ou'i uid'una scritta,
Che diceua, ~~Anastasio Papa guardo,~~
~~Lo qual trasse Fotin de la uia dritta~~.

Land. IN quest'undecimo canto descriue la discesa nel settimo cerchio. Ma acciò che habbiamo piena notitia di quello che seguita, l'auttore nel vij. viij. & ix. cerchio pone i supplici de' uiolenti, & de' fraudolenti. Et perche amendue questi peccati procedono da malignità, non è dubbio, che'l fin di quelli è l'ingiuria. Et l'ingiuria per uiolẽza si fa, o al prossimo, o a se medesimo, o a Dio. Al prossimo si fa ingiuria, o in se, come è batterlo, ferirlo, ucciderlo. O nelle sue cose, come inferir in quelle incendi, furti, rapine. A se medesimo similmente si fa ingiuria uccidendosi, e dilapidando i propri beni. Fassi nel terzo luogo ingiuria a Dio bestemmiandolo, negandolo, o facendo contra le sue cose, cioè, alla natura. La onde questo settimo si distingue in tre cerchietti, ouer tre gironi. Et nel primo, & piu superiore son puniti quelli c'hanno usato uiolenza contra il prossimo. Nel secondo contra di se. Nel terzo contra Dio, contra la natura, & l'arte. Dopo seguiteremo l'ottauo, & il nono cerchio, doue si punisce la fraude. Questa si commette, o contra quelli che non si fidano, & questi si puniscono nell'ottauo cerchio. O contra quelli che si fidano, a' quali è instituito il nono, perche è piu graue. Conciosia che rompe due gradi d'amore, cioè il naturale, & l'uniuersale, & l'accidentale, & particolare. IN su l'estremità d'un'altra ripa. Dimostra per questo

in quãto precipitio caggino tali peccatori, perche rouinano dall'eccellẽza dell'huomo a la profondità bestiale. Nessun animal è piu alto, che l'huomo, perche nessun'animale è rationale se non l'huomo, la qual ragione se si cõuerte al uitio, nessun'animal è piu uitioso. GRAN pietre. Perche il terreno nõ sosterrebbe. Et per la durezza de le pietre intendi l'habito fermo, & immutabile di questi uitij, & il gran pondo di questi peccatori, cioè, quanto son aggrauati dalla cõscienza. CON maggior stipa, cioè, siepe che circonda i peccatori, degni di piu chiuso carcere. Ouero stipa, cioè stiua, perche stipare in latino significa circõdare, & stiuare, & diremo stiua, quasi grande empimẽto di crudeltà, come meglio di sotto intenderemo. Pone in questo luogo il puzzo per l'abominatione, la quale è di questi peccati, & per l'infamia somma, nella quale tali peccatori incorrono; percioche, se come dice Agostino. Fama bona est odor bonus. Seguita che l'infamia sia graue fetore. ~~VIDI una scritta che diceua io guardo Anastasio Papa. Fotino cherico di Thessaglia, insieme con Acacio furon heretici, & teneuano che lo spirito santo non procedesse dal padre, & che'l padre fusse maggior che'l figliuolo, & tal heresia persuasero ad Anastasio Pontefice. Costui fu Romano, & sedè al tempo di Theodorigo Imperatore, & facendo aperta profession di tal heresia, & essendone ripreso da molti prelati uenne in tanta ostinatione, che uolle [illegible] in publico concistoro: [illegible] che disputando fu costretto dalla necessità del uentre d'andare a porgio il peso, doue a un tratto gl'uscirono tutte l'interiora, & così perì. Et non senza cagione pone la scritta a questa tomba, perche dinota che l'heresia in un sommo Pontefice [illegible], perche quanto piu è eccellente chi pecca, tanto piu è noto il peccato. Onde Giuuenale, come piu uolte [illegible]. Omne animi uitium tanto conspectius in se crimen habet, quanto maior qui peccat habetur.~~

a well-educated, literate clergy. In time, a compromise was reached in which trained Inquisition officials would "cleanse" those passages of text deemed offensive, inking out words or entire passages of unacceptable text and allowing the expurgated editions to circulate.

The copy of *The Divine Comedy* at Brandeis contains an original document pasted on the back of the title page, signed by a cleric, that states that the necessary cancellations have been made. But the passage of time has taken a toll—the ink used in the redaction has faded, and the printed words beneath have reappeared, enabling the reading of the entirety of the original passages.

The commentaries to this edition suffered a great deal more redaction than the poem itself. Specifically, the commentaries of Landino and Vellutello, and a few verses of the *Inferno* and *Paradiso*, were condemned. Why the inquisitor chose to completely ignore Sansovino's commentary is unknown, yet one variable may shed light on the matter: his edition of the poem was dedicated to Pope Pius IV.

Dante's exile from Florence lasted the rest of his life, and the influence of this dislocation on *The Divine Comedy* is evident throughout—in his views of politics on the peninsula, prophecies of his exile, and the eternal damnation of some of his opponents.

Description by Aaron Wirth, M.A. 2009, PH.D. 2014

DONATED BY HENRY AND HANNAH HOFHEIMER

Shakespeare Collection

The Shakespeare Collection—the core of which was acquired from Ruth M. Baldwin, combined with other Shakespeare acquisitions—includes many rare and fascinating editions, compilations, and critical material from the Renaissance through the early twentieth century. In December 1961, Allan Bluestein, a member of the philanthropic Brandeis Bibliophiles, donated what is perhaps the most brilliant gem in the collection: a First Folio edition of Shakespeare's works from 1623. To underscore the rarity of this treasure, fewer than 240 copies of the First Folio are known to exist today, and roughly one-third of these are in the Folger Shakespeare Library. Bluestein also donated a copy of the Second Folio and a Fourth Folio; another Fourth Folio was donated by Henry and Hannah Hofheimer. In all, 4 folios, 74 copies of single plays, 119 editions of multiple "complete" works, 13 works of poetry, and 58 critical, analytical, descriptive, and illustrative works comprise the Shakespeare holdings.

William Shakespeare lived from about 1564 to 1616; the First Folio was created in 1623, seven years after his death. Printed in London by Isaac Jaggard and Edward Blount, this represented the first time that theatrical works were compiled and released in such a way to the public. Due to the popularity of Shakespeare's plays in the theater, people also wanted to have a physical copy of the text for their own. The compilation of thirty-six plays, an immense amount of work for a printer to produce in large format, was not a luxury every home could afford. The copy includes an engraved image of the playwright by Martin Droeshout, the first inclusion of Shakespeare's portrait in his work.

One of the most significant issues with Renaissance drama, particularly that of Shakespeare, and one of the major reasons a collection such as this one is so important, is the question of reliability. Shakespeare wrote down the plays only to hand to the actors, and never compiled or revised his works in the polished manner that later came into style and is the norm today. Shakespeare had no true ownership over his works—they became the property of the theatrical company, and were not circulated due to fear of rival companies' potential profit. Oftentimes the versions that were printed as quartos or folios were written down by audience members and subject to individual nuances or mistakes. The show might change slightly from performance to performance, and there was always a chance that the actors would introduce a variance from the texts. It was therefore impossible to create an edition that matched what initially emerged from the pen of Shakespeare.

A CATALOGVE
of the ſeuerall Comedies, Hiſtories, and Tragedies contained in this Volume.

COMEDIES.

HISTORIES.

TRAGEDIES.

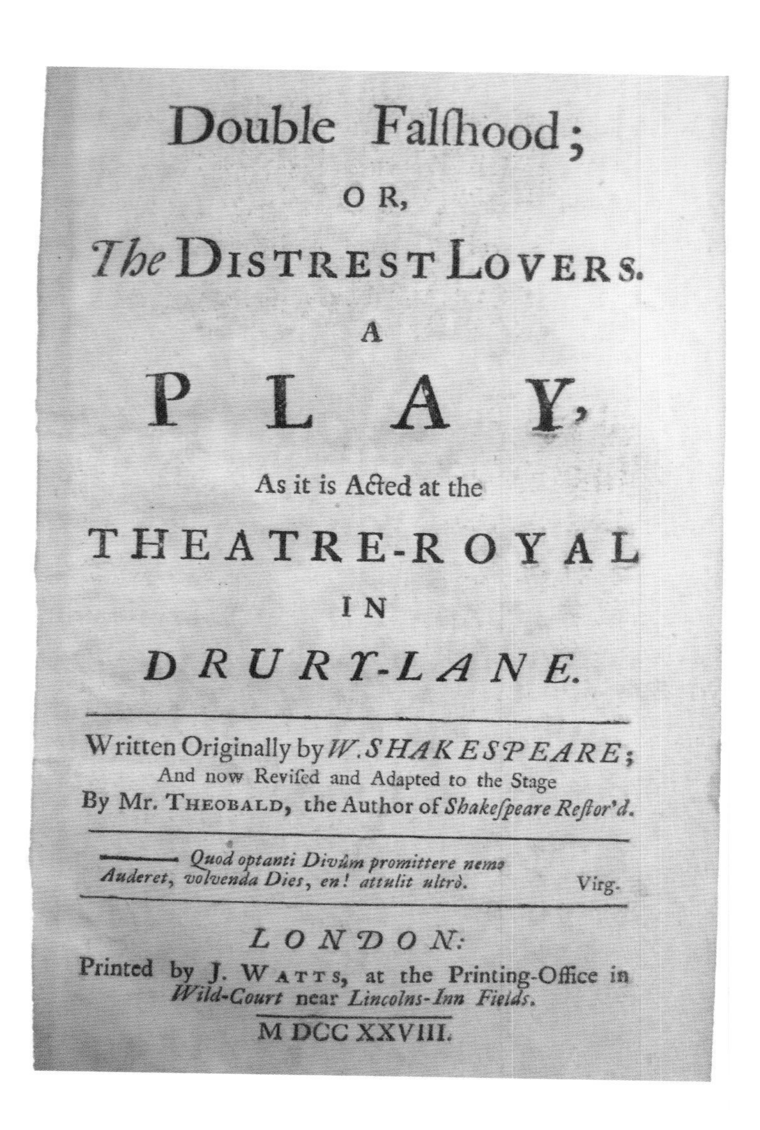

Double Falſhood;

OR,

The DISTREST LOVERS.

A

PLAY,

As it is Acted at the

THEATRE-ROYAL

IN

DRURY-LANE.

Written Originally by *W. SHAKESPEARE*;
And now Reviſed and Adapted to the Stage
By Mr. THEOBALD, the Author of *Shakeſpeare Reſtor'd.*

—— *Quod optanti Divûm promittere nemo*
Auderet, volvenda Dies, en! attulit ultrò. Virg.

LONDON:
Printed by J. WATTS, at the Printing-Office in
Wild-Court near *Lincolns-Inn Fields.*
M DCC XXVIII.

For the modern scholar, this translates into the necessity to compare multiple versions. The implications of variance between editions cannot be overemphasized. Small changes in wording can result in large differences in meaning, and many small differences add up to interpretations of the text that are still highly debated more than four hundred years after Shakespeare's death. Even the most famous lines have multiple versions. The texts reflect this preoccupation with reliability, with some even questioning Shakespeare's authorship.

One of the most sensational parts of the Shakespeare Collection is *Double Falshood; Or, The Distrest Lovers*: "A play, as it is acted at the Theatre-Royal in Drury-Lane. Written originally by W. Shakespeare; and now revised and adapted to the stage by Mr. Theobald, the author of Shakespeare restor'd." The collection includes three copies of this rare 1728 work. To paraphrase the title-page description, "Mr. Theobald" presents to the public a work based on a play of

Shakespeare, which is now lost if the claim holds true. Theobald introduces his work in such a way as to make the authorship ambiguous. The idea of a lost work of Shakespeare is not unreasonable; a play titled *The History of Cardenio* has been cited as another possible "lost play," with Cardenio suspected to have been based on a character in Cervantes's *Don Quixote*. Indeed, the characters in *Double Falsehood* (as the spelling now appears) all sport Spanish names, and the setting is Seville. Scholars disagree on the veracity of Theobald's claims; many write off Shakespeare's original authorship as a ploy to gain an audience, while the Arden Shakespeare edition went so far as to publish *Double Falsehood* as part of its Shakespeare series in 2010.

The variety of ways in which to present Shakespeare is almost as large as the collection itself. The range of texts available grants insight into Shakespeare's works and his popularity, but also into publishing trends over four centuries. A 1709 six-volume set introduces the idea of looking at the author alongside the works by including biographical text. Divisions emerged in the trajectories of texts, as some "early editions" were revised in their own right rather than reverting to the originals. Soon after, editions began to include the opinions of their editors.

Shakespeare was quickly canonized. In 1752, little more than a century after his death, *The Beauties of Shakespeare* was published; this reference work functions as a database of Shakespearian quotations, treating them as commonly known maxims. Other works compare similar passages of Shakespeare, in addition to providing explanations. Zachary Grey's *Critical, Historical, and Explanatory Notes on Shakespeare*, published in 1754, offers modern readers a view into the eighteenth century. Grey's work proceeds play by play, commenting on the allusions, to contribute a foundational text for critics and analysts to build upon.

Shakespeare was, of course, a poet as well as a playwright. The earliest version of his poems available in the collection was published in 1710, almost a century after his plays were released to the public, and includes the poetry only as a supplement to a compilation of the plays. Many poems in the works represented in the Brandeis collection have been given titles, most likely as an addition of the editor, whereas in today's compilations they are referred to simply by numbers.

The rarity and quality of the works alone would make the Shakespeare collection stand out, but the number and breadth of topics covered signifies the truly magnificent nature of this scholarly collection.

Description by Margo Kolenda-Mason, B.A. 2014

Three Books of Renaissance Cryptography and the Secret of Shakespearean Authorship

Invisible ink. Hidden messages. Codes in text. All provide context for three rare and important examples of the Renaissance craft of cryptography, with one of the volumes having the added distinction of being cited as a central piece of evidence in a controversy over the authorship of Shakespeare's plays.

The *Cryptographia* of Johannes Balthazar Friderici, the classic treatise on cryptography, was first published in 1684; it contains a survey of the field, including information on ciphers in letters, gestures, signs, and music, as well as instructions for the preparation and use of invisible ink. Brandeis University's copy of the *Cryptographia* is from the 1685 edition, the second of four. With text in German, the book includes an engraved added title page and several appended plates by Johann Friedlein, as well as numerous letter-set and woodcut illustrations within the text, showing the various cryptographic systems.

The second volume is the *Polygraphie, et universelle escriture Cabalistique de M.I. Tritheme Abbé*, a French translation with commentary by Gabriel de Collange of the work of the Würzburg abbot Johannes Trithemius, whose *Polygraphia* was placed on the *Index of Prohibited Books* by the Catholic Church in 1609. Trithemius was rumored to be a magician, and his three-volume *Steganographia* did nothing to repair this reputation, although a decryption key to the first two volumes was published in 1606 and showed them to be genuinely concerned with steganography, the study of hidden messages, as the title claimed. The *Polygraphia* text features woodblock head- and tailpieces and initials throughout. Most interesting is a series of cipher disks, called volvelles, within the body of the text, each consisting of a movable wheel that turns to create various alignments of letters or symbols for creating coded messages.

The third volume, and perhaps the most famous due to its importance to several prominent adherents to the Baconian theory of the authorship of Shakespeare's plays, is the ninth book of the *Systema integrum cryptographiae* of Gustavus Selenus, *Cryptomenytices et cryptographiae.* Gustavus Selenus, which roughly translates to "man of the moon," is the pseudonym of the book collector August, Duke of Braunschweig-Lüneburg (1579–1666), the founder of a famous library in Wolfenbüttel that bears his name. The original aim of Duke August was

LA tierce figure extensiue de la table auerse, en sa qualité, forme & espece, ne contient ny cō-

Gustavi Seleni
CRYPTOME-
NYTICES ET CRY-
PTOGRAPHIÆ
Libri IX.
In quibus & planiſſima
STEGANOGRAPHIÆ
a
Johanne Trithemio,
Abbate Spanheymenſi & Herbipolenſi,
admirandi ingenij Viro, magicè &
ænigmaticè olim con-
ſcriptæ,
ENODATIO
traditur.
Inſperſis ubiquè Authoris ac
Aliorum, non contemnendis
inventis.
CIↃ IↃ CXXIIII.

to elucidate the writings of Trithemius, including those found in the *Polygraphia*. However, this soon morphed into an effort to create an encyclopedic account of the science of cryptography as it was then practiced.

Duke August's work has been called the first encyclopedia of cryptography, and it aims for a full description of the science, with chapters on everything from simple inverted and transposed alphabet codes to accounts of cryptography in music and the visual arts. A large schema detailing the relationship of various parts of the field to one another is included on a folding plate just before the first chapter.

It is not this schema but rather the title page that has attracted the most interest in this volume; several scholars have claimed that hidden within the engravings is the key to discovering the real author of the Shakespeare plays. Theories as to the identity of the "true" author of the Shakespeare corpus have long been a part of the study of the poems and plays and have often been expressed by well-respected scholars of Elizabethan literature, especially during the early decades of the twentieth century. A 1910 work by Edwin Durning-Lawrence, *Bacon Is Shakespeare*, devotes a chapter to the Selenus volume, with an analysis of the title page.

While interest in the topic has died down somewhat in academic circles, in 2007 Mark Rylance, artistic director of Shakespeare's Globe Theatre from 1995 to 2005, caused a bit of a stir by issuing a "Declaration of Reasonable Doubt About the Identity of William Shakespeare," which was accompanied by a list of prominent doubters, including Sigmund Freud, Henry James, Walt Whitman, and Charles Dickens.

Description by Adam Rutledge, PH.D. 2017

DONATED BY SAMUEL NASS

Judaica Materials in Special Collections

With extensive holdings in subjects as diverse as Bible, rabbinics, Jewish philosophy and mysticism, and Hebrew and Yiddish literatures, the Judaica research collections at Brandeis provide a treasure trove of materials in Jewish history, dating from ancient times through the modern era. A number of rare (or unique) books, documents, and objects are of special interest.

A small sampling of the rare books in the areas of hagadot, prayer books, rabbinics, Bible commentaries, Hebrew grammar, and philosophy and history includes: *Seder Hagadah shel Pesah* (Venice, 1629), following the Roman ritual tradition, with a translation into Spanish; the multi-volume mahzor for the holidays, *Sha'ar Bat Rabim* (Venice, 1711–1715); Levi ben Gershon (Gersonides), 1288–1344: *Perush al ha-Torah* (Venice, 1547); Maimonides, 1135–1204: *Sefer ha-Mitsvot* (Venice, 1550) and *Hilkhot Bikurim* (Leiden, 1702); Levi ben Gershon: *Milhamot ha-Shem* (Riva di Trento, 1560); David Kimhi, ca. 1160–ca. 1235: *Sefer ha-shorashim* (Venice, 1529); and David Gans, 1541–1613: *Tsemah David* (Frankurt am Main, 1692).

Other rare works are Josephus's *De Antiquatibus ac de Bello Judaico* (Venice, 1499) and *Orden de oraciones de los cinquo ayunos del anyo* (Amsterdam, 1618). Facsimiles of medieval illuminated manuscripts include examples of hagadot and prayer books. One of these reproductions, the Rothschild Miscellany, numbers 948 pages containing 70 religious and secular works stunningly illustrated.

Among the highlights relating to Jewish life in Europe is the Leon Lipschutz Collection of Dreyfusiana and French Judaica, which documents the Dreyfus Affair in turn-of-the-century France and also features materials that relate to those in the Consistoire Central Israélite de France files, together providing a sweeping view of the French and worldwide Jewish communities from the mid-eighteenth through the first third of the twentieth century.

The American Jewish community is also well represented. Correspondence and news articles shed light on the life of Leo Frank, whose trial and lynching led to the formation of the Anti-Defamation League. The papers of Rabbi Stephen S. Wise, owned jointly with the American Jewish Historical Society, reflect Wise's life as a leading Reform rabbi and leader of the American Zionist movement. Rare books relating to the American Jewish community include a number of volumes by Isaac Leeser, a nineteenth-century author and communal leader; Isaac Mayer

Wise's *Tefilot Bene Yeshurun: Minhag Amerika* (1870); and David Einhorn's *Book of Prayers for Israelitish Congregations* (1872).

Among a large collection of the personal and professional papers of Louis D. Brandeis are many documents relating to the justice's Zionist work, while a major focus on Jewish feminism is distinguished by the papers of Aviva Cantor, E.M. Broner, Ma'yan: The Jewish Women's Project, Marcia Freedman, and the feminist magazine *Lilith*.

The Holocaust literature comprises several collections, including papers relating to Helmut Hirsch, which preserve the life and work of a young German Jewish artist murdered in 1937 for his anti-Nazi activities. The Jewish Resistance Collection contains examples of propaganda, individual testimonies, newsletters, and other documents pertaining to Jewish resistance movements during World War II. One particularly fascinating German antifascist pamphlet from 1933 is disguised as an owner's manual for an Electrolux vacuum cleaner. Beneath that cover, the pamphlet's real topic is "From Arson to Murder — The Rise and Fall of the National Socialist [Georg] Bell." The Theresienstadt concentration camp files consist of 200 daily bulletins of the camp's "Jewish Self-Administration," while the Spitzer family papers tell the story of a Czech Jewish family before, during, and after World War II, bearing witness to the fullness of their lives before the Holocaust.

Some of the more unusual holdings are a large Yiddish sheet-music trove and the Bernice and Henry Tumen Collection of Jewish religious and ceremonial ob-

Bayle

Elektrolux der beste Staubsauger

Gegen bequeme Monatsraten

Staubsauger: schont die Gesundheit
Staubsauger: ist hygienisch
Staubsauger: spart Zeit
Staubsauger: spart Kraft
Staubsauger: spart Geld
Staubsauger: der beste ist Elektrolux

Elektroluxvertrieb: ....

....

1933

Von der Brandstiftung zum Fememord!

Glück und Ende des Nationalsozialisten Bell

jects, with everything from a Scroll of Esther and Havdalah spice boxes to amulets and Kiddush cups.

Completing the Judaica holdings are a number of collections relating to the history of Brandeis University itself, including the Near Eastern and Jewish Studies faculty papers of Alexander Altmann, Marvin Fox, Nahum Glatzer, Benjamin Halpern, Leon Jick, and Marshall Sklare, and of longtime chaplain Albert Axelrad.

Description by Jim Rosenbloom, Judaica Library, 1976–2019

L'Encyclopédie

It is a rare to see a complete and original issue of one of the most important publications in modern history, the thirty-five-volume *Encyclopédie, ou Dictionnaire raisonné des sciences, des arts et des métiers* (Encyclopedia, or a systematic dictionary of the sciences, arts and crafts). Published between 1751 and 1780, this general encyclopedia, edited by Denis Diderot and Jean le Rond d'Alembert, consists of twenty-one volumes of text (seventeen original and four supplemental), twelve volumes of illustrations (eleven original and one supplemental), and a two-volume index. While the supplemental volumes and the index were neither written nor edited by Diderot or by d'Alembert, they are often considered to be part of the first full issue. In 1775, Charles Joseph Panckoucke was granted permission to reissue the work, and when he did so, he added seven volumes: the five supplements and the two-volume index.

Printed by the Société typographique de Neuchâtel, entries in the original twenty-eight volumes (text and illustrations) were written by a number of authors, all experts in their fields. This method of presenting accurate and comprehensive information fit in with Diderot and d'Alembert's vision. The original editors were fully aware that the enterprise of collecting knowledge was inherently unending. According to Diderot's entry on encyclopedias: "When one considers the immense material for an encyclopedia, the only thing one perceives distinctly is that it cannot be the work of a single man. How could a single man, in the short span of his life, manage to comprehend and develop the universal system of nature and art?" Previous dictionaries and encyclopedias had been written by one person—they represented a single vision and a single set of ideas. The *Encyclopédie* comprised a multitude of voices.

Nevertheless, there was certainly a driving philosophical/political/intellectual agenda, and it is the careful laying out of Enlightenment ideals (especially in the "Preliminary Discourse") for which *L'Encyclopédie* is most well-known. As scholar Philipp Blom wrote in the prologue to his book about the encyclopedia, "What makes it the most significant event in the entire intellectual history of the Enlightenment is the particular constellation of politics, economics, stubbornness, heroism, and revolutionary ideas that prevailed, for the first time ever, against the accumulated determination of Church and Crown, of all established forces in France taken together, to become a triumph of free thought, secular principle, and private enterprise. The victory of the *Encyclopédie* presaged not only the Revolution, but the values of the two centuries to come."

Previous attempts at the organization of universal knowledge were often

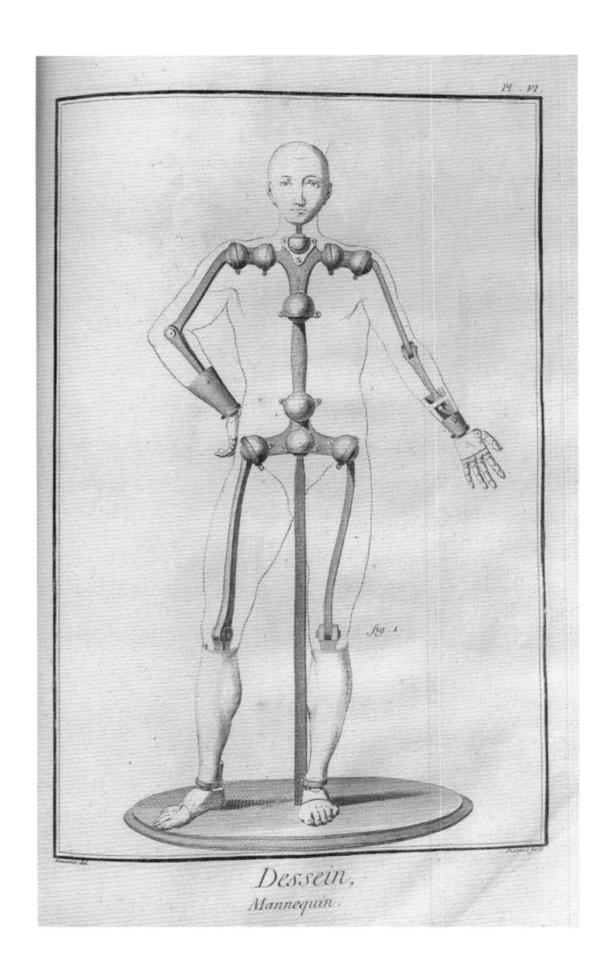

single-minded, myopic, and inaccessible. Perusing *L'Encyclopédie* today means not just accessing information, or even learning about what was important and understood a quarter of a millennium ago. It means understanding what the presentation of such vast swaths of knowledge meant, especially considering accessibility. Access to information was far less egalitarian in the eighteenth century than it is today, and it was often so directed and controlled that the purpose of its presentation was far less about educating and liberating than it was about controlling and subjugating.

For Diderot, the purpose of an encyclopedia was far more universal: "to collect knowledge disseminated around the globe; to set forth its general system to the men with whom we live, and transmit it to those who will come after us, so that the work of preceding centuries will not become useless to the centuries to come; and so that our offspring, becoming better instructed, will at the same time become more virtuous and happy, and that we should not die without having rendered a service to the human race."

Description by Surella Evanor Seelig, M.A. 2005,
Outreach and Special Projects archivist

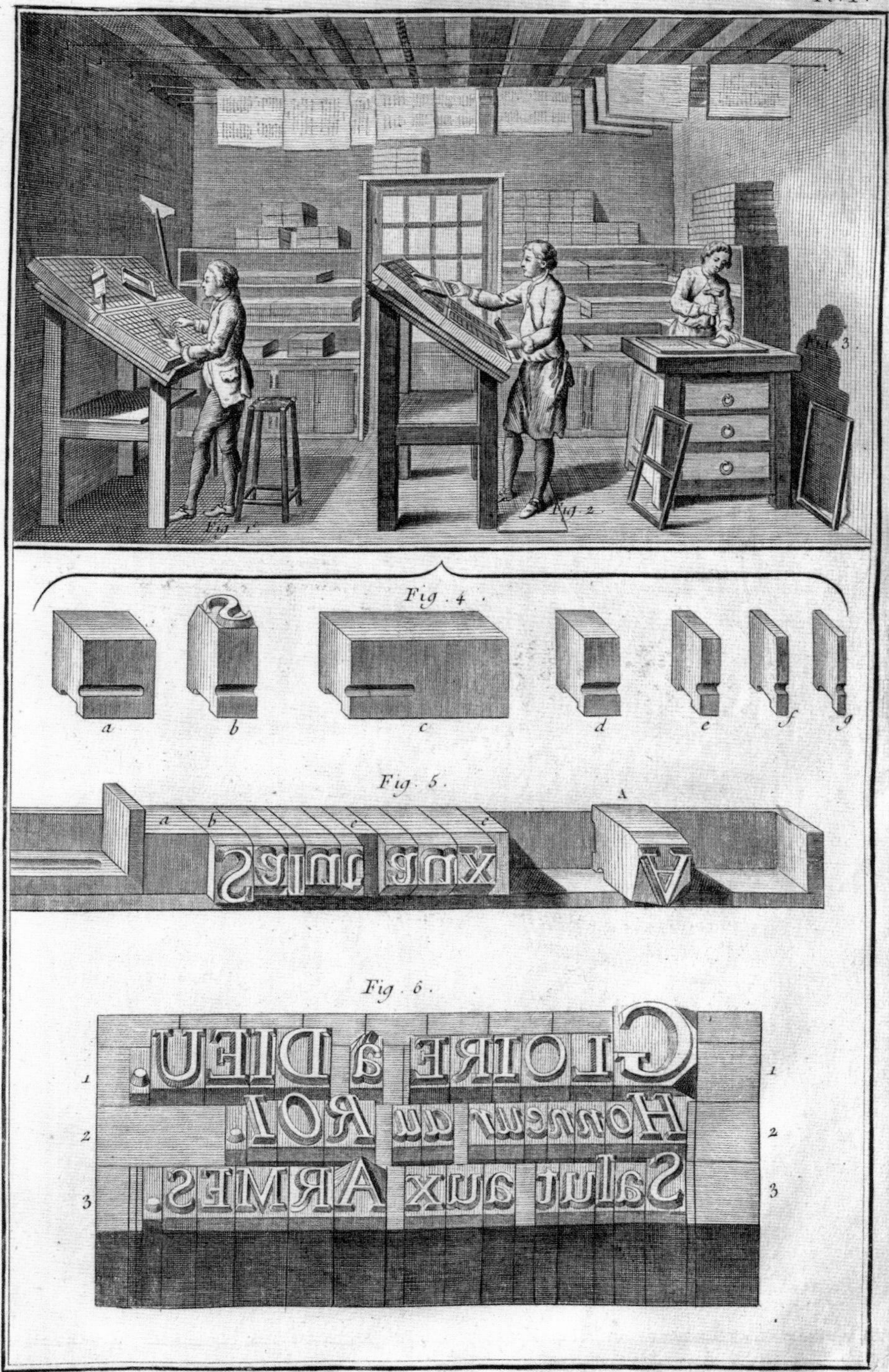

Goussier Del. Benard Fecit.

Imprimerie en Lettres, L'Operation de la Casse.

More Than Just a John Hancock

THE SIGNERS OF THE DECLARATION OF INDEPENDENCE AND THE CONSTITUTION COLLECTIONS

Nothing looms larger than the Declaration of Independence and the United States Constitution in the pantheon of great American texts; they are the foundation of the nation. These documents seem chiseled in stone, modern-day Ten Commandments. But what is often overlooked is that the texts were crafted by individuals, men with unique thoughts and beliefs. The founders sought to shape the nation, but they did so based on a personal and collective understanding of liberty and freedom forged by oppression and war. They were drawn together in a common cause that had lasting consequences.

Together, the two collections contain over one hundred autographed documents from virtually all of the key American founders. The papers began arriving at Brandeis University in the early 1960s, before being completed as a set in the early 1970s in time for the nation's Bicentennial.

While eye-catching enough just for the famous autographs, including those of John Adams, Benjamin Franklin, Thomas Jefferson, George Washington, and John Hancock, the collections' true prominence lies in their vast samplings of

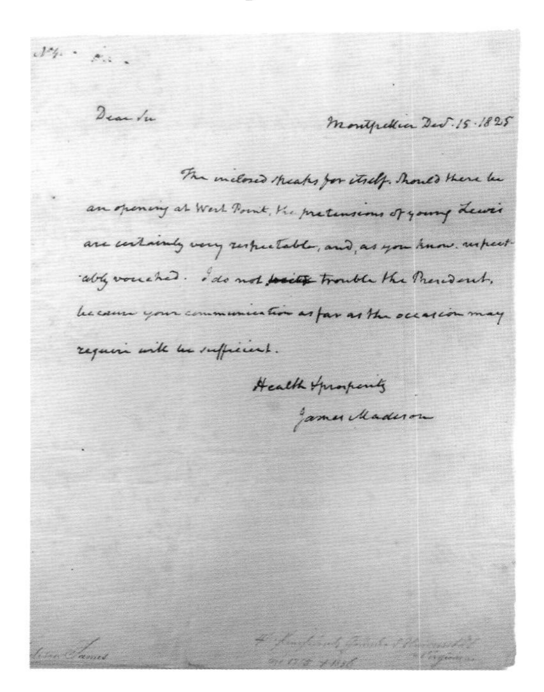

Dear Sir

Montpellier Decr. 15. 1825

The inclosed speaks for itself. Should there be an opening at West Point, the pretensions of young Lewis are certainly very respectable, and, as you know, respectably vouched. I do not trouble the President, because your communication as far as the occasion may require will be sufficient.

Health & prosperity

James Madison

Head Quarters Morris Town 18th April 1777

Dear Sir

I am fav.d with yours of the 15th. I have wrote fully to Congress upon the inexpediency and indeed danger of forming a Camp at Bristol before I am reinforced more strongly here, and I hope they will accord with me.

I am of opinion with you, that General Howe will never attempt Philad.a without first making a Stroke at the Army collected here. At the same time that I thank you for the desire you express for serving in this depart:ment, I applaud your Resolution of submit:ting chearfully to whatever post is assigned to you.

I am Dear Sir
with great Regard
Y.r most ob.t Serv.t
G.o Washington

x 224

full documents and manuscripts penned by the signers' own hands. Much more than brief handwriting snippets or historical relics, many of the records provide a glimpse into the minds and experiences of important individuals in the history of the nation.

From the oath of loyalty given by Thomas Lynch, Jr. (a South Carolina delegate), to fellow Continental Congress member Arthur Middleton's instructions to the peace commissioners in France, the collections feature personalized and chronologically advancing portraits of the Revolutionary War. In Boston during 1778, Massachusetts delegate Robert Treat Paine worried about what to do with the British prisoners of war from General John Burgoyne's army (gained after the American victory at the Battle of Saratoga), fearing that they could rise up during an invasion. Perhaps the prize is a letter from General George Washington, written during the New Jersey campaign in 1777, that reveals the commander-in-chief's understanding of the motives and tactics of his British counterpart, General William Howe.

The scope of these documents reaches beyond the war itself, and is quite expansive across American history, from the Colonial era through the early republic—including a government form signed by Massachusetts governor Samuel Adams and a Colonial legal paper fining two individuals for fornication.

The documents also provide the opportunity to examine some of the less well-known founders, including Charles Carroll, who, by 1832, was the last surviving signer of the Declaration of Independence.

Description by Craig Bruce Smith, M.A. *2009,* PH.D. *2014*

THE GIFT OF ELISE O. AND PHILIP D. SANG

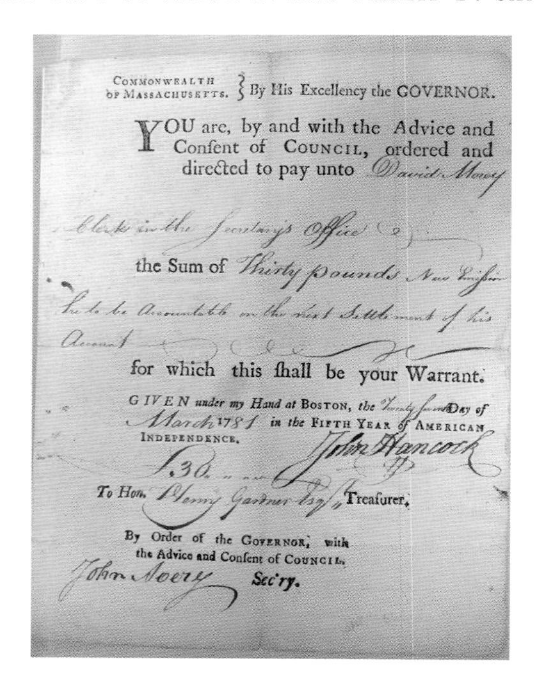

COMMONWEALTH OF MASSACHUSETTS. } By His Excellency the GOVERNOR.

YOU are, by and with the Advice and Conſent of COUNCIL, ordered and directed to pay unto David [illegible]

Clerk in the Secretary's Office

the Sum of Thirty pounds New Emission

he to be Accountable on the next Settlement of his Account

for which this ſhall be your Warrant.

GIVEN under my Hand at BOSTON, the [illegible] Day of March 1781 in the FIFTH YEAR of AMERICAN INDEPENDENCE.

£30 .. ..

John Hancock

To Hon. Henry Gardner Esq. Treaſurer.

By Order of the GOVERNOR, with the Advice and Conſent of COUNCIL.

John Avery Sec'ry.

Jack J. and Therese G. Katz Collection of Chinese Snuff Bottles

Snuff bottles gained widespread popularity in China after the introduction of tobacco by Europeans in 1537. The Chinese used snuff—finely pulverized tobacco—as a form of medication and often converted old medicine bottles into snuff carriers. The production of the bottles flourished between 1622 and 1795, reflecting their use as both a luxury item and a common gift. Most snuff bottles were small—between 2 inches and 3 inches high—and designed to be carried on the person in a small silk pouch. They came in various shapes and were made from several different types of material, including glass, ivory, jade, metal, porcelain, quartz, and coral, as well as turquoise, mother of pearl, and lacquer. Most included a tight stopper and a small spoon used to withdraw snuff from the bottle.

Forty-seven Chinese snuff bottles from the eighteenth and nineteenth centuries make up the Brandeis collection. After 1882, a highly skilled technique called "inside painting" became fashionable. In one of the bottles, the inside-painted images show, on one side, a scholar in a blue robe admiring a chrysanthemum spray in bloom below a short poem. On the other side, the artist, Ma Shao-Hsuan, included a longer verse:

> It is not so that I love the chrysanthemum more than the other flowers;
> But I believe that there will be no more flowers after this one has bloomed.
> Poets' ease it is to write nature poems in the spring,
> But if they look for a brocade-like flower garden in the fall
> When willow's green is half-turned to gold;
> All they will be are ill-successful flower seekers.

Glass represents one of the more common materials of Chinese snuff bottles; glass bottles appear in several forms, including monochrome, painted, cameo, mottled, or glass imitations of other stones. A glass snuff bottle with interior painting shows a portrait of a Manchu man wearing a winter coat and round hat. While most bottles were created in flattened, oval, or tubular shapes, some resembled human figures.

The collection also features a jade snuff bottle in the shape of the creature that symbolized reincarnation, a large cicada, or locust, with a greenish stomach, reddish-brown wings, and a head with black spots. Jade was a favorite stone in

不是花
中偏愛菊
此花開
盡更無花

China and used in many decorative arts; the Chinese word for jade, *yu*, means "gem supreme." The jade of this bottle dates to the Sung period (960–1279 C.E.).

In addition to the forty-seven snuff bottles, the collection also contains several hand-carved wooden stands. One displays a carved turquoise snuff bottle with a chained cover; carved dragon-head handles adorn this bottle with a chain of links connected to a Fu lion. The bottle also shows a mother and her two small children at a table before a window. Another example is a rare gold lacquer and pietra dura bottle made with amber lacquer, with a tessellated gold ground depicting a scene of three small boys picking peaches.

It is these beautiful designs and ornate decorations that account in large part for the enduring popularity and collectability of Chinese snuff bottles.

Description by Alexandra Wagner Lough, PH.D. 2013

BRANDEIS ACQUIRED THIS COLLECTION FROM
JACK J. AND THERESE G. KATZ IN DECEMBER OF 1964

Bernice and Henry Tumen Collection

The history of Jewish ceremonial art and objects expresses itself within the experiences of Jews living among diverse cultures in dynamic and complex lands. As Jews constructed and interpreted their various identities, they did so as a minority group attempting to reconcile traditional religious duty within a surrounding folk-art influence. The works of Jewish ceremonial art in the Bernice and Henry Tumen Collection reflect this tension and shed light on the artistic expression that blossomed under the constraints.

The 177 Jewish ceremonial objects, as well as rare Israeli coins and books on Judaica, principally showcase nineteenth- and twentieth-century religious artifacts, along with Roman glass and clay pieces from the first to the fourth century. The ceremonials originate from many parts of Europe and the Near East, as well as from areas of North Africa and North America.

Individually, these items illustrate the significance of the use of beauty in the performance of commandments. Collectively, they illuminate the communities and environments that informed, challenged, and stimulated their creation and application.

As public displays of religious observance, these ceremonials were carefully and beautifully constructed. The collection contains intricate silverwork and incorporates precious gemstones: a nineteenth-century Torah crown fashioned from red velvet includes seed pearls and floral designs, and an ivory European Torah pointer is decorated in silver with an inset turquoise stone. None of these Torah ornaments would have been viewed as simply everyday articles but were considered works of art befitting the place of the Torah in Jewish life.

This yearning for holy beauty on earth continued with the emergence of Kabbalah, Jewish mysticism, as amulets and talismans grew in popularity among the medieval European and early modern Mediterranean Jewish populations. Jewish amulets, emphasizing religious texts and names, were worn for purposes of protection (against sickness, misfortune, and the "evil eye"). Many of the pieces can be worn as ornaments and contain the word *Shaddai* or the Hebrew letter *shin*. It should be noted that while amulets were quite popular, they have been denounced by some rabbinical authorities as mere superstition.

The various intercultural factors that inspired Jewish ceremonial art are also well documented in the collection, including Christian, Dutch, Greek, and Islamic influences: a nineteenth-century Christian censer transformed into a Jewish spice

box, a hexagonal Dutch dreidel inscribed with Latin letters, and a nineteenth-century Near Eastern menorah backplate with nine mihrabs. (In the mosque, a mihrab indicates the direction of the Kaaba in Mecca, and therefore should be the direction of prayer.) Indeed, the spice containers display an unmatched receptiveness to outside influence. There is no Jewish law that dictates what kind of box should be used and no rule describing which type of spice should be contained.

The objects in the collection speak to a living tradition, one that demonstrates the complex interactions between tradition and continuity, art and beauty, in the substance of everyday life.

Description by Zachary Fine Albert, M.A. 2012

DONATED BY BERNICE AND HENRY TUMEN IN 1981

Burmese Palm-Leaf Manuscripts

The practice of using palm leaves as material for manuscripts has a long tradition, dating to the pre-paper era; it is believed they were being utilized as far back as 5 C.E. Two nineteenth-century Burmese Buddhist texts, handwritten on palm leaves, are part of the collections at Brandeis. Although the language of both manuscripts is Burmese, the exact dates and origins are unknown. The more complete of the two manuscripts is composed of sixty-six leaves—rectangular, dried, cut, and smoked palmyra palm leaves, or *peisa*—on which, using ink, a scribe has copied what is most likely a Buddhist text. The handwriting is beautifully clear, with little decorative flourish. The leaves measure roughly 5 centimeters wide by 50 centimeters long, and the manuscript is bound on each side with a wooden board. The edges of the two protective boards are painted red and maroon, and the edges of the manuscript leaves themselves are gilded. The piece is held closed with two fabric cords that pierce the leaves and wood at either end and allow the reader to open the manuscript like a fan. The second manuscript is a fragment of twenty-five palm leaves tied with fabric cords threaded through the leaves but without the protective boards. This is believed to be a Buddhist history of priests.

Likely having originated in India, palm-leaf manuscripts appeared throughout South and Southeast Asia. Perhaps it was the durability and toughness of

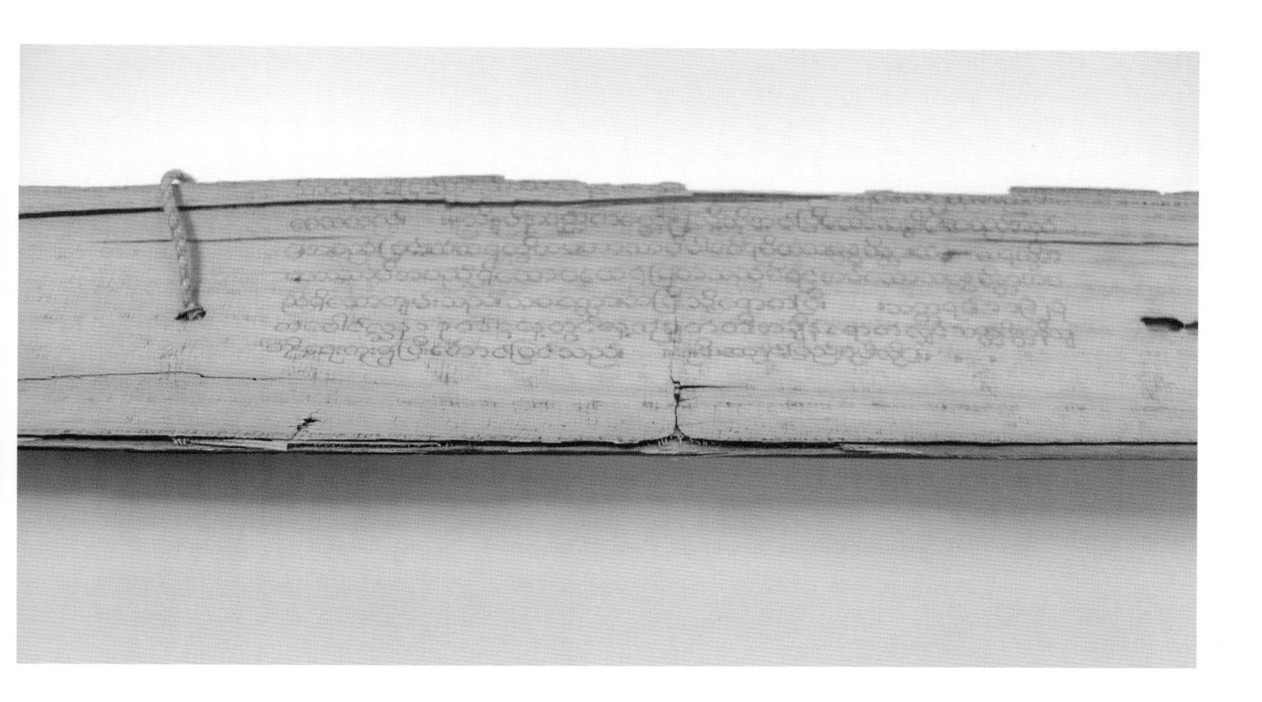

palm leaves that made them ideal for Buddhist monks and others to use as a writing surface. Unfortunately, due to the high humidity of the climate in Southeast Asia, palm leaves decay rapidly, and therefore it is rare to find examples of these delicately constructed manuscripts that are more than two hundred years old. In fact, it was common practice to copy the manuscripts to new palm leaves as the old ones weakened and began to disintegrate. This custom only came to an end relatively recently, in the nineteenth century, with the advent of industrial-scale printing presses. Most of the older examples that have been preserved are generally those that were carried by Buddhist missionaries to Central Asia, where a colder, drier climate—one less destructive to the materials—was prevalent. The earliest surviving palm-leaf manuscript dates to ninth-century Nepal, and the most recent examples to be found, like the manuscripts in this collection, date to the nineteenth century.

Some scholars believe that the physical nature of the palm leaves was actually a central factor in the development of rounded scripts in Southeast Asia: rounded writing would have been easier to copy onto leaves without causing damage to the writing surface, while more angular scripts were likely to split the leaf. As well, the shape of the palm leaf itself was replicated and can be seen in manuscripts made from a wide variety of materials, including birch bark (India), cotton cloth (Burma), and copper-plate charters (South and Southeast Asia).

Description by Max Close, B.A. 2016

DONATED BY PHILIP PINSOF

Fore-edge Paintings

Twenty-two volumes featuring a rare, hidden, and little-known art form, fore-edge painting, are among the gems of the more than 10,000 rare books at Brandeis.

While bibliophiles may be familiar with the gilt edges often found on antique books, many may not know that this gold finishing sometimes hides a secret painting or two: images of children playing in the snow, a lovers' embrace, a family crest, a landscape, or a famous landmark.

A book has four edges: the spine, top edge, bottom edge, and fore edge, the last being the one used to thumb through the pages. Fore-edge paintings are artistic decorations meant to enhance a volume's beauty, added by artists to individual copies and sometimes with little or no relationship to the subject of the book itself. Single fore-edge paintings, whether hidden under gilt or not, provide only one image. A double fore-edge painting displays one image that appears when the pages are fanned in one direction, and a second when the fanning is reversed. The triple fore-edge painting adds a third image, which takes the place of the gilt edging and is visible when the book is closed. There are also "panoramic fore-edge paintings," which occur not only on the fore edge but also on the top and bottom edges.

Depending on the artist's employer (the bindery or the owner of the volume), these paintings could be added before or long after binding. Rarely signed, the work of fore-edge artists and the dates of completion are usually identified by style. The Brandeis collection consists mostly of nineteenth-century examples with contemporary and later paintings.

Believed to have originated in the title markings applied to fore edges in the tenth century, the art of fore-edge painting began as a utilitarian procedure—mostly a method for identification rather than beautification. Before book spines were regularly marked with titles, the fore edges faced outward with the titles visible. Later, when titles were shifted to the spines, the fore edge began to be used as a place to list the owner's name (or their family mottoes, coats of arms, or monograms).

When the sixteenth-century Italian engraver and painter Cesare Vecellio (cousin to Titian) began painting the fore edges, the purpose of fore-edge markings shifted—from identification to beautification. Vecellio's paintings, like the early markings of title and owner, were painted on the very edge of the pages so as to be visible when the book was closed. Around a century later, English bookbinder Samuel Mearne added a new skill to the art: he began to paint not on the absolute edge of the text block but within the inner edges of the pages. This shift in technique resulted in artwork that was visible only when the pages were fanned

and undetectable when the book was closed. Thus, the "disappearing fore-edge painting" was born.

As fore-edge paintings grew in popularity, artists were employed to paint landscape scenes with country estates on the fore edges of volumes, which were then bound in painted vellum covers or exotic leather bindings. While they continue to be a relatively rare art form, fore-edge paintings are still being created today, usually added to antiquarian books.

Perhaps due to their hidden nature, relatively little has been known about these pieces of secret art. Owners of books adorned with fore-edge paintings may not even be aware of the treasures they hold. This small but stunning collection provides a peek into this special art form.

Research by Hansol Lee, former undergraduate; research and description by Surella Evanor Seelig, M.A. 2005, Outreach and Special Projects archivist

SIXTEEN OF THE WORKS OF THIS TYPE AT BRANDEIS ARE FROM THE REUBEN M. AND REGINE GINSBERG COLLECTION OF FORE-EDGE PAINTED BOOKS, DONATED BY MICHAEL GINSBERG (CLASS OF 1970) IN HONOR OF HIS PARENTS

Walter E. Fernald Developmental Center's Samuel Gridley Howe Library Collections

Founded in South Boston in 1850 by physician and abolitionist Samuel Gridley Howe and medical activist Dorothea Dix, the Massachusetts School for Idiotic and Feebleminded Youth, later known as the Walter E. Fernald State School, became the United States' first such institution. All types or grades of mental, moral, and physical disabilities made up the population, from the "idiot" (a term then used for those with mental disabilities) to individuals who possessed attributes only a little below the normal standard of human intelligence.

By the late 1860s, Howe's educational reforms for his mentally disabled patients were quite successful and influenced similar institutions throughout North America. Howe's method of education provided the residents with the means to earn wages, live freely, and return to their respective communities and live independently. Yet many believed because these "idiots" did so well that they should remain in the school. Howe, the school's superintendent, vehemently opposed permanent institutionalization, as he believed that once the students learned basic education, they could be rehabilitated back into society as "decent" citizens.

When Howe retired in 1874, Edward Jarvis, an authority on vital statistics, became the school's second superintendent. After observing the school rehabilitate residents with mental subnormalities into high-functioning disabled youths, the Massachusetts government encouraged the institution to admit disabled adults, delinquent youths, and even children from broken or poor homes. In fact, if a poverty-stricken family decided that the best place for one or all of their children was outside the home, the likelihood of them residing at the school was high.

With government pressure to add adults and wayward children to the program, it became clear that more space was needed. So, in 1887, with a legislative appropriation of $25,000, the school moved to a hilly neighborhood in Waltham, Massachusetts, that would eventually encompass over 190 acres. What started as a school became a self-contained community, with courses for farm and industry work; mandatory daily education; shoe repair, rug making, knitting, sewing, weaving, and housekeeping classes; and dancing and athletics for fitness. All the

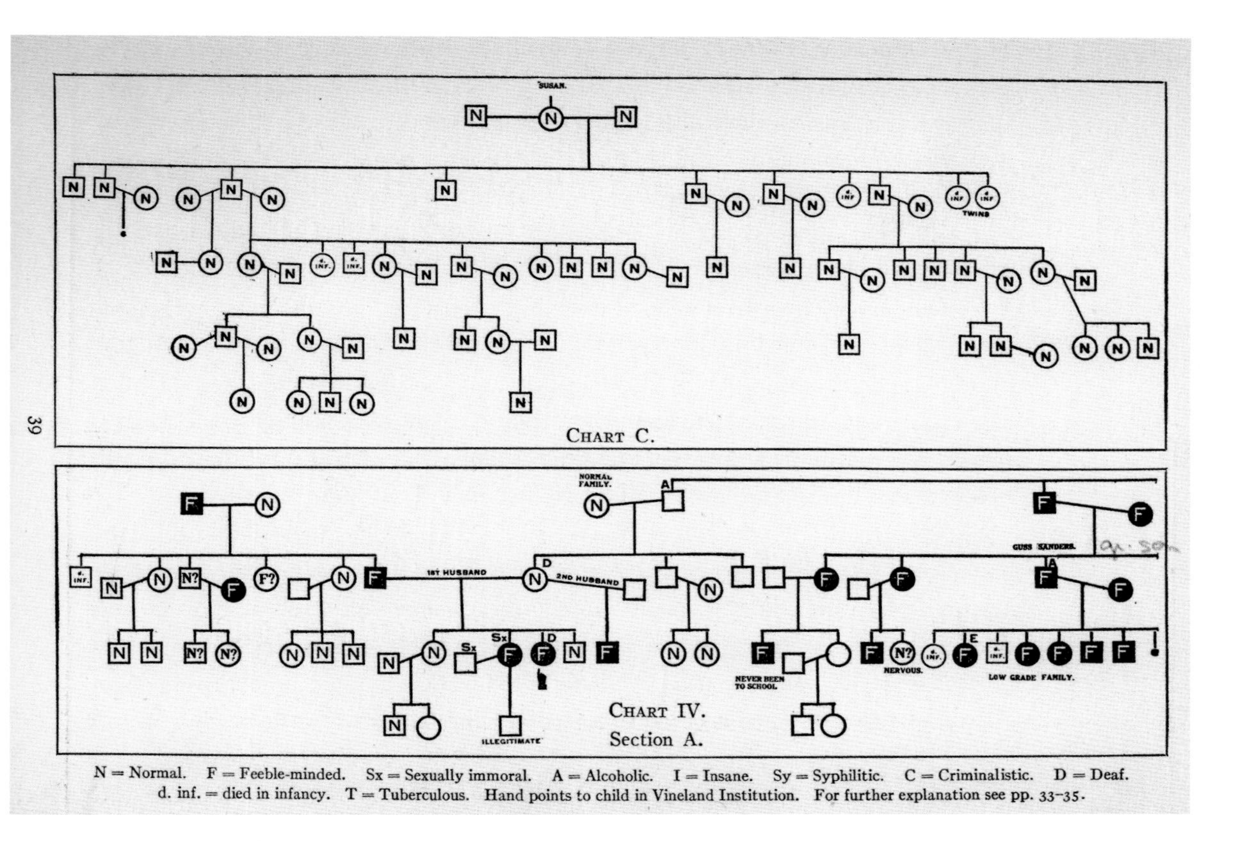

N = Normal. F = Feeble-minded. Sx = Sexually immoral. A = Alcoholic. I = Insane. Sy = Syphilitic. C = Criminalistic. D = Deaf. d. inf. = died in infancy. T = Tuberculous. Hand points to child in Vineland Institution. For further explanation see pp. 33–35.

while the objective was the same—after acquiring basic academic and job skills, residents were expected to graduate to a life beyond the institution.

While the Howe approach continued to be effective, medical arguments and public opinion began to change around the turn of the twentieth century. The school's third superintendent, Walter E. Fernald, a world-renowned expert on mental retardation, did not agree with Howe's rehabilitation program. By the 1910s, Darwin's theories of natural selection and a revived interest in Mendelian genetics had led many scientists to argue that human traits such as intelligence and morality were biologically rooted. Moreover, under Fernald's guidance, the school took a more "scientific" stance on the mentally disabled, specifically, the fast-rising international bio-social movement called eugenics.

Eugenicists had rediscovered the work of Gregor Mendel, who, in the mid-1800s, recorded the results of crossbreeding pea plants and found a very regular statistical pattern for features like height and color, thus introducing the concept of genes. One branch of genetics developed into the study of social theory known as eugenics. It was presented as a mathematical science that could be used to predict the traits and behaviors of humans and to control human breeding so that individuals with the best genes would reproduce, thereby improving the species.

At the same time, officials began to encourage social-service agencies, courts, and police to send suspected "morons" for IQ testing: people of color, Jews, southern Europeans, developmentally disabled people, and the rural poor were particularly vulnerable to being labeled as "polluting the gene pool of society." Those who scored below normal would be admitted to state schools, as they were deemed a danger to the public, and would, as a matter of public policy, be prevented from reproducing.

Several states created so-called traveling clinics that administered IQ tests at public schools around the nation. Many of the clinics labeled children as feebleminded, even though their teachers and parents insisted that they were normal. The clinics separated the children from their families by convincing the parents that an institution offered the best possible future. Those families who did not volunteer their children for admission often lost custody of them in court.

After Fernald's death, in 1924, his mission of "scientific" investigation and the inclusion of poor, delinquent, orphaned, and epileptic people continued under the next superintendent, Ransom Greene. It is worth noting, however, that this period in science and medicine was not filled entirely with specialties that history now deems quackery and pseudoscience—major positive breakthroughs occurred in fields such as war neurosis, endocrinology, and rights for the handicapped.

But it was not until decades later, in the 1960s, that support for the rights of the disabled gained momentum, encouraged by the civil rights and women's rights movements. People with different disabilities—mental and physical handicaps, along with hearing and visual impairments—came together to fight for a common cause. In the forefront of this effort, and with ties to both the Howe Library and Brandeis University, were Irving Kenneth Zola and Gunnar Dybwad.

An internationally renowned sociologist, Zola specialized in medical sociology and disabilities studies. As the Mortimer Gryzmish Professor of Human Relations at Brandeis from 1963 until his death in 1994, he was a founding member of the Society of Disability Studies. The Zola collection contains materials on aging and disability, the disabled in literature, and disability in the workplace.

Gunnar Dybwad was a celebrated human-rights advocate, lawyer, administrator, and authority on autism, retardation, and cerebral palsy. A professor of human development at Brandeis and founder of the Starr Center for Mental Retardation at the university's Heller School, Dybwad was one of the first to frame mental disability as a civil rights matter rather than as a medical or social-work problem. His collection holds a vast amount of international literature.

The Samuel G. Howe Library Collection's scope is vast, including thousands of pamphlets, case studies, and journals on topics ranging from what were once known as feeblemindedness and cretinism to eugenics and crime. The material dates from the 1810s to the 1950s and is related primarily to North America and the United Kingdom.

There are materials on self-advocacy, awards and photographs, and works from world-renowned practitioners such as psychologists Alfred Binet and Edgar A. Doll, polymaths Francis Galton and Karl Pearson, Walter E. Fernald, Dorothea Dix, Ellis Island medical officer Howard Knox, and eugenicists Charles B. Davenport and Henry H. Goddard.

The Fernald Center closed in 2014.

Description by Aaron Wirth, M.A. 2009, PH.D. 2014

Trustman Collection of Honoré Daumier Lithographs

Though one can view Honoré Daumier's nineteenth-century lithographs from a purely artistic or purely political standpoint, they were often a blend of both. An artist whose work was characterized by whimsical and often surrealist imagery, Daumier (1808–1879) frequently made political statements with his art but always sought to entertain. While Daumier's works (which, in addition to lithographs, include numerous paintings, drawings, sculptures, and wood engravings) are found at institutions and museums across the globe, the Benjamin A. and Julia M. Trustman Collection is one of the major Daumier repositories in the United States, comprising as it does nearly all (3,878) of the 4,000 known Daumier lithographs, and several proofs, illustrated books, and woodcuts.

Born in Marseilles in 1808, Daumier moved to Paris with his family in 1814, eventually becoming a part of and drawing inspiration from the cosmopolitan scene there. Daumier first used his talents in lithography on behalf of music publishers and advertisers at the young age of thirteen, before quickly expanding into political cartoons and other artistic endeavors. Early in his career, Daumier received work and commissions from two magazines run by Charles Philipon, *La Caricature* and then *Le Charivari*.

While Daumier's star has risen in the art world since his death, he was well known during his lifetime for his sometimes grotesque and otherworldly caricatures of French politicians and various fellow countrymen. In fact, he was once thrown in jail for a controversial cartoon titled *Gargantua*. One example of his tongue-in-cheek portraiture is a lithograph depicting Agricol Perdiguier (1805–1875)—a French socialist politician and a deputy after the 1848 Revolution—who was forced into exile following the rise of Napoleon III in 1851. The caricature lampoons the salary of 25 francs the deputy received, which was an outrageous sum for the day.

Perhaps one of Daumier's most moving and most scathing pieces is an 1871 work captioned (translated from the French) "Other Candidates," in which political candidates come to scavenge on the carcass of a woman, labeled "France." Such seriousness is present in many of Daumier's drawings, paintings, and lithographs and exemplifies his more overtly political work.

Daumier did not, however, maintain a serious facade at all times, and there are examples of his lithographs being employed for less political ends. Among

h. Daumier
Gargantua.
Lith de Delaporte

H.D.
RUE TRANSNONAIN, LE 15 AVRIL 1834

artwork lampooning the French economy and politics, there are lithographs of polkas and poodles. One such piece, *Une Terrible Rencontre*, is a cartoon of an urban family encountering a frog on a walk in the country, the husband shielding his wife and child as though confronted by a monster. While not explicitly political, the image does gently rib the city dwellers of Paris for their increasing alienation from nature as the Industrial Revolution's engines begin to turn.

Alongside Daumier's cartoons and caricatures stand some of the advertisements he created, including one for the magazine *Le Charivari* to help draw in new subscribers. The ad is not without Daumier's token humor, as the title's letters are repeated in a caption, in all capitals, as though one is being shouted at through the image: "VOILLLLLLLLLA! GRRRRRRAND GALOP."

One of Daumier's most famous prints is his *Rue Transnonain, 15 de Avril 1834*, depicting the aftermath of a bloody French National Guard attack on the French citizenry. The controversial lithograph stone was destroyed by the French government, which also did away with as many copies of the prints as it could find. The only duplicates were hidden from the state by Parisians, and Brandeis holds a copy of this rare work.

Description by Max Close, B.A. 2016

BENJAMIN A. AND JULIA M. TRUSTMAN COLLECTION

Michael Lally Civil War Letters

Michael Lally, an immigrant to Massachusetts from Ireland, fought for the Union in more than a dozen major battles of the Civil War, including the first and second Bull Run (Manassas), the Siege of Yorktown, Williamsburg, Fredericksburg, Chancellorsville, and Gettysburg. A soldier in the Eleventh Massachusetts Regiment, Lally wrote letters from Maryland and Virginia to his wife and children in Roxbury, Massachusetts, chronicling his experiences on the front.

Lally's fifty-seven letters in the collection, the first dated July 16, 1861 (just before the first battle of Bull Run), and the last on June 6, 1865 (after Lee's surrender), describe particulars of battle as well as more mundane matters, such as the need for postage stamps, handkerchiefs, a flannel shirt, and whiskey (which, to his great dismay, was removed from one of the boxes sent by his wife). Lally writes often about sending money home and asks for news of the family as well as of friends and neighbors; his letters are sprinkled with prayers for his and his family's safety and words of reassurance.

According to the casualty sheet, Lally was "slightly wounded" on May 5,

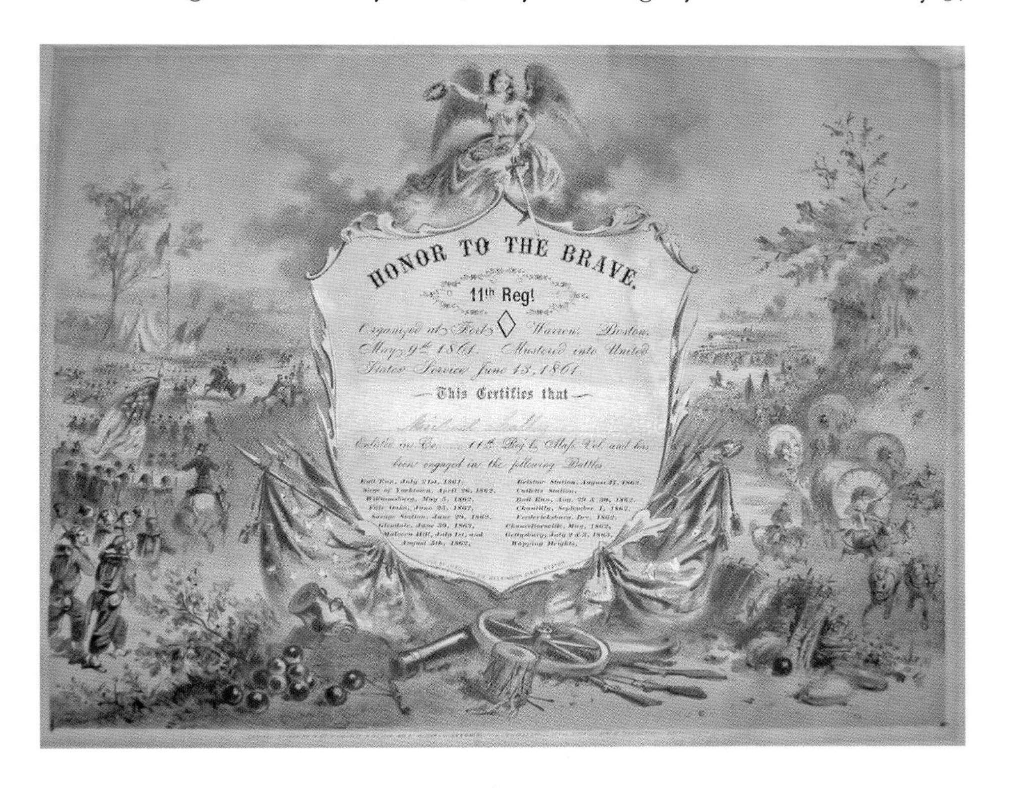

HONOR TO THE BRAVE.

11th Reg!

Organized at Fort ◇ Warren: Boston. May 9th 1861. Mustered into United States Service June 13, 1861.

—This Certifies that—

Enlisted in Co. ... 11th Reg't Mass. Vol. and has been engaged in the following Battles

Bull Run, July 21st, 1861.
Siege of Yorktown, April 26, 1862.
Williamsburg, May 5, 1862.
Fair Oaks, June 25, 1862.
Savage Station, June 29, 1862.
Glendale, June 30, 1862.
Malvern Hill, July 1st, and August 5th, 1862.
Bristow Station, August 27, 1862.
Catletts Station.
Bull Run, Aug. 29 & 30, 1862.
Chantilly, September 1, 1862.
Fredericksburg, Dec. 1862.
Chancellorsville, May, 1862.
Gettysburg, July 2 & 3, 1863.
Wapping Heights.

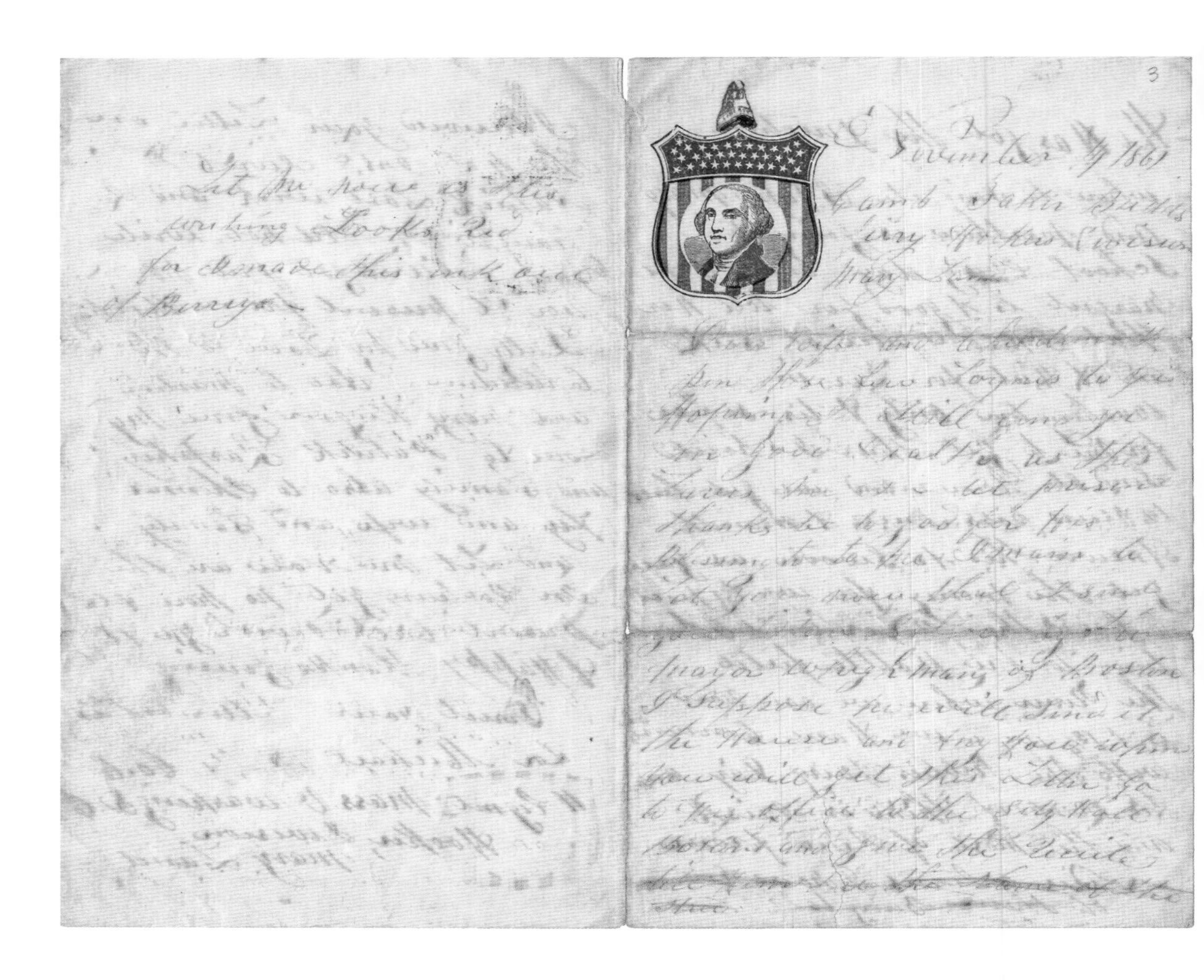

1862, after which he wrote these lines from Williamsburg, Virginia (excerpted from two separate letters):

> Dear wife and children thanks be to God I have the opportunity of writing to ye once more. Hoping that it will find ye in good health as this [leaves] me in at present. Thanks be to God for bringing me safe through the battle on Munday the 5 ins which was a hard day between blood and rain from 7 in the morning till 7 in the eve which I have left a good many of my comrades lying in a desolate condition before night. But thank the Lord for my safety through it. Now I sertantly hope that I will have the pleasure of seeing my little ones once more for I think the back of Sesses is broke now for we have drove them some 30 miles a through the woods, What we did not kill or woond, and the most of our Army is in hot pursuit after them on the Richmond which I think they will make another stand. But our division will not be there for the don their part of the fighting now and as swoon as ye here that Richmond falls and Northfolk the next thing you will here of going

hom playing Patrick's day [?] through Boston. . . . Now I have to rest for I am falling asleep writing these few loynes. I wish ye good look until I see you onc mor

Your Respectly
Michael Lally

A 1961 certificate from the Military Division of the Adjutant General's Office, War Records Section, of the Commonwealth of Massachusetts, states that Lally was enlisted on June 13, 1861, and began active duty as a private in the Army that day: "[W]ounded May 5, 1862, at Williamsburg, Va.; reenlisted March 11, 1864. Active service terminated as Sergeant, Company C, 11th Regt. Mass. Volunteer Infantry on July 14, 1865, Having been honorably mustered out of service."

Lally's letters provide a glimpse into the day-to-day wants, sufferings, triumphs, and small comforts of an ordinary soldier trying to provide for his family and live through the war so that he can join them at home again.

Description by Sarah Shoemaker, head of Archives and Special Collections

DONATED BY MRS. BEATRICE THOMSON IN HONOR OF
MR. AND MRS. EDWARD ROSE

Diary (1859–1886) of William Ayrton

The entries in the earnest and meticulously handwritten diary of William Ayrton ("My Diary of My Mental Life from My Age of 21 and during My Public Life in Business Having left my Native Village in AD 1856 when I was 18 and beginning at Manchester") tell the story of a young man finding his way in life and grappling with the contradictions between his faith and the modern world he sees around him. In one hundred pages, Ayrton transcribes his inner monologue from the age of twenty-one, when he was just starting out in business, to age forty-four, when he has become an ordained deacon with a wife and children.

Much of the diary focuses on Ayrton's relationship with God, and on his struggles to succeed at his work while maintaining a life that adheres to a strict moral and religious code. As the diary opens, the year has just turned 1859, and Ayrton is celebrating his birthday. He outlines what makes a good party and tells of his frustration with having already broken his New Year's resolutions. The diary follows Ayrton as he finds his footing as a clerk and travels for business throughout England, and, at one point, to France.

Two particularly interesting moments describe the intersection of Ayrton's life with major public figures and events. In one entry he writes of running into Charles Dickens on the street, and later, in a subsequent account, he describes getting caught up with the Paris Commune uprising. On page 84, he tells of how this began: "I happened to lodge in a house where there was another man lodging who, I sometime after, found he was connected with the Revolutionists."

Ayrton is a great observer of those around him: "As my great subject in all my experience of life, has always been to observe earnestly and interestedly the various circumstances of the population, wherever I might be so that I might notice and learn all the various doubts, difficulties, and problems of life, and also all their conduct, with regard to the natural world, the Universe and their own humanity."

Ultimately, Ayrton is searching for the meaning of life, something which he professes to find though does not explain in this diary: "I never heard from any leaders and teachers, a real correct, and complete solution of the problem of life. It thus naturally enforced itself upon me for a thorough solution, and ever remained in a prominent position in my mind. I was thus mentally compelled to solve it for myself in A.D. 1886 in Manchester, when I had been appointed a Churchwarden, at St. Clements Church in Greenheys."

Lamartine on his Mothers Diary. —

"It was the household history of the day, the annals of the passing hour, the fugitive recollections of facts and impressions seized in their flight, and arrested in their course, before the night should disperse them for ever; happy or unfortunate dates, inward events, the fall of the sands of time arrested in the hour glass, outpourings of anxiety or sadness, bursts of gratitude and joy, prayers ascending still warm from the heart to GOD, all the vibrating chords of a nature that lives, that loves, that rejoices, that suffers, blesses, invokes, adores, in one word, a written "Seal."

(also see the preface to his "Memoirs of my Youth." by his Mother)

My Diary.
OF
My Mental Life.
FROM
My Age of 21
AND DURING
My Public Life in Business
Having left my Native Village
in AD 1856 when I was 18
and beginning at
MANCHESTER.

and merited punishment. Therefore, be cautious, patient, teachable, respectful to elders, and discreet persons. No studies, or readings answered several letters, therefore I retired — with hopes and aspiration for Improvement.

February 23rd. Rose at 7.30, in slothfulness, wandering and distracting thoughts. No French or Elocution till evening. I read Beard's "Self Culture", Lamartine's "Voyage" for an hour, then retired at X. 45. ———

Wilcox. Advice on **ACTION.**

" Do something; do it soon! with all thy might;"
"An angel's wing would droop, if long at rest;"
"And GOD inactive, were no longer blest."
" Some high or humble enterprise of "Good" "
" Contemplate, till it shall possess thy mind, "
" Become thy study, pastime, rest, and food, "
" And kindle in thy heart a flame refined; "
" Pray heaven for firmness, thy whole soul to bind "
" To this high purpose; to begin, pursue, "
" With thoughts all fixed, feelings purely kind; "
" Strength to complete, and with delight review, "
" And Strength to give the praise where all is due "

My General Course, — now to be Pursued. ——

TIME.	DUTIES.
A.M. 4.	Rise.
4. to 5.	Wash, dress, Exercise, Devotions.
5. to 7.	Business study. French and others.
7. to 8.	General Culture. Physiology.
8. to 9.	Breakfast, private business, or general culture exercise
9. to 12.	My daily labour.
P.M. 12. to 1½.	Dinner, private business, or general culture exercise.
1½. to 7.	My daily labour.
7. to 8½.	Tea. private business. general culture, exercise.
8½. to 9½.	Business study. French. Translation Tuitions.
9½. to 10.	Diary. Devotions. then to Rest and sleep.

February 24th Rose at 7. In better spirits, through rising earlier. studying French then to business, nothing particular to be remarked. From Mr James conduct in "E"s* case; those who are often the readiest at threatening and bullying, are the soonest cowed when opposed. Therefore be kind, civil and thoughtful and respectful to all, and beware of rash words. Met with Cousin Thexton at home, at 9, tea, and study until X.30. and

* a trade traveller

While Ayrton's language leans toward the stiff and formal, his style of writing belies the open and unflinching way in which he bares his soul. Readers can reflect on this man's thorough examination of his own self and watch how, between descriptions of his business affairs and his frequent exhortations to God, he does battle with his lesser inclinations.

Description by Surella Evanor Seelig, M.A. 2005,
Outreach and Special Projects archivist

PURCHASED WITH A GRANT FROM THE
ANN AND ABE EFFRON FUND

Paris Commune Posters

"Liberté, Equalité, Fraternité"—the motto of the French Republic, from its origins in the French Revolution to official adoption during the Third Republic—was appropriated by both the government at Versailles and the coalition of revolutionary Communards to publicize the events of the 1871 Paris Commune. The short-lived revolutionary government body was formed in Paris upon France's defeat in the Franco-Prussian War and the undoing of Napoleon III's Second Empire. The posters displayed during that time proclaimed orders and communiqués as well as information and propaganda relating to the military and political events of the uprising.

The defeat of the French army and the capture of Emperor Louis Napoleon Bonaparte in the battle at Sedan in September 1870 came after desperate and bloody fighting led by Prussian Field Marshal Helmuth von Moltke and King Wilhelm I. It accorded the French Republicans the opportunity to depose Louis Napoleon and bring an end to the Second Empire. Committed (at least at first) to carrying on the war, a new republic was declared at Versailles before German forces occupied a significant proportion of French territory, including the contested border region of Alsace-Lorraine, and laid siege to Paris. The "Government of National Defense" at Versailles soon realized the hopelessness of its situation and renewed armistice talks with the newly declared German Empire.

As rumors of the negotiations trickled into Paris, left-wing groups, including the socialist followers of Louis-Auguste Blanqui and radical Republicans (Jacobins), began to organize resistance to the armistice with the support of the National Guard, the citizens' militia of Paris. Distrust of the Versailles government—dominated by monarchists and suspected of planning to restore the monarchy—spurred the revolutionaries. In response to efforts by the Versailles government to disarm the National Guard and pacify Paris, a council calling itself the Central Committee of the National Guard prepared to defend the city. From early April to late May 1871, the Communards battled troops loyal to the government. The bloody repression of the insurrection by government troops and the execution of its leaders followed.

Of the seven posters associated with notable events in the history of the Commune, one details the first outbreak of violence, on April 2, 1871, framing it as an act of aggression by "royalist conspirators," who, "unable to count on the French army, have ATTACKED with Papal zouaves [soldiers] and Imperial police." The message concludes by pledging that "Elected by the population of Paris, our duty

RÉPUBLIQUE FRANÇAISE

N° 54 LIBERTÉ — ÉGALITÉ — FRATERNITÉ N° 54

COMMUNE DE PARIS

A LA GARDE NATIONALE

DE PARIS

Les conspirateurs royalistes ont ATTAQUÉ.

Malgré la modération de notre attitude, ils ont ATTAQUÉ.

Ne pouvant plus compter sur l'armée française, ils ont ATTAQUÉ avec les zouaves pontificaux et la police impériale.

Non contents de couper les correspondances avec la province et de faire de vains efforts pour nous réduire par la famine, ces furieux ont voulu imiter jusqu'au bout les Prussiens et bombarder la capitale.

Ce matin, les chouans de Charette, les Vendéens de Cathelineau, les Bretons de Trochu, flanqués des gendarmes de Valentin, ont couvert de mitraille et d'obus le village inoffensif de Neuilly et engagé la guerre civile avec nos gardes nationaux.

Il y a eu des morts et des blessés.

Élus par la population de Paris, notre devoir est de défendre la grande cité contre ces coupables agresseurs. Avec votre aide, nous la défendrons.

Paris, 2 avril 1871.

La Commission exécutive :

BERGERET, EUDES, DUVAL, LEFRANÇAIS, Félix PYAT, G. TRIDON, E. VAILLANT.

is to defend the great city [la grande cité] against the guilty aggressors. With your help, we will defend it."

A poster from the last days of the uprising announces plans of the Commune's leadership to confiscate the home and property of Adolphe Thiers, leader of the Versailles government. With the action to be carried out on May 13, the declaration itemizes what is to be done with Thiers's property, from sending art objects and precious books to national libraries and museums, to appropriating linen for use by ambulances, to establishing a public park on the grounds of the residence.

In the end the Communards did not prevail. Since then, the Commune has held special importance for political theorists of the left, perhaps most notably Karl Marx, who viewed the events as the first historical example of rule by the working class.

Description by Drew Flanagan, M.A. 2011, PH.D. 2018

RÉPUBLIQUE FRANÇAISE

N° 329 LIBERTE — EGALITÉ — FRATERNITE N° 329

COMMUNE DE PARIS

DIRECTION DES DOMAINES

Sur la délibération approuvée du Comité de Salut public, le citoyen Jules Fontaine, Directeur général des Domaines,

En réponse aux larmes et aux menaces de Thiers, le bombardeur, et aux lois édictées par l'Assemblée rurale, sa complice,

ARRÊTE :

ARTICLE PREMIER.

Tout le linge provenant de la maison Thiers sera mis à la disposition des ambulances.

ART. 2.

Les objets d'art et livres précieux seront envoyés aux bibliothèques et musées nationaux.

ART. 3.

Le mobilier sera vendu aux enchères, après exposition publique au garde-meuble.

ART. 4.

Le produit de cette vente restera uniquement affecté aux pensions et indemnités qui devront être fournies aux veuves et orphelins des victimes de la guerre infâme que nous fait l'ex-propriétaire de l'hôtel Georges.

ART. 5.

Même destination sera donnée à l'argent que rapporteront les matériaux de démolition.

ART. 6.

Sur le terrain de l'hôtel du parricide sera établi un square public.

Paris, 25 floréal an 79.

Le Directeur général des Domaines,

J. FONTAINE.

IMPRIMERIE NATIONALE. — Mai 1871.

Buffalo Bill Dime Novels

Buffalo Bill (né William Cody) was already a legendary figure and bona fide international celebrity by the time the Buffalo Bill dime novels were published at the turn of the last century. First introduced in 1860 by Beadle & Adams, the dime novel exploited cheap printing, newly efficient distribution, and a broader reading public hungry for sensational yarns involving detectives, cowboys, and romantic heroines. America's move toward mass-market publishing is well represented through the more than one thousand items in the Brandeis dime-novel collection.

The *Buffalo Bill Stories*, for instance, present the reader with a wellspring of enduring iconography and storytelling tropes. After stints as a cattle driver, teamster, innkeeper, and military scout, Cody found his calling as a guide to wealthy Easterners desiring a "true" experience of the West and caught the eye of Ned Buntline, an early dime-novel impresario who prevailed upon Cody to play himself in a Chicago stage melodrama called *Scouts of the Prairie* in 1873. Cody soon formed his own touring company, and from there it was a few short steps to Buffalo Bill's Wild West, a popular pageant of historical melodrama and spectacular displays of marksmanship, riding, and other feats of derring-do.

Authenticity was a key element of the Wild West's publicity machine: Eastern audiences could see skirmishes reenacted by actors well before the actual conflicts had been settled. The cycle of history, performance, and myth could become quite dizzying, as when Cody interrupted a Wild West tour to join up with the Fifth Cavalry at the first news of Custer's Last Stand.

Given this backdrop, it's hardly surprising that many of the issues of the *Buffalo Bill Stories* should come with a prefatory note admonishing the reader to "Beware of Wild West imitations of the Buffalo Bill stories. They are about fictitious characters. The Buffalo Bill weekly is the only weekly containing the adventures of Buffalo Bill, (Col. W.F. Cody), who is known all over the world as the king of the scouts."

This air of realism extends to the back matter, featuring how-to guides of dubious practicality to the largely urban readership ("How to Tie a Wire") and pseudo-ethnographic excursions ("The False-Face Dance").

If the dime novels were somewhat late arrivals to the burgeoning Wild West industry, their cover illustrations and dialogue-rich scenarios provided a crucial link between the touring circuit and the coming nickelodeon boom. With an emphasis on action and heroic figures, the genre proved natural fodder for the new medium—even as early Westerns like *The Great Train Robbery* (1903) were filmed

No. 418
MAY 15, 1909
BUFFALO BILL AT BABYLON BAR
or THE MOUNTAIN PIRATES
FIVE CENTS
THE BUFFALO BILL STORIES
A Weekly Publication devoted to Border History
"Cheat a forlorn an' lone woman with yer thieving tricks, will ye?" screamed the irate female as she belabored the tall Yankee who had been running the shell game. "Well, you'll find, Mister, that I'm able ter pertect myself."
Street & Smith Publishers New York

BUFFALO BILL STORIES

ISSUED EVERY TUESDAY **BEAUTIFUL COLORED COVERS**

There is no need of our telling American readers how interesting the stories of the adventures of Buffalo Bill, as scout and plainsman, really are. These stories have been read exclusively in this weekly for many years, and are voted to be masterpieces dealing with Western adventure.

Buffalo Bill is more popular to-day than he ever was, and, consequently, everybody ought to know all there is to know about him. In no manner can you become so thoroughly acquainted with the actual habits and life of this great man, as by reading the BUFFALO BILL STORIES.

We give herewith a list of all of the back numbers in print. You can have your news-dealer order them or they will be sent direct by the publishers to any address upon receipt of the price in money or postage-stamps.

162—Buffalo Bill's Canyon Cache 5
177—Buffalo Bill in Morenci 5
210—Buffalo Bill's Blind Lead 5
211—Buffalo Bill's Sacrifice 5
212—Buffalo Bill's Prison Feud 5
213—Buffalo Bill's Diamond Hunt 5
214—Buffalo Bill's Avenging Hand 5
217—Buffalo Bill's Cheyenne Comrades 5
218—Buffalo Bill's Fiery Trail 5
219—Buffalo Bill's Sioux Foes 5
221—Buffalo Bill's Iron Fist 5
223—Buffalo Bill's Florida Foes 5
224—Buffalo Bill's Grim Climb 5
225—Buffalo Bill's Red Enemy 5
226—Buffalo Bill on a Traitor's Track 5
228—Buffalo Bill's Air Voyage 5
229—Buffalo Bill's Death Thrust 5
230—Buffalo Bill's Kiowa Foe 5
232—Buffalo Bill's Wyoming Trail 5
235—Buffalo Bill's Apache Round-up 5
236—Buffalo Bill's El Paso Pard 5
237—Buffalo Bill on the Staked Plains 5
238—Buffalo Bill's Border Raid 5
239—Buffalo Bill's Bravest Fight 5
240—Buffalo Bill's Heathen Pard 5
241—Buffalo Bill's Dakota Dare-devils 5
242—Buffalo Bill's Arapahoe Alliance 5
243—Buffalo Bill on Special Service 5
244—Buffalo Bill on a Treasure Hunt 5
245—Buffalo Bill's Lost Quarry 5
246—Buffalo Bill Among the Comanches 5
247—Buffalo Bill's Stockade Siege 5
248—Buffalo Bill's Creek Quarrel 5
249—Buffalo Bill Among the Pawnees 5
250—Buffalo Bill on a Long Hunt 5
251—Buffalo Bill's Wyoming Trail 5
252—Buffalo Bill and the Redskin Wizard 5
253—Buffalo Bill's Bold Challenge 5
254—Buffalo Bill's Shawnee Stampede 5
255—Buffalo Bill's Worst Foe 5
256—Buffalo Bill on a Desert Trail 5
257—Buffalo Bill's Rio Grande Feud 5
258—Buffalo Bill in Tight Quarters 5
259—Buffalo Bill's Daring Rescue 5
261—Buffalo Bill's Treasure Train 5
262—Buffalo Bill Among the Blackfeet 5
263—Buffalo Bill's Border Beagles 5
264—Buffalo Bill and the Bandits in Black 5
265—Buffalo Bill and the Indian Tiger 5
266—Buffalo Bill on the Deadwood Trail 5
267—Buffalo Bill in the Cañon of Death 5
269—Buffalo Bill and the Robber Ranch King 5
270—Buffalo Bill in the Land of Wonders 5
271—Buffalo Bill and the Traitor Soldier 5
272—Buffalo Bill's Dusky Trailers 5
273—Buffalo Bill's Diamond Mine 5
274—Buffalo Bill and the Pawnee Serpent 5
275—Buffalo Bill's Scarlet Hand 5
276—Buffalo Bill Running the Gantlet 5
277—Buffalo Bill's Leap in the Dark 5
278—Buffalo Bill's Daring Plunge 5
280—Buffalo Bill's Ghost Raid 5
282—Buffalo Bill's Camp-fires 5
283—Buffalo Bill Up a Stump 5
284—Buffalo Bill's Secret Foe 5
285—Buffalo Bill's Master-stroke 5
286—Buffalo Bill and the Masked Mystery 5
287—Buffalo Bill and the Brazos Terror 5
288—Buffalo Bill's Dance of Death 5
289—Buffalo Bill and the Creeping Terror 5
290—Buffalo Bill and the Brand of Cain 5
291—Buffalo Bill and the Mad Millionaire 5
292—Buffalo Bill's Medicine-lodge 5
293—Buffalo Bill in Peril 5
295—Buffalo Bill in the Death Desert 5
296—Buffalo Bill in No Man's Land 5
297—Buffalo Bill's Border Ruffians 5
298—Buffalo Bill's Black Eagles 5
299—Buffalo Bill's Desperate Dozen 5
300—Buffalo Bill's Rival 5
301—Buffalo Bill's Ice Chase 5
302—Buffalo Bill and the Boy Bugler 5
303—Buffalo Bill and the White Specter 5
304—Buffalo Bill's Death Defiance 5
305—Buffalo Bill and the Barge Bandits 5
306—Buffalo Bill, the Desert Hotspur 5
307—Buffalo Bill's Wild Range Riders 5
308—Buffalo Bill's Whirlwind Chase 5
309—Buffalo Bill's Red Retribution 5
310—Buffalo Bill Haunted 5
311—Buffalo Bill's Fight for Life 5
312—Buffalo Bill's Death Jump 5
313—Buffalo Bill and the Pit of Horror 5
314—Buffalo Bill in the Jaws of Death 5
315—Buffalo Bill's Aztec Runners 5
316—Buffalo Bill's Dance with Death 5
318—Buffalo Bill's Fiery Eye 5
319—Buffalo Bill's Mazeppa Ride 5
320—Buffalo Bill in the Land of Spirits 5
321—Buffalo Bill's Gypsy Band 5
322—Buffalo Bill's Maverick 5
323—Buffalo Bill, the White Whirlwind 5
324—Buffalo Bill's Gold Hunters 5
325—Buffalo Bill in Old Mexico 5
326—Buffalo Bill's Message from the Dead 5
327—Buffalo Bill and the Wolf-master 5
328—Buffalo Bill's Flying Wonder 5
329—Buffalo Bill's Hidden Gold 5
330—Buffalo Bill's Outlaw Trail 5
331—Buffalo Bill and the Indian Queen 5
332—Buffalo Bill and the Mad Marauder 5
333—Buffalo Bill's Ice Barricade 5
334—Buffalo Bill and the Robber Elk 5
335—Buffalo Bill's Ghost Dance 5
336—Buffalo Bill's Peace-pipe 5
337—Buffalo Bill's Red Nemesis 5
338—Buffalo Bill's Enchanted Mesa 5
339—Buffalo Bill in the Desert of Death 5
340—Buffalo Bill's Pay Streak 5
341—Buffalo Bill on Detached Duty 5
342—Buffalo Bill's Army Mystery 5
343—Buffalo Bill's Surprise Party 5
344—Buffalo Bill's Great Ride 5
345—Buffalo Bill's Water Trail 5
346—Buffalo Bill's Ordeal of Fire 5
347—Buffalo Bill Among the Man-eaters 5
348—Buffalo Bill's Casket of Pearls 5
349—Buffalo Bill's Sky Pilot 5
350—Buffalo Bill's "Totem" 5
351—Buffalo Bill's Flat-boat Drift 5
352—Buffalo Bill on Deck 5
353—Buffalo Bill and the Bronco Buster 5
354—Buffalo Bill's Great Round-up 5
355—Buffalo Bill's Pledge 5
356—Buffalo Bill's Cowboy Pard 5
357—Buffalo Bill and the Emigrants 5
358—Buffalo Bill Among the Pueblos 5
359—Buffalo Bill's Four-footed Pards 5
360—Buffalo Bill's Protégé 5
362—Buffalo Bill's Pick-up 5
363—Buffalo Bill's Quest 5
364—Buffalo Bill's Wolf of the Plains 5
366—Buffalo Bill Among the Mormons 5
367—Buffalo Bill's Assistance 5
368—Buffalo Bill's Rattlesnake Trail 5
369—Buffalo Bill and the Slave-Dealers 5
370—Buffalo Bill's Strong Arm 5
371—Buffalo Bill's Girl Pard 5
372—Buffalo Bill's Iron Bracelets 5
373—Buffalo Bill's Ranch Riders 5
374—Buffalo Bill's Jade Amulet 5
375—Buffalo Bill's Magic Lariat 5
376—Buffalo Bill's "Paper-Talk" 5
377—Buffalo Bill's Bridge of Fire 5
378—Buffalo Bill's Bowie 5
379—Buffalo Bill's Pay-streak 5
380—Buffalo Bill's Mine 5
381—Buffalo Bill's Clean-up 5
382—Buffalo Bill's Ruse 5
383—Buffalo Bill Overboard 5
384—Buffalo Bill's Ring 5
385—Buffalo Bill's Big Contract 5
386—Buffalo Bill and Calamity Jane 5
387—Buffalo Bill's Kid Pard 5
388—Buffalo Bill's Desperate Plight 5
389—Buffalo Bill's Fearless Stand 5
390—Buffalo Bill and the Yelping Crew 5
391—Buffalo Bill's Guiding Hand 5
392—Buffalo Bill's Queer Quest 5
393—Buffalo Bill's Prize "Getaway" 5
394—Buffalo Bill's Hurricane Hustle 5
395—Buffalo Bill's Star Play 5
396—Buffalo Bill's Bluff 5
397—Buffalo Bill's Trackers 5
398—Buffalo Bill's Dutch Pard 5
399—Buffalo Bill and the Bravo 5
400—Buffalo Bill and the Quaker 5
401—Buffalo Bill's Package of Death 5
402—Buffalo Bill's Treasure Cache 5
403—Buffalo Bill's Private War 5
404—Buffalo Bill and the Trouble Hunter 5
405—Buffalo Bill and the Rope Wizard 5
406—Buffalo Bill's Fiesta 5
407—Buffalo Bill Among the Cheyennes 5
408—Buffalo Bill Besieged 5
409—Buffalo Bill and the Red Hand 5
410—Buffalo Bill's Tree-trunk Drift 5
411—Buffalo Bill and the Specter 5
412—Buffalo Bill and the Red Feathers 5
413—Buffalo Bill's King Stroke 5
414—Buffalo Bill, the Desert Cyclone 5
415—Buffalo Bill's Cumbres Scouts 5
416—Buffalo Bill and the Man-wolf 5
417—Buffalo Bill and His Winged Pard 5
418—Buffalo Bill at Babylon Bar 5
419—Buffalo Bill's Long Arm 5
420—Buffalo Bill and Old Weasel Top 5
421—Buffalo Bill's Steel Arm Pard 5
422—Buffalo Bill's Aztec Guide 5
423—Buffalo Bill and Little Firefly 5
424—Buffalo Bill in the Aztec City 5
425—Buffalo Bill's Balloon Escape 5
426—Buffalo Bill and the Guerrillas 5
427—Buffalo Bill's Border War 5
428—Buffalo Bill's Mexican Mix-up 5
429—Buffalo Bill and the Gamecock 5
430—Buffalo Bill and the Cheyenne Raiders 5
431—Buffalo Bill's Whirlwind Finish 5
432—Buffalo Bill's Santa Fe Secret 5
433—Buffalo Bill and the Taos Terror 5
434—Buffalo Bill's Bracelet of Gold 5
435—Buffalo Bill and the Border Baron 5
436—Buffalo Bill at Salt River Ranch 5
437—Buffalo Bill's Panhandle Man-hunt 5
438—Buffalo Bill at Blossom Range 5
439—Buffalo Bill and Juniper Joe 5
440—Buffalo Bill's Final Scoop 5
441—Buffalo Bill at Clearwater 5

If you want any back numbers of our weeklies and cannot procure them from your news-dealer, they can be obtained direct from this office. Postage-stamps taken the same as money.

STREET & SMITH, PUBLISHERS, 79-89 SEVENTH AVE., NEW YORK CITY

no farther west than New Jersey. In the cover illustrations of the *Buffalo Bill Stories* we find the basic repertoire of gestures and compositional framings familiar from thousands of Western movies. Cody's body is invariably outstretched, and the corresponding text boxes offer a complementary burst of excitable talk ("'Up with that left hand of yours, quick, Death Notch Dick, or my bullet hunts your heart!' cried Buffalo Bill"). Even in those illustrations not depicting daring rescues, action remains paramount. Take the cover of Number 418 (May 15, 1909), in which the only weapon being brandished is the umbrella of an "irate female."

Cody would find himself on the sidelines when the film medium encroached upon his territory. His 1913 film epic, *The Indian Wars*, was by all accounts a flop, and Cody eventually fell back upon a series of ill-advised business ventures and cut-rate performances. So, too, did the dime novels give way to the neatly packaged narratives available via radio and cinema. But even with their all-but-inevitable obsolescence, the issues of the *Buffalo Bill Stories* remain not only as fascinating objects in themselves but as documents of a popular culture still very much with us.

Description by Max Goldberg, Archives and Special Collections reference assistant, 2014

BUILT WITH MAJOR DONATIONS BY EDWARD G. LEVY, EDWARD T. LEBLANC, AND FORMER SPECIAL COLLECTIONS LIBRARIAN VICTOR BERCH (M.A. 1966)

Louis Dembitz Brandeis Collection

With a wealth of primary-source materials relating to the university's namesake and his immediate family, the Louis D. Brandeis Collection offers an array of documents on American legal history, the progressive and Zionist movements, the U.S. Supreme Court, and the founding and early years of Brandeis University. The files chronicle the development of Brandeis's political, legal, and intellectual views and include early-edition copies of many of his most famous publications and speeches.

Personal correspondence provides insights into Brandeis's relationships with his wife, Alice, and children, Susan and Elizabeth. A committed writer, Brandeis penned several letters on most days; they were brief and pragmatic but often contained interesting observations on contemporary events. The papers of Susan Brandeis and her husband, Jacob Gilbert, reflect their own activities in American Zionism and the creation of Brandeis University, while the files of Elizabeth Brandeis and her husband, Paul Rauschenbusch, are small but provide important glimpses of the family history.

Louis Brandeis was born in Louisville, Kentucky, on November 13, 1856. His parents, Adolph and Frederika, were Bohemian Jews from Prague who had immigrated to America in 1848 following the wave of revolutions across Europe. Adolph proved a successful businessman, and the young Louis grew up in relative comfort. After a three-year trip to Europe with his family, during which he attended classes in Dresden, Brandeis returned to America in 1875 and enrolled at Harvard Law School at the age of nineteen. His decision to embark on a legal career was influenced by his uncle, Louisville attorney Lewis Dembitz, whom Brandeis would later honor by adopting his name. Brandeis excelled academically, graduating from Harvard in 1877 as the law school valedictorian. The collection holds several notebooks from his time at Harvard that illustrate the development of his legal thinking there.

After graduation, Brandeis spent a brief stint practicing law in St. Louis, Missouri, before returning to Boston in 1879 and founding the Warren & Brandeis law firm with Harvard classmate Samuel Warren. With the success of the firm (it continues today as Nutter McClennen and Fish), Brandeis's own reputation as a litigator grew.

In December 1890, Brandeis and Warren published "The Right to Privacy" in the *Harvard Law Review*. Observing that photography and other recent innovations had diminished the level of protection accorded individuals' private lives, they claimed the law should recognize and police the boundary between the public and the private. A similar devotion to "the right to be let alone" later led Brandeis to his famous dissent in *Olmstead v. United States* (1922), in which he argued that warrantless government wiretaps violated the U.S. Constitution's Fourth and Fifth Amendments. This dissent became a touchstone of modern privacy jurisprudence.

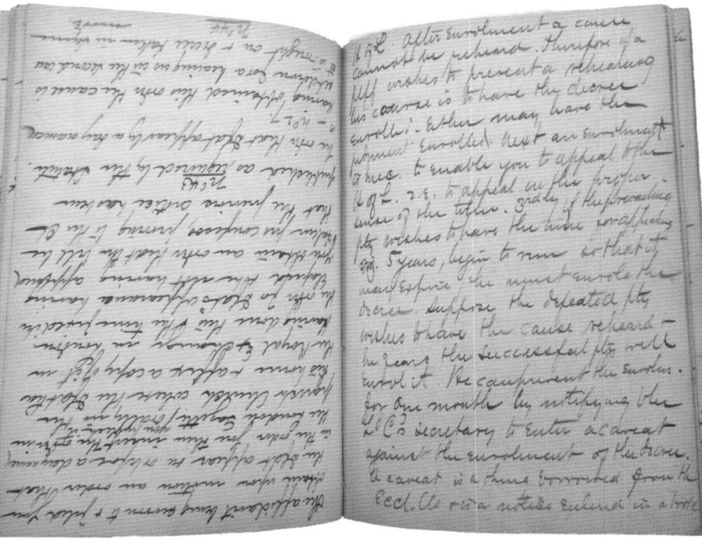

Form followed function in Brandeis's litigation practice, as he introduced the use of extensive social science information as an integral part of appellate briefs. This innovative technique reflected Brandeis's faith in the scientific study and control of social forces. Using information compiled by his sister-in-law Josephine Goldmark, Brandeis first employed what became known as the "Brandeis Brief" in *Muller v. Oregon* (1908), a decision that upheld hours regulations for female workers based in part on evidence that long workweeks had deleterious effects on women.

Brandeis later attracted national attention when he successfully fought J.P. Morgan's attempted monopolistic merger of New England railroad companies. The collection boasts hundreds of pages of material (much of it handwritten) on his crusade against the New England railroad merger.

Increasing fame and his strong support for Democrat Woodrow Wilson's presidential candidacy in 1912 led Brandeis to help shape Wilson's "New Freedom" agenda. This service was rewarded in 1916 when President Wilson nominated Brandeis to the U.S. Supreme Court. The selection proved politically divisive, with Brandeis's Jewish background and social activism working against him. The confirmation hearings were testy and infused with a palpable antisemitism in some quarters. Nevertheless, Brandeis was confirmed by a Senate vote of 47–22.

Once he arrived on the court, Brandeis carved out a unique place in America's judicial canon. Along with his friend and fellow associate justice Oliver Wendell

Holmes, Jr., he crafted several notable dissenting opinions designed to protect the First Amendment free-speech rights of political dissidents. Brandeis wrote several important opinions that developed an increasingly sophisticated set of procedures governing the federal court system. In the most famous of these opinions, *Erie Railroad Co. v. Tompkins* (1938), Brandeis fundamentally altered the balance of judicial federalism in America by reversing nearly a century of precedent in holding that federal courts could not create their own judge-made rules and had, instead, to defer to state court judgments on such matters.

Brandeis's record on racial issues presented to the court was arguably more ambiguous and less distinguished. While his voting patterns showed a clear aversion to racially biased criminal trials, he twice voted with the majority in upholding "all-white" primaries. He also sided with the majority in cases upholding denials of U.S. citizenship to persons of Japanese and Indian ancestry, and he voted to sustain "separate-but-equal" educational facilities for students on the basis of race.

The collection includes first-print copies of several of Brandeis's Supreme Court opinions, many bearing his handwritten editorial comments, in cases as diverse as those dealing with Native American affairs, commercial law, antitrust regulation, probate law, immigration and naturalization, property, and free speech.

Throughout his career, Brandeis devoted increasing amounts of his attention and time to supporting progressive social and economic causes, and to pro bono work as "the people's attorney." This commitment continued during his tenure on the bench. While he had been largely disinterested in Judaism in his youth, the antisemitism he suffered as he became an increasingly public figure, coupled with his professional involvement with Jewish groups, led to an interest in Zionism. He eventually became a leader in the movement to establish a Jewish state and continued to press the Zionist cause throughout his judicial career and for the rest of his life.

In January 1931, New York Zionist Abraham Sakier proposed to Brandeis the idea of "an American strictly secular first-class university whose faculty and student body shall be predominantly Jewish. . . . [T]he name of this university," Sakier suggested, "should be the 'Brandeis University,' because you are the greatest Jew in the history of this country." Brandeis appears to have balked at the idea, as indicated in a later follow-up letter from Sakier preserved in the collection.

In 1932, at the age of eighty-two, Brandeis retired from the bench. Spending much of his remaining time at his vacation home in Chatham, Massachusetts, he continued to correspond with and advise influential figures. He died from a heart attack in Washington, D.C., on October 5, 1941.

On May 14, 1948, the State of Israel was established. The university that bears the Brandeis name enrolled its first class in September of that year.

Description by Winston Bowman, M.A. 2011, PH.D. 2015

The Recuyell of the Historyes of Troye and the Kelmscott Press

One of the most beautiful books Brandeis owns is the Kelmscott Press edition of *The Recuyell of the Historyes of Troye* by Raoul Le Fèvre. When William Caxton first printed the *Recuyell* in Bruges in 1473–1474, it became the world's first printed English book. William Morris's decision to bring it out in the second year of the Kelmscott Press—and the way that he and his team produced the book—makes a remarkable story. It sheds light not only on the Arts and Crafts movement but also on the entire history of modern bookmaking, which was born with one eye on history and the other glued to the latest technology.

The story of this spectacular book begins on November 15, 1888, when Morris went to a slide lecture by the skilled typographer Emery Walker at the Arts and Crafts Society. That night changed Morris's life—and the course of the modern book arts. It was on that night that he saw a series of brilliantly colored magic-lantern slides of *photographs* of illuminated books, projected through one of the powerful gas lanterns that were soon to revolutionize bookmaking as well as the study of art history. It was not the pages themselves but seeing how well these modern enlargements and illuminations conveyed the beauty of the originals that decided Morris. The following morning he went to visit Walker and the provisional plans for the press were drawn up; less than three years later, in January 1891, the first book was printed, a copy of Morris's own medieval-inspired romance, *The Story of the Glittering Plain*.

William Morris, writer, designer, socialist, and founder of the Arts and Crafts movement, is the most talented and influential of those polymaths who flourished in the age of Darwin. Like Darwin, there was little he was not interested in and almost nothing he did not turn his hand to. Stained glass, house design, furniture, fabrics, and wallpapers are only a few of the "lesser arts" that he mastered.

Morris has been called the father of modern design. Although his theories went on to become the basis of modern design, and perhaps one of the key foundations of modernist art generally, he was history-obsessed in a way that few who followed him were. Morris looked backward to medieval and early modern workers for inspiration, not because they were made authoritative by the gap of centuries that yawned between, but because their struggles with their medium impressed him, as an artist, as the finest kind of aesthetic effort. His credo—

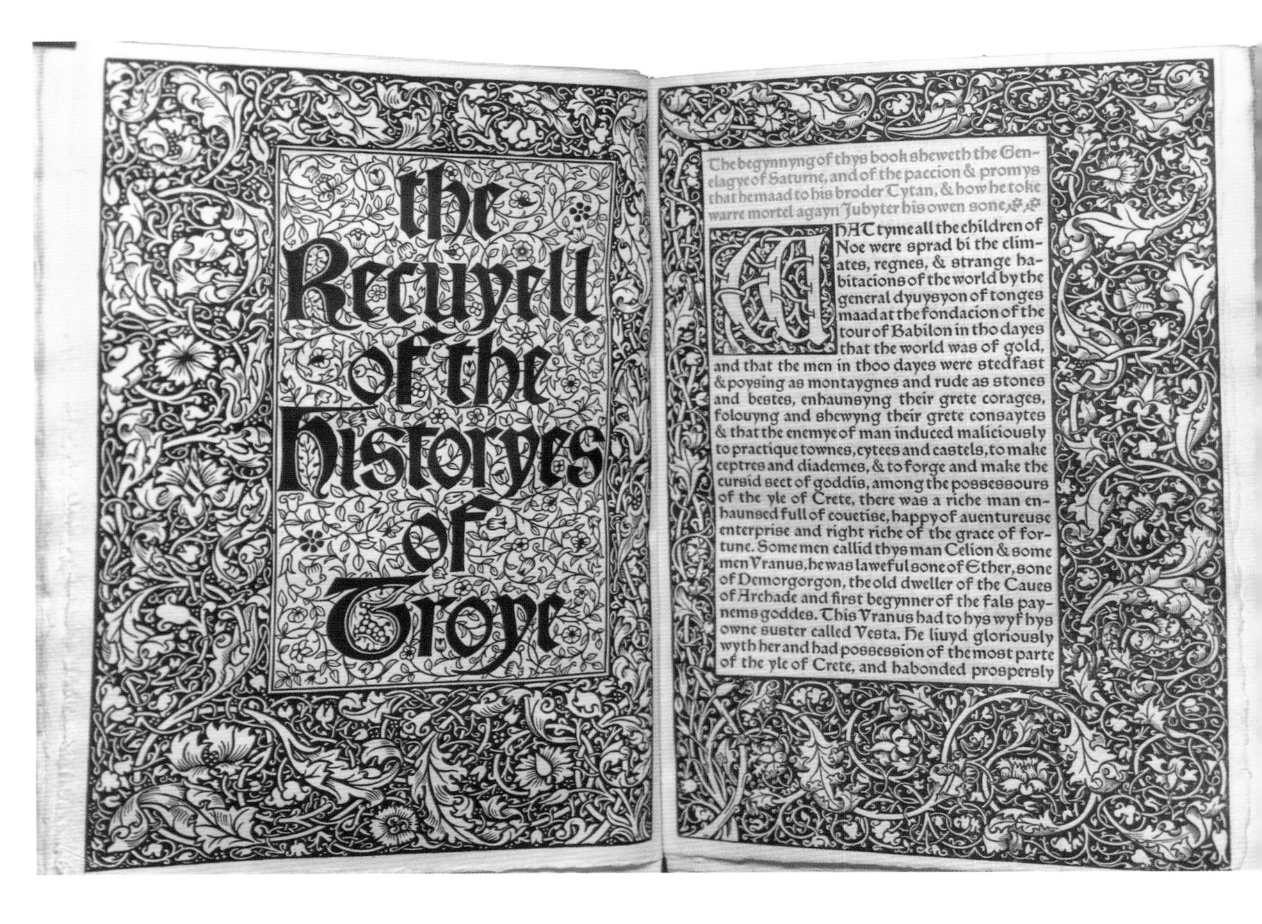

the Recuyell of the Historyes of Troye

The begynnyng of thys book sheweth the Genelagye of Saturne, and of the paccion & promys that he maad to his broder Tytan, & how he toke warre mortel agayn Jubyter his owen sone.

WHAT tyme all the children of Noe were sprad bi the climates, regnes, & strange habitacions of the world by the general dyuysyon of tonges maad at the fondacion of the tour of Babilon in tho dayes that the world was of gold, and that the men in thoo dayes were stedfast & poysing as montaygnes and rude as stones and bestes, enhaunsyng their grete corages, folouyng and shewyng their grete consaytes & that the enemye of man induced maliciously to practique townes, cytees and castels, to make ceptres and diademes, & to forge and make the cursid sect of goddis, among the possessours of the yle of Crete, there was a riche man enhaunsed full of couetise, happy of auentureuse enterprise and right riche of the grace of fortune. Some men callid thys man Celion & some men Vranus, he was laweful sone of Ether, sone of Demorgorgon, the old dweller of the Caues of Archade and first begynner of the fals paynems goddes. This Vranus had to hys wyf hys owne suster called Vesta. He liuyd gloriously wyth her and had possession of the most parte of the yle of Crete, and habonded prospersly

"Have around you nothing that you do not know to be useful or believe to be beautiful"—remains an inspiration.

He was also the de facto leader of English socialism during the unhappy late 1880s, when a string of disappointments, internal divisions, and brutal government clampdowns left the hopes of the radical left near total extinction. Morris, though, never defined himself solely as a socialist. Moreover, the grim news of the late 1880s turned him away from outright activism. He left party politics but without ever giving up on his ideals, or his efforts.

And so we come back to the choice that Morris made, a year into Kelmscott production, to reprint Caxton's *Recuyell*. Morris's formative encounter with John Ruskin's 1853 *The Nature of the Gothic* had persuaded him to look back to the creative efforts of medieval workers for inspiration; Morris saw genius in the way that they had devoted themselves to expressing their individual insights in a durable medium that spoke to the hopes, fears, and desires of all.

His reasons for admiring medieval work had everything to do with Kelmscott's curious double identity as half antiquarian, half radically new. In fact, medieval books struck him as differing radically from their modern successors, being *at once* visually compelling (what he called "ornamental") and narratively absorbing ("epical").

It was Morris's infatuation with medieval bookmakers like Caxton that inspired him, after Emery Walker had opened his eyes, to found Kelmscott Press. The press was Morris's effort, in collaboration with artists of all aspects of bookmaking, to find in the early days of printed books inspiration for a thoroughly modern kind of beautiful object.

The Recuyell of the Historyes of Troye is a crucial transition for the Kelmscott Press. Earlier experiments led to the first typeface that Morris designed, the Golden font. Though beautiful in its own right, Golden in some ways suffers from the laborious process of magnification, comparison, and inspiration that went into its making. It suffers principally because although Morris took as his model Italian types, in his heart he was more drawn to the German (Gothic or blackletter, the latter name deriving from their thickness and blackness on the page).

With *The Recuyell of Troye* in 1892 (about the sixth book Kelmscott produced), Morris, for the first time, turned wholeheartedly to Gothic antecedents. The result was two separate typefaces, both seen in this book for the first time: the Troy and the Chaucer. One was an 18-point type that produces the remarkably vivid pages; the other a 12-point version, used for the index and table of contents. This would later become the central font for the acknowledged masterwork of the Kelmscott Press, the book known as "The Kelmscott Chaucer."

A book is not a mere carrier of text, as Morris stressed, nor an accidental vehicle in which you can find your favorite stories. Look at a book in that dismembered way and you miss a crucial dimension that adds depth to an otherwise flat artwork. This was the credo that he and Walker shared throughout their collaboration—and it explains why pages of his letters and writings are filled with musings on the correct ratio of white space to text on the page (high), on the ratios between inner and outer, and upper and lower margins (the lower margin must be the largest), and on the darkness of ink (as black as possible).

Description by John Plotz, professor of English and
Barbara Mandel Professor of the Humanities

GIFT OF ARTHUR VERSHBOW

Consistoire Central Israélite de France Collection

While the Consistoire Central Israélite de France collection provides a sweeping view of the French Jewish community from the mid-eighteenth through the first third of the twentieth century, perhaps the most fascinating aspect is its provenance and relation to an ongoing debate in the academic world regarding the line between preservation and appropriation. Purchased in good faith by Brandeis some decades ago from Zosa Szajkowski, this is one of several similar collections held by institutions around the United States.

Szajkowski, a prolific scholar of Jewish history, spent much of his life collecting French Judaica and selling or donating it to interested institutions. One of the many Jewish scholars who traveled to Europe in the years surrounding World War II to save European Judaica from destruction, Szajkowski was in good company in these endeavors, and much of his work during this era can be seen as the liberation or preservation of endangered and vital materials. But he continued removing artifacts long after the war was over and long after the danger was gone. Scholar Lisa Leff, author of a book on Szajkowski, suggests that while the objective threat may have faded during much of his collecting period, Szajkowski strongly believed postwar Europe to be an unsafe and unhealthy home for Jews and their history, and continued to think of himself as a rescuer of the Jewish experience. Leff points out that although it is all but impossible to know, document by document, the origin of these materials with any certainty, Szajkowski was twice arrested for (and once convicted of) theft, and those legal issues raise questions about the collection's provenance. While there is good reason to think that much of what Szajkowski sold to Brandeis was not come by honestly or openly, what can certainly be said about both his work and this collection is that they have allowed scholars extraordinary access to the workings of a fundamental institution of French Jewish history.

The Consistoire Central Israélite de France was an administrative body (modeled on the Catholic and Protestant consistories) through which the Jewish community organized, self-governed, and interacted with the French state. It was created by Napoleon in the early years of the nineteenth century and exists (in altered form) to this day. Despite having a complicated and none-too-altruistic relationship with the Jews of France, Napoleon, in creating the Consistoire, brought

Art. 27.

Les rabbins membres du grand-sanhédrin seront préférés, autant que faire se pourra, à tous autres pour les places de grands rabbins.

Décret du 17 Mars 1808, qui prescrit des mesures pour l'exécution du réglement.

Art. 1.er

Pour l'exécution de l'art. 1.er du réglement délibéré par l'assemblée générale des Juifs, exécution qui a été ordonnée par notre décret de ce jour, notre ministre des cultes nous présentera le tableau des synagogues consistoriales à établir, leur circonscription & le lieu de leur établissement.

about a stronghold of Jewish life, religion, and culture, one that would sustain its community through two centuries of religious, political, and military turmoil.

PRIME OFFERTE PAR LE CALENDRIER ISRAELITE FRANÇAIS
LE GRAND SANHÉDRIN (1807)

In 1806, Napoleon gathered an assembly of Jewish notables led by Rabbi David Sinzheim of Strasbourg and posed twelve questions through which he established the relationship between the laws of the Jewish community and the laws of France. The answers laid the groundwork for the future consistorial statutes. In 1807 he established a Grand Sanhedrin (supreme legal body of Jewish law), an institution that had not sat for roughly 1,500 years, and in 1808, in conjunction with a committee of Sanhedrin members, he organized the Consistoire. Through this organizational framework, every department where at least 2,000 Jewish people lived could create a consistory and appoint a chief rabbi; those with fewer than 2,000 could combine with others to form a regional consistory. All were to be overseen by a central consistory and the chief rabbi of France.

This collection documents the workings of the many provincial consistories, as well as the Central Consistory in Paris, and gives a detailed picture of the ways in which these authorities oversaw the religious and secular aspects of French Jewish life. With documents dating from long before the French Revolution to the interwar years of the twentieth century, this collection tells the complicated story of the relationship of the Jewish community both to itself and to the French state. While many of the records revolve around French Jewry, there is a significant section devoted to its relationships with Jewish societies in countries around the world, opening a window onto the interactions of the worldwide Jewish community, both within itself and with the secular community.

Description by Surella Evanor Seelig, M.A. 2005,
Outreach and Special Projects archivist

Léon Lipschutz Collection of Dreyfusiana and French Judaica

A matter vital to understanding recent French history, politics, and culture, the Dreyfus Affair of 1894 remains relevant more than a century after it occurred. In that year a young and successful Alsatian Jewish captain in the French military named Alfred Dreyfus was accused of sharing French military secrets with the Germans, a charge based on flimsy evidence backed up by a military establishment terrified of looking weak in the face of treason. The accusations were based on the "bordereau"—a ripped piece of paper offering information on French artillery developments that was found by a French spy in the German embassy. Relying on poor handwriting analysis, the listing was erroneously attributed to Dreyfus. Additional validation was either trumped up or fabricated entirely. In short order Dreyfus was convicted and sentenced to Devil's Island.

Terrified from its recent defeat by the Germans in the Franco-Prussian War, the nation imploded following the conviction and quickly divided into pro- and anti-Dreyfus camps. While many aspects of French culture at the turn of the twentieth century laid the groundwork for the national debacle that was to become the Dreyfus Affair, widespread antisemitism was a major factor. Dreyfus's professional success and his wealthy Alsatian background made him an easy scapegoat and target of hatred, but it was his being a Jew that was the most damning.

In reaction to the injustice, Émile Zola, the famous author and ardent supporter of Dreyfus, wrote "J'accuse!," a scathing open letter to the French president, which was published with the help of journalist Georges Clemenceau, later prime minister of France. The letter virulently attacked members of the government and military leadership, implicating them in a massive conspiracy. Zola's hope, which came to fruition, was that this letter would bring to light previously hushed-up details of the Dreyfus case and force a retrial. The French military attempted to protect itself by declaring a law of amnesty, making it virtually impossible to prosecute any of those who had been involved in the initial false conviction, forgery of documents, and coverup. The handwritten manuscript draft of Clemenceau's forceful argument against this law is preserved in the Brandeis collection, as are materials from other famous Dreyfus supporters such as the writer Anatole France.

Although Dreyfus was not exonerated until twelve years later, the appearance of "J'accuse!" stood as a pivotal moment in the Affair and in French and Jewish

Desachy 229

DREYFUS EST UN TRAITRE

Vive la France!

VIVE LA RÉPUBLIQUE!

Général MERCIER

Le général Mercier est né à Arras, le 8 décembre 1833. Sorti le deuxième de l'École polytechnique en 1853.

En 1862, M. Mercier partait, comme capitaine, au Mexique, où il y fit preuve, à Puebla, des plus brillantes qualités militaires, et reçut la croix de la Légion d'honneur.

En 1870, le général Mercier combattit à l'armée de Metz. Depuis, le général Mercier fit toute sa carrière dans les armes savantes. Il fut directeur de l'École centrale de pyrotechnie militaire.

Il ne songeait pas à s'occuper de politique lorsque plusieurs de ses collègues le recommandèrent pour le poste de ministre de la Guerre, dans le cabinet Dupuy. Comme tel, le général Mercier eut à connaître toute l'affaire Dreyfus à ses débuts.

Le général Mercier, qui est un patriote, a été injurié par les ennemis de l'armée et de la France. Il n'en est que plus estimé par les bons citoyens.

Cliché Pierre Petit.

« Des notes que j'ai eues en ma possession m'ont révélé qu'un officier des bureaux de l'État-Major avait communiqué à une puissance étrangère des documents dont il avait eu connaissance en vertu de ses fonctions.

« Je l'ai fait arrêter. »

Général MERCIER, Ministre de la Guerre.
(Novembre 1894.)

Général BILLOT

Né à Chaumeil (Corrèze), le 15 août 1828, le général Billot est inspecteur de corps d'armée, membre du Conseil supérieur de la Guerre.

La guerre de 1870-71 le trouva chef d'état-major de la division Lavaucoupet. Il combattit à Sarrebruck, Spicheren, Borny, Noisseville, s'échappa après la reddition de Metz et reprit du service à Tours. Il devint général et prit une part importante à la victoire de Villersexel.

Le général Billot fut élu député de la Corrèze, puis nommé sénateur inamovible.

Comme ministre de la Guerre, à plusieurs reprises, il a affirmé de la façon la plus catégorique et la plus solennelle la culpabilité du traître Dreyfus.

Cliché Pierre Petit.

« Dreyfus, en mon âme et conscience de soldat et de chef de l'armée, Dreyfus est coupable! Dreyfus est un traître! »

Général BILLOT, Ministre de la Guerre.
(Décembre 1896. — Déclaration à la Chambre des Députés.)

M. CAVAIGNAC

M. Cavaignac est né à Paris le 21 mai 1853. Il est le fils du célèbre général républicain qui tenta de s'opposer au coup d'État de 1857.

Engagé volontaire en 1870, M. Cavaignac fut décoré de la médaille militaire pour sa belle conduite. Il passa par l'École polytechnique.

C'est seulement en 1882 que M. Cavaignac entra dans la politique, comme représentant du département de la Sarthe. Il fut ministre de la Guerre en 1895, puis encore en 1898. Il démissionna, parce qu'il n'admettait point qu'on pût discuter l'innocence du traître Dreyfus et procéder à la revision de son procès, — estimant que cette revision, qui aboutira à une condamnation nouvelle, ne peut être qu'une cause de conflits, d'agitations et de ruines pour le pays.

Cliché Reutlinger

« J'ai la certitude absolue de la culpabilité de Dreyfus! »

CAVAIGNAC, Ministre de la Guerre.
(7 juillet 1898. — Discours à la Chambre des Députés.)

« Je demeure convaincu de la culpabilité de Dreyfus et aussi résolu que précédemment à combattre la revision du procès. »

CAVAIGNAC, Ministre de la Guerre.
(4 septembre 1898. — Lettre de démission adressée au Président du Conseil, M. Brisson.)

VIVE L'ARMÉE!

A BAS LES TRAITRES!

Général ZURLINDEN

Le général Zurlinden, né à Colmar, le 3 novembre 1837, élève à dix-neuf ans à l'École polytechnique. Lieutenant d'artillerie en 1860, capitaine en 1866.

M. Zurlinden se conduisit si vaillamment aux batailles de Rezonville et de Saint-Privat qu'il fut nommé chevalier de la Légion d'honneur.

Prisonnier, détenu à Wiesbaden, il s'évada, au péril de sa vie, revint à Tours où Gambetta le nomma chef d'escadrons.

Depuis la guerre, le général Zurlinden a gravi tous les grades de l'armée. Il est grand officier de la Légion d'honneur, ancien commandant de corps d'armée et gouverneur militaire de Paris. A démissionné, comme ministre de la Guerre, parce qu'il s'opposa à la revision du procès du traître Dreyfus.

Cliché Pierre Petit.

« L'étude approfondie du dossier judiciaire de Dreyfus m'a trop convaincu de sa culpabilité pour que je puisse accepter, comme chef de l'armée, toute autre solution que celle du maintien intégral du jugement. »

Général ZURLINDEN, Ministre de la Guerre.
(17 septembre 1898. — Lettre au Président du Conseil, M. Brisson.)

Général CHANOINE

Le général Chanoine était à Lille, commandant une division, lorsqu'à la suite de la démission du général Zurlinden lui fut offert le portefeuille de la Guerre.

Le général Chanoine a de superbes états de service. Entré à Saint-Cyr en 1852, il passa aux zouaves, fut envoyé en Chine comme chef d'état-major du corps expéditionnaire. En 1869, il était aide de camp du général Bourbaki. Pendant la guerre, il prit part à la bataille de Rezonville et à divers combats, comme chef d'escadrons.

Il fit campagne en Orient, en Afrique et en Chine. A vingt ans, il était chevalier de la Légion d'honneur.

A démissionné parce qu'il se refusait à s'associer aux manœuvres antipatriotiques qui tendent à la revision du procès Dreyfus.

Cliché Lafery et Dinolé.

« Puisqu'on a parlé de cette affaire néfaste devant laquelle mes prédécesseurs se sont retirés, je déclare que je respecte la séparation des pouvoirs politique et judiciaire : j'ai le respect de la chose jugée. Mais j'ai le droit aussi d'avoir mon opinion. Elle est conforme à celle de mes prédécesseurs.

Général CHANOINE, Ministre de la Guerre.
(25 Octobre 1898. — Discours à la Chambre des Députés.)

En dépôt : 3, rue Saint-Joseph.

Sceaux. — Imprimerie E. Charaire.

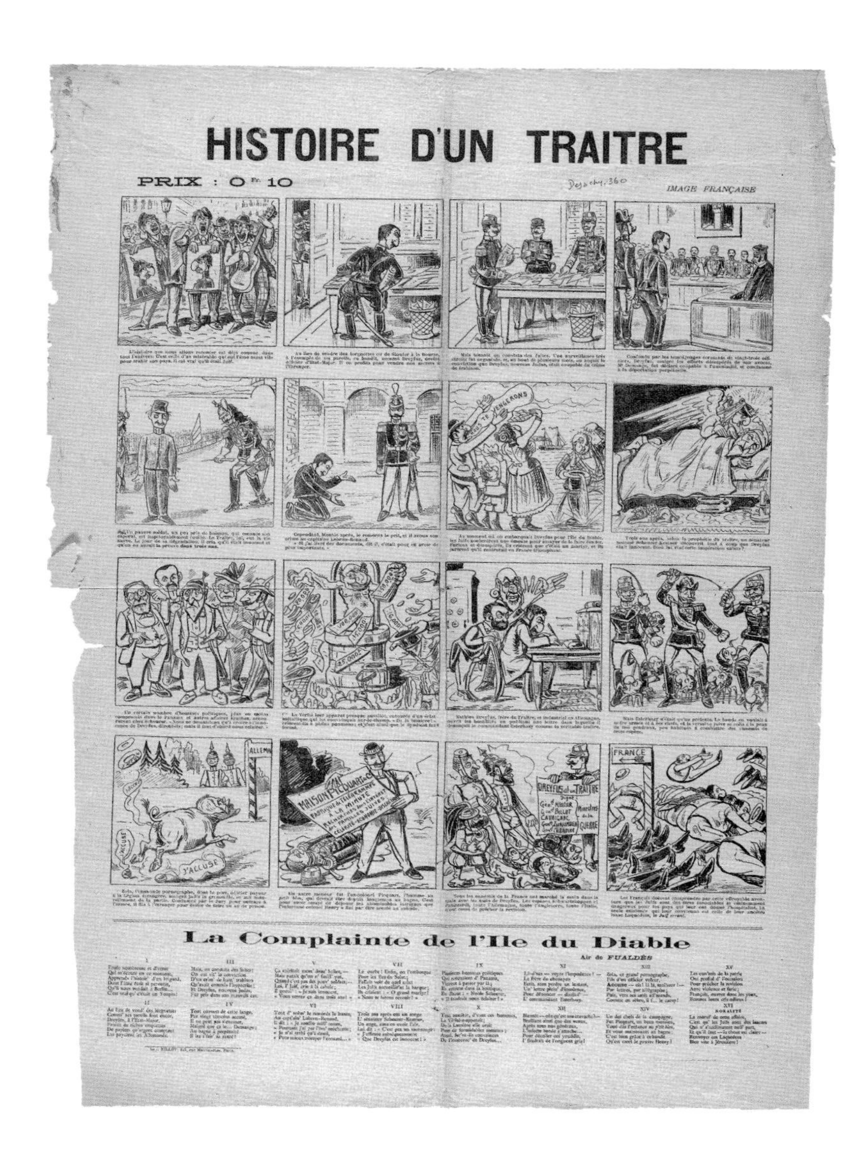

history. As Jacques Chirac, president of France, noted in a public address to the families of Dreyfus and Zola on the centennial of the letter's publication: "a man stood up against lies, malice and cowardice. Outraged by the injustice against Captain Dreyfus, whose only crime was to be a Jew, Émile Zola cried out his famous 'I Accuse . . . !'" In consequence, Chirac went on, "this text struck minds like lightning and changed the fate of the Affair within a few hours. Truth was on the march."

Key to understanding the collection is the guide written by Léon Lipschutz, who spent much of his life in Paris studying and collecting Dreyfusiana and Judaica, then donating his acquisitions to various institutions. More than an index, the guide organizes and analyzes the holdings and is a source of critical scholarship.

Deuxième Année. — Numéro 87 — Cinq Centimes — JEUDI 13 JANVIER 1898

Directeur ERNEST VAUGHAN

L'AURORE

Littéraire, Artistique, Sociale

J'Accuse...!

LETTRE AU PRÉSIDENT DE LA RÉPUBLIQUE

Par ÉMILE ZOLA

LETTRE A M. FÉLIX FAURE

Président de la République

Monsieur le Président,

The Dreyfusiana collection is divided into four series: books; letters/manuscripts; newspaper clippings; and photographs. The material follows how the Affair and its aftermath continued to play out in France and abroad, long after many of the major players had died. While most of the materials are specifically related to the Dreyfus Affair, there is also a small but notable group of documents that focuses more generally on Jewish life and intellectualism in France from the late 1700s to the mid-twentieth century.

Description by Surella Evanor Seelig, M.A. 2005,
Outreach and Special Projects archivist

DONATED BY LÉON LIPSCHUTZ

Native American Watercolors

The works of well-known Native American artists from the San Ildefonso Pueblo just north of Santa Fe, New Mexico, are well represented in the thirty-eight original watercolor paintings in the Brandeis collection, which range in size from 6 inches by 7 inches to 24 inches by 36 inches. Along with Tibetan and Indian artworks, the watercolors came to the university in 1971 when the Riverside Museum of New York City closed its doors. Opened in 1922 on Riverside Drive, the museum concentrated on ethnographic and contemporary art.

Many of the paintings reflect the themes encouraged by the Euro-American patrons who invested resources to uncover artifacts and preserve Pueblo culture in the early decades of the twentieth century. Several of the watercolors depict festivals, scenes of everyday life, and ceremonial dances, including *Winter Animal Dance* by Julian Martinez (1897–1943), an artist well known for his pottery decorations. After a 1908 excavation of San Ildefonso uncovered several pieces of ancient pottery, Martinez (also known as Pacano) and his wife, Maria, used polychrome and experimented with different firing techniques to reproduce the original vessels. The result of their efforts produced the black-on-black pottery for which San Ildefonso is famous.

In addition to several paintings by Martinez, the collection also holds works by other successful Pueblo artists, including Alfonso Roybal (1898–1955), Abel Sanchez (1899–1971), and Romando Vigil (1902–1978). Roybal, who signed his paintings "Awa Tsireh," began his career decorating pottery before developing his talent in watercolor. After seeing some of Roybal's work, Edgar Hewitt, the anthropologist in charge of the early-twentieth-century San Ildefonso excavation, hired him to paint at the Museum of New Mexico, which led to the inclusion of his work in several other Native American art exhibitions around the country.

Sanchez, also known as "Oqwa Pi," which means "Red Cloud," developed one of the two distinctive artistic styles associated with the San Ildefonso school. In his paintings of native ceremonies and festivals, Sanchez used bright and vibrant colors, which other San Ildefonso artists later adopted. In addition to a long and successful artistic career, Sanchez enjoyed success in public office, serving six terms as governor of the San Ildefonso Pueblo.

Vigil similarly contributed to the development of the San Ildefonso school by combining the decorative style of painters like Sanchez and Martinez with one that emphasized realism. As a result, Vigil's paintings are both abstract and

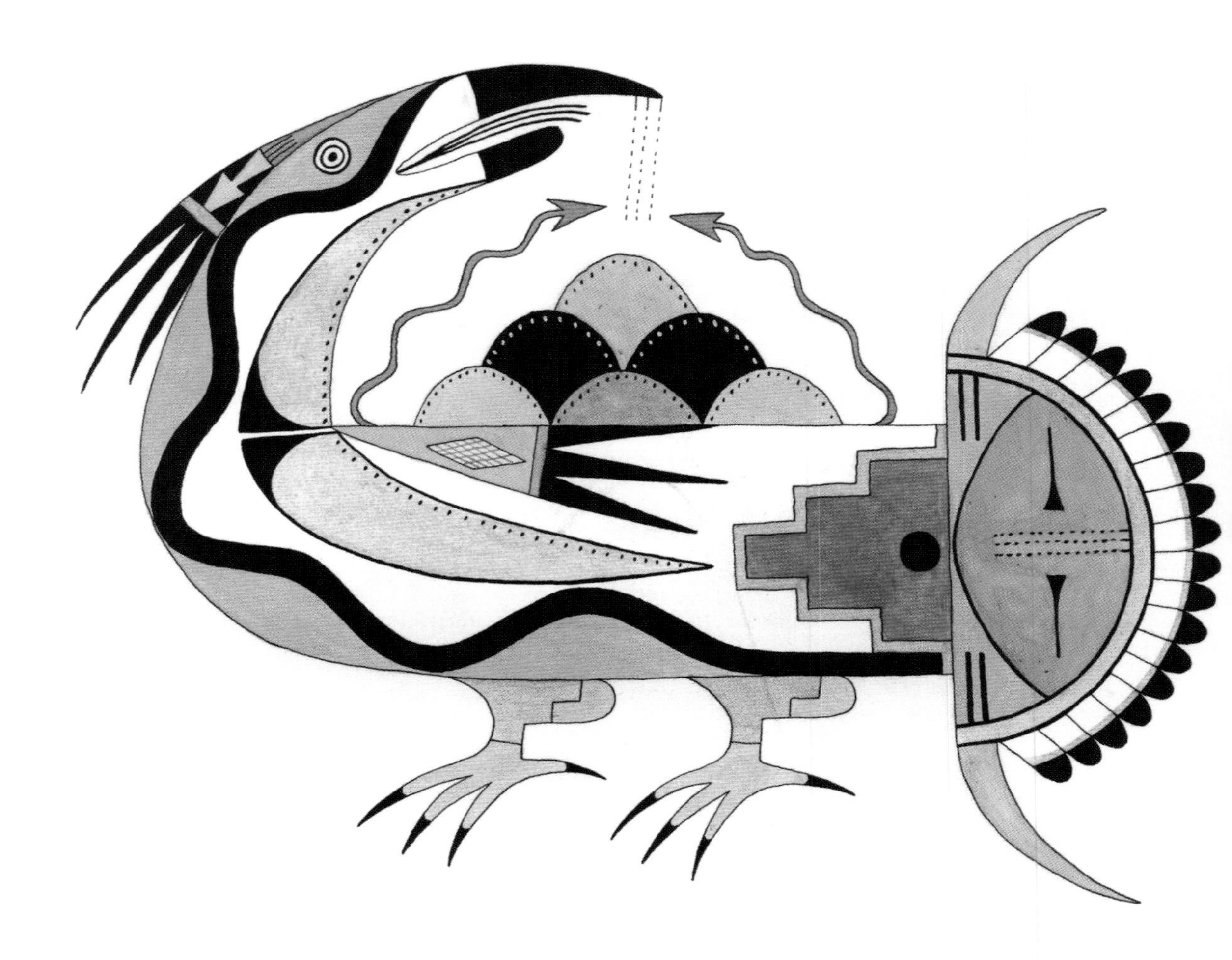

descriptive of Pueblo culture. In 1933, the Corcoran Gallery in Washington, D.C., hired Vigil, or "Tse Ye Mu," along with several other San Ildefonso artists, to paint murals for the Exposition of Indian Tribal Arts. Later in his life, Vigil worked for Walt Disney Studios.

Description by Alexandra Wagner Lough, PH.D. 2013

Pauline Trigère Papers

Acclaimed fashion designer Pauline Trigère—a French Jew of Russian descent who immigrated to the United States just before World War II—made an indelible mark on the industry for well over fifty years. Ranging from her 1908 birth certificate to a clipping of her 2002 *New York Times* obituary, the papers provide an intimate look at the life and work of the woman once described as "the grande dame of American fashion." The collection includes a mixture of correspondence, both personal and professional, reflecting how inextricably linked these worlds were for Trigère.

With a tailor father and a dressmaker mother, the future designer had fashion in her blood. Growing up in Paris, the young Trigère assisted her parents and trained as a cutter at Martial and Armand in Place Vendôme before marrying Lazar Radley, also of Russian-Jewish extraction. In 1937, she, Radley, and their sons, Jean-Pierre and Philippe, left a Europe that had become increasingly unsafe for Jews and settled in New York. Having fallen in love with Manhattan, Trigère, her husband, and her brother, Robert (often called Sioma), opened a tailoring shop. When she and Radley separated in 1941, Trigère went to work assisting at the Hattie Carnegie fashion brand while teaming up with Sioma to build the Pauline Trigère line. In 1942, she created a collection of eleven looks, and, with

her brother by her side, took the fashion world by storm. Within a few years, Pauline Trigère designs were prized for the style and innovations she introduced. Sioma continued as her business partner, and, in time, son Jean-Pierre also came to play a key role in his mother's fashion house.

Appropriate to the designer's intertwining world of family and work, the collection is largely made up of letters, memos, and notes to, from, and among her two sons, brother, former husband, and longtime friend Julio Werthein. Written in both French and English, they detail the life of a woman who was a trendsetter not just in fabric, draping, and cut but on social issues as well. Among the many industry accolades—she won the coveted Coty American Fashion Critics' Award three times and, in 1993, was given the Council of Fashion Designers of America lifetime achievement honor—one of Trigère's most lasting achievements came without ceremony. In 1961, she was the first major designer to send an African American model—Beverly Valdes—down the runway.

The collections at Brandeis include both the Pauline Trigère papers and the Trigère family papers, the latter centering on Robert (Sioma) Trigère.

Description by Surella Evanor Seelig, M.A. 2005,
Outreach and Special Projects archivist

PAULINE TRIGÈRE PAPERS DONATED BY THE FAMILY;
TRIGÈRE FAMILY PAPERS DONATED BY JANE TRIGÈRE

Leo Frank Trial Collection

One of the most notorious capital-punishment cases in early-twentieth-century America was that of Leo Frank, a pencil-factory superintendent in Atlanta, Georgia, and a Northern Jew. The account of Frank's trial and subsequent lynching reverberate to this day.

Born in Texas in 1884, Frank spent his formative years in Brooklyn. He attended Cornell University, graduating with an engineering degree in 1906, and married Lucille Selig, a Georgia native, four years later. The Franks lived in Atlanta, where Leo was the superintendent of the National Pencil Factory. In April 1913, a young employee of the factory named Mary Phagan was found murdered. Based on circumstantial evidence, Frank was accused of the crime; the trial was widely considered a mockery of justice, with crowds shouting "hang the Jew" outside the courtroom. Jim Conley, the pencil factory's custodian and an early suspect in the case, gave damning testimony that ultimately sealed Frank's conviction. (Many years later, Conley's lawyer proclaimed his belief in Frank's innocence.)

After Frank was sentenced to death, new evidence came to light. In response to this information and to widespread public outcry and petitioning, Georgia governor John Slaton commuted Frank's sentence to life in prison. That decision inspired a mob—composed in part of prominent individuals, including a former state governor—who kidnapped Frank from prison and lynched him on August 17, 1915. The events surrounding the Leo Frank case were instrumental in the founding of the Anti-Defamation League; they also spurred the rebirth of the Ku Klux Klan.

At the heart of the collection is the correspondence between Frank, writing mostly from prison, and his wife, Lucille, as well as Governor Slaton. Many of Frank's missives to his wife describe the day-to-day needs and doings of prison life, the state of his health, and his affection for her. In the last letter from Frank in the collection, he writes to his mother-in-law after an attempt on his life was made by another inmate: "I hope you did not yesterday or today hear the rumor I heard—viz: that I was dead. I want to firmly and decisively deny that rumor. I am alive by a big majority." This letter was written on August 4, 1915, two weeks before Frank was lynched.

One letter to Frank in prison, postmarked April 20, 1915, did not reach him before his death. In it, a person signing himself "A Friend of Connelly's [sic]," wrote: "Sir I know in my very heart and soul that it was Connelly that killed the

Fairbanks, Alaska, June 11, 1915

Hon. J. M. Slaten,
Governor of Georgia,
Atlanta, Ga.

Your Excellency:

The undersigned most respectfully approaches you in behalf of Lee Frank, convicted in your city and state. It does not behoove any citizen of the United States to mention the justice of a verdict on the part of its fellow citizens, any decision of a regularly constituted court of justice, but in the question of mercy, no man should be backward in asking the same for any unfortunate who has come under the jurisdiction of the law.

Therefore, the undersigned begs to intercede with Your Excellency to bestow clemency upon the said Leo Frank, if your judgement, combined with human compassion, will allow you to do so.

Very Respectfully yours

Phagan girl." It goes on: "the white folks never did treat me good so I need not cair [sic] whether you live or die but before me and my god Connelly killed Mary Phagan as true as death he did."

A month after her husband's death, Lucille wrote to Thomas Loyless, a Georgia newspaper editor who believed in her husband's innocence. "I only pray that those who destroyed his life will realize the truth before they meet their God—they perhaps are not entirely to blame, fed as they were on lies unspeakable, their passions aroused by designing persons. . . . But those who inspired these men to this awful act, what of them? Will not their conscience make for them a hell on

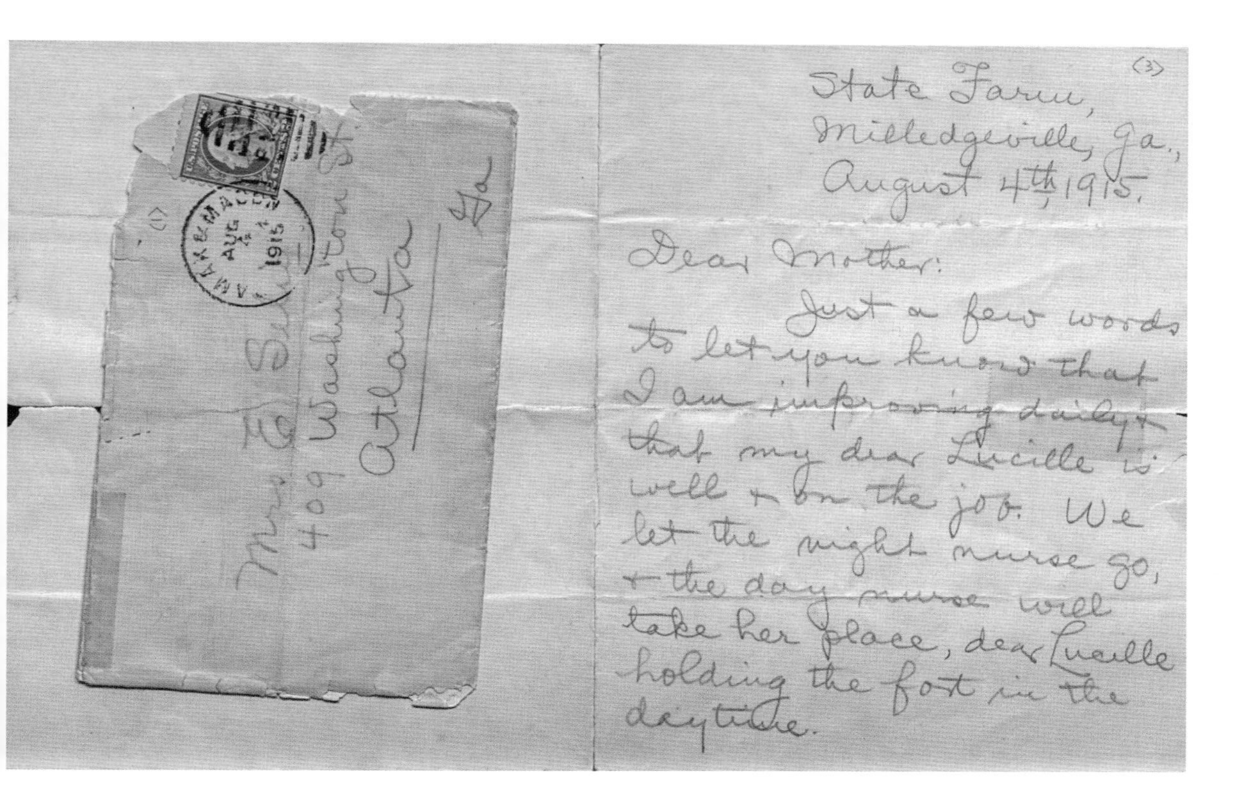

(3)

State Farm,
Milledgeville, Ga.,
August 4th, 1915.

Dear Mother:

Just a few words to let you know that I am improving daily & that my dear Lucille is well & on the job. We let the night nurse go, & the day nurse will take her place, dear Lucille holding the fort in the daytime.

earth, and will not their associates, in their hearts, despise them? . . . If there is a God—and I know there is—truth will prevail."

In 1986, seventy-one years after his death, Leo Frank was pardoned by the state of Georgia.

Description by Sarah Shoemaker, head of Archives and Special Collections

THIS COLLECTION WAS DONATED TO BRANDEIS IN 1961 BY HAROLD E. AND MAXINE MARCUS. THESE MATERIALS WERE GIVEN TO THEM BY HAROLD'S AUNT, LUCILLE FRANK, WHO DIED IN 1957. THE MARCUSES WERE ACTIVE DONORS TO THE UNIVERSITY (BEGINNING IN THE 1950S), AND MAXINE WAS A FOUNDING MEMBER OF THE ATLANTA CHAPTER OF THE BRANDEIS UNIVERSITY NATIONAL WOMEN'S COMMITTEE AND A PERMANENT MEMBER OF THE NATIONAL BOARD.

Nahum Goldmann Collection

Nonconformity marked the political career of Zionist and Jewish activist Nahum Goldmann. Born in the Russian Empire in 1895 and raised in Germany, he lived most of his life in Europe and the United States. A politically aware teenager, he began publishing articles and making public speeches when he was only fourteen, and first attended a Zionist congress at age sixteen. His first book, *Eretz Israel: Reisebriefe aus Palästina*, was published in 1913, when he was just eighteen.

Goldmann lived in Geneva from 1933 to 1940; it was there he married and had two sons. During this time, he headed the Comité des Délégation Juives, represented the Jewish Agency at the League of Nations, and cofounded the World Jewish Congress. In 1940, Goldmann and his family moved to America, where he continued his work in Zionist politics and efforts on behalf of the Jewish refugees and victims of World War II. After the war, Goldmann cofounded the Conference on Jewish Material Claims Against Germany (commonly known as the Claims Conference) and negotiated with West Germany for billions of dollars in reparations payments for the Jewish victims of Nazi war crimes. He served as president of the World Jewish Congress from 1949 to 1978 and president of the World Zionist Organization from 1956 to 1968, and he had a hand in founding and leading several other Jewish organizations.

היהודי המעופף ד"ר נחום גולדמן

Although he spent much of his adult life working to establish the State of Israel, Goldmann never took up permanent residence in the very country he helped to create, nor did he pursue a career in its government. In his preface to the book *Nahum Goldmann: Statesman Without a State*, historian Mark A. Raider (Brandeis PH.D. 1996) notes that Goldmann's beliefs differed drastically from the established Zionist leadership. According to Raider, despite his accomplishments, Goldmann often angered the established Jewish, Zionist, and Israeli leadership by opposing and subverting mainstream policies. Goldmann saw Israel as an important cultural center and a much-needed homeland for the Jewish refugees of World War II, but he also believed in cultivating a healthy diaspora. He argued for a peaceful approach to relations with the Arabs, and even proposed that Israel become an officially neutral state.

Manuscripts, audiovisual recordings, personal papers, press clippings, awards, and artifacts make up the heart of the collection. The materials range from 1910 to 2004, although the majority date to Goldmann's later years, from 1960 to 1982. The correspondence, writings, and speeches document Goldmann's diplomatic work, family life, and political beliefs, while scrapbooks and photo albums record his numerous visits to Jewish communities in Europe, Latin America, and Israel, and the events he participated in there. Material from the late 1970s and early 1980s shows that even in his later years Goldmann was still very much engaged in Jewish public life, as he reflected upon the ideals he mastered early on: "I can hardly say, for instance, when I became a Zionist. Even as a child I was a Zionist without knowing it, inasmuch as I took over my father's concepts and his positive attitude to everything Jewish as axioms of my heritage."

Description by Emily Lapworth, B.A. 2012, former project archivist for the Nahum Goldmann Collection

DONATED BY NAHUM GOLDMANN'S SON,
DR. GUIDO GOLDMAN

Marcel Proust Letters

In search of letters by Marcel Proust at Brandeis University? *Mais oui!*

Among the gems of literary history housed at Brandeis are twenty-three original letters penned between 1913 and 1916 by Marcel Proust, the writer many consider the greatest French novelist of the twentieth century. Although these letters represent only a fraction of those that Proust wrote during this pivotal period, they are among some of the most important documents in the publication history of his 3,000-page tome, *À la recherche du temps perdu* (*In Search of Lost Time*). The letters articulate concerns that he had about the editing process and, in turn, they serve to illuminate larger dimensions of Proust's novel and his literary aesthetics.

The earliest letters date from February 1913, the year that saw the publication of *Du côté de chez Swann* (*Swann's Way*), the first volume of the *Search*. They include key negotiations with his first editor and publisher, Bernard Grasset, and reveal Proust's preoccupations with the shape and format of his novel, the reception that he envisioned for his book, and the truths that he hoped readers would discover within its pages. In addition, the letters bear witness to ups and downs in the personal and professional relationship between Proust and Grasset. The opening and closing formulas that Proust uses in his written exchanges with Grasset from 1913 to 1916 reflect the evolution of their partnership. We see the happy beginnings of their collaboration and the gradual slide toward distanced politeness that precedes the dissolution of their business dealings. The last letter dates from 1916, the year that Proust leaves Éditions Grasset for Gaston Gallimard's Nouvelle Revue Française.

Of the twenty-three letters, all are handwritten by Proust on cream-colored laid paper, except for one, which is typed on stationery bearing the letterhead of the French newspaper *Le Figaro*. Twenty-two are addressed to Grasset, and one, dating from April 1914, to Louis Brun, Grasset's friend and business partner. Although twenty of the letters are undated, they appear—with dates—in the writer's correspondence that was published (in French) between 1971 and 1992 by the Proust scholar Philip Kolb. Three of the letters are accompanied by typed transcriptions in French, and one of those also includes a typed English translation.

Because the provenance of the letters is unclear, this collection has a certain air of mystery about it. Kolb's bibliographic citations do not provide clues, and the records at Brandeis are a bit murky regarding their acquisition, although a 1966 *Brandeis University Bulletin* announces the acquisition of the letters and quotes Milton Hindus, then the Peter and Elizabeth Wolkenstein Professor of English, on their scholarly value.

Many of Proust's peculiar graphic habits show up in his letters. Like his manuscripts that devolve into a maze of paragraphs sprouting in divergent directions on a single page, Proust's letters tend to unfurl in unusual ways. Typically, a horizontal sheet of stationery is folded into halves and the right-hand side covered with words flowing from top to bottom; page two continues in the same manner on a separate sheet of paper, also folded into two sections. For page three, Proust turns page two vertically and writes along the fold, continuing to the bottom of the sheet of paper; page four begins at the halfway fold of page one and continues to the bottom of that page. Proust often adds notes in the blank areas at the beginning and end of his letters. These meticulous efforts to fill the space available anticipate Proust's suggestions, spelled out in later letters, for extending into the margin the text of his too-lengthy first volume in an attempt to squeeze his manuscript into the number of pages prescribed by Grasset.

102 boulevard Haussmann

Monsieur,

M. René Blum m'a écrit pour me résumer la conversation qu'il avait eue avec vous et je tiens avant tout à vous dire quel grand plaisir c'est pour moi d'être édité chez vous. Ainsi que M. Blum vous l'a dit (c'est parce que je crains que le livre, surtout le premier volume, soit une mauvaise affaire pour un éditeur, je le rends mal) mon désir est que vous ne fassiez pour lui aucuns frais. Je ferai tous les frais de l'édition, ainsi que la

le presse où elle ne nuise pas à la clarté contienne beaucoup de lignes et les lignes beaucoup de lettres afin que le volume ne soit pas trop "volumineux". Les pages de l'Éducation sentimentale de Fasquelle me semblent à ce point de vue assez bonnes mais je n'en aime pas les caractères typographiques. À mon goût personnel, ce qui me plairait mieux comme caractères, ce sont ceux que le Mercure de France a employés pour la Double maîtresse d'Henri de Régnier ou les Éditions de la Revue Blanche pour Charles Louis Philippe. Vous verrez si vous jugez possible de vous en rapprocher. Mon second volume que nous publierons dans les mêmes conditions sera peut-être d'une meilleure vente car il est infiniment plus narratif et peut-être aussi parce qu'il est fort indécent. Mais je regretterais que ce fût là la cause de son succès. Le premier n'est qu'une interminable préparation. Je vous ai écrit une fort longue lettre pour expliquer que dans mon état de santé actuel je ne peux recevoir de visite, vivant dans les fumigations, et difficilement en faire pour aucune. Si par hasard un soir je suis mieux, j'en profite, je me lève et sors, mais sans que mes crises ne permettent de savoir d'avance quand ces accalmies, fort rares, se produisent. Si cependant vous me dites qu'on peut toujours

One of the most moving aspects of these letters is their representation in metaphorical terms of the substantial obstacles that Proust had to overcome in order to publish *Swann* and the rest of his novel. As Proust's thoughts unfold on paper and his sinuous sentences deplete the ink in his fountain pen, the fading words are a physical reminder of his struggles against poor health, dwindling financial reserves, and, of course, the passage of time. When, after a stretch of fading text, suddenly dark, bold words reappear, reinforced and strengthened from a fresh dip of the pen, the reader senses that Proust, having taken a deep breath, is ready to continue observing, assessing, reflecting, and, above all, writing.

A closer look at the earliest letter in the Brandeis collection gives a good idea of the layers of information for which many of these pages of correspondence can be mined. In this letter, written on February 24, 1913, Proust has concluded a deal that makes Grasset the publisher of what will eventually become *Swann's Way*. By this time, Proust had already met with rejection from five other editors, so it is not surprising that he seems thrilled to be working with Grasset. The author expresses concerns about the editing and publication process, especially the negative effect that it may have on the format of his novel. Particularly worrisome to him is the problem posed by its excessive length. Determined to squeeze more words into the limited number of pages, Proust suggests a smaller font size. (Despite his efforts to invent more ways to reduce the book's heft, *Swann* eventually will appear with no fewer than 523 pages).

To avoid becoming a financial drain on Grasset and to retain some control over the eventual configuration of his book, Proust states his clear intention to pay the full cost of advertising and publishing the novel. Above all, the author wishes to preserve the intrinsic coherence of his work, whether or not it is immediately obvious to his readers. He is confident that the second volume—at this point, there are only two on the immediate horizon—will sell more easily because it is a more traditional narrative and contains a scandalous scene, but he hopes that its element of licentiousness does not prove to be the only reason for its financial success.

Du côté de chez Swann is finally published in November of 1913, but world events delay the balance of Proust's plans. By August 1914, Europe is engulfed in war, Grasset has been drafted, and the publication of Proust's novel is suspended indefinitely. The second volume of *In Search of Lost Time* eventually finds its way into print in 1918, published by Gallimard's Nouvelle Revue Française. This invaluable collection of letters enables the reader to retrace key moments in the publication history of *In Search of Lost Time*, to relive Proust's anxieties about and aspirations for his book, and to gain a new level of understanding about how the production process ultimately shaped the first volume of this groundbreaking French novel.

Description by Hollie Harder, professor of French and Francophone studies and director of the French and Italian language programs

Diary of a World War I Aid Worker

Among a number of archival materials documenting twentieth-century European conflicts, including the two world wars, is the diary of an American Red Cross worker, Anna Weimar (b. 1869), who was stationed at the U.S. Navy base in Nantes, France, during the final months of World War I. Weimar's diary spans a full year—June 28, 1918 to July 7, 1919—and ends just eight days after the establishment of the League of Nations.

A volunteer worker with the American Red Cross in Chicago, Weimar was forty-nine when she sailed to Europe in the summer of 1918. Though her assigned duties were primarily clerical, Weimar spent much of her time tending to patients at the naval hospital in Nantes: writing letters for them, bringing treats, and even placing flowers at their gravesites when they died. The emotional upheaval of her work and her sadness pervade many entries. Weimar is also candid about the

PEACE. signed NOVEMBER 11 Today.

Today was a happy day in France - Peace
19 Germany & the allies was signed today or rath
armistice - The P.M. was made a holiday -
women and children danced in the stre
Nantes - they played "Ring around the Rosy"
an American soldier in the middle for the "Rosy"
all acted like happy children, the dropp
shroud, they have worn for 4 yrs - Tonight
a train of wounded men came in from the
19 it was the worst train load we have had.
train was late, got in at 2 in the mornin
While waiting I sat in my barrack windo
large silvery moon shown over the 3 bro
Pines near our barracks - a heavy vap
from the earth, at first thin & spiral like
it floated softly until it was about 4 ft

gruesomeness of the war. In one entry, from October 12, 1918, she writes: "Today I saw the worst case I've seen thus far a very nice blond boy had his whole chin, a piece of his tongue, his right cheek—and just as the shrapnel struck him he was in the act of pulling his helmet down & it took off his right thumb—he can only take liquids his front teeth & lower jaw being gone—he tried to tell me he wanted some coca—the kind you pour hot water on & drink—he can't get enough to eat."

In another note, from November 6, 1918—five days before the armistice—Weimar observes: "I feel half sick today and have the blues a lot of boys came in today in the rain & they had to be put into those cold, bare wards—they had had no food for 24 hrs & were almost overlooked—one is desperately sick with pneumonia & they cant find Hicks to look after him—it has poured rain for two days & nights. The place is a mud hole—& all the pneumonias are worse."

There are moments of levity in Weimar's diary, though they, too, are sometimes punctuated by sobering reality. In her entry for November 11, 1918, Weimer writes in bold at the top of the page: "PEACE signed Today." She continues:

> Today was a happy day in France—Peace between Germany & the allies was signed today or rather an Armistice—The P.M. was made a holiday—men, women and children danced in the streets of Nantes—they played "Ring around the rosy" with an American soldier in the middle for the "Rosy" They all acted like happy children, the[y] dropped the shroud they have worn for 4 yrs—Tonight we had a train of wounded men come in from the front. It was the worst train load we have had—the train was late, got in at 2 in the morning—While waiting I sat in my barrack window—a large silvery moon shown over the 3 beautiful pines near our barracks—a heavy vapor rose from the earth, at first thin & spiral like and it floated softly until it was about 4 ft from the ground, when it became denser & moved from side to side—I imagined it was the spirits of our boys who had played "Hookey" [sic] from heaven to celebrate the good news—

Weimar was stationed in Europe for another seven months following the armistice, and her journal is filled with descriptions of her travels and her impressions as a tourist, all of which provide a valuable first-person account of life in the European theater during the final phase of World War I.

Description by Karen Adler Abramson, B.A. 1985, M.A. 1994; university archivist, 2003–2005; head of Archives and Special Collections, 2005–2010

Colonel Edward H. McCrahon Family Collection of World War I Posters

A fascination with artistic propaganda was the inspiration behind the more than five hundred World War I posters collected by Colonel Edward H. McCrahon. Born in Brooklyn, New York, McCrahon signed up with the French army and engaged in World War I two years before the United States entered the conflict. When his country began fighting alongside the Allies, McCrahon joined the U.S. Army and rose to the rank of colonel. Captivated by the poster art he saw throughout his service abroad, McCrahon began to collect these pieces of agitprop when the war ended; by the 1930s he had developed the largest known collection of war posters.

The artworks differ widely in terms of country of origin, language, message, and physical state. Many are American, though there are a significant number of examples from other countries. An initial count shows one Canadian, three Italian, fifteen British, twenty-one German, and sixty-five French. The collection includes several non-English-language posters that were printed in America but directed at immigrant communities, providing a fitting representation of the propagandistic messages disseminated throughout the war.

A theme common to almost all, no matter the language or country of origin, was the public's monetary involvement in the war. The posters called on the citizens of the various warring countries to support the war financially through the purchase of war bonds and loans. Many German examples feature the term *Kriegsanleihe*, or "war loan," similar to the Liberty Bonds and Loans advertised in the American effort. The message is that money funds war and almost everything else must fall in line with that reality. This is apparent in other themes common to many of the collection's works, including the need to save food to feed soldiers and the encouragement of women to aid in the war effort.

American posters generally presented a more threatening attitude than their European counterparts. For example, the American representations tended to portray racist, xenophobic attitudes toward the German people, with statements such as "Keep these [boots] off the U.S.A." and "Beat back the Hun with Liberty Bonds." Other images depicting ruined monuments played on the American fear of the European dystopia encroaching on U.S. soil. A poster with the words "That liberty shall not perish from the earth / Buy liberty bonds / Fourth Liberty Loan" presents an image of America, specifically the Statue of Liberty and New

AMERICANS ALL!

HONOR ROLL

Du Bois
Smith
O'Brien
Cejka
Haucke
Pappandrikopolous
Andrassi
Villotto
Levy
Turovich
Kowalski
Chriczanevicz
Knutson
Gonzales

Howard Chandler Christy 1919

Victory Liberty Loan

4-C

Forbes

York City, being engulfed in flames. The sentiment suggests this disaster to be an inevitability without the American citizenry's support for the war.

The images and words used are intense, forceful, and often incredibly disturbing and frightening. No matter where the posters originated, they were designed to encourage a beleaguered populace to support a violent and costly war and were intended to bring the citizenry in line with the government's war footing. There was no room for gentle encouragement. Despite the military objectives, the images are often stunningly beautiful and were created by some of the best artists of the time. Whatever their country of origin, World War I poster artists used alluring paintings, telling photos, and shocking text to grab the viewer's attention and to illustrate the messages their governments wanted to impart.

Description by Rochelle Fayngor, B.S. *2017, and Adam Gurfinkel,* B.A. *2017*

THIS COLLECTION WAS GENEROUSLY DONATED TO BRANDEIS BY THE FAMILY OF COLONEL MCCRAHON. NEW YORK AUCTION HOUSE GUERNSEYS AND THE ETTINGER FAMILY WERE INSTRUMENTAL IN THE DONATION.

World War I and World War II Propaganda Posters Collection

Influenced by examples from Western European countries, the creation and production of visually stunning pictorial publicity yielded a high level of artistry and industrial application in the United States, especially when applied to wartime efforts. Nearly one hundred images illustrating a variety of war-related topics highlight this World War I and World War II posters collection.

World War I created demands on both physical and human resources on a larger scale than thought necessary before. The war was one of industrial competition, in which the manufacture of arms and munitions became essential; it was a war in which recent inventions like the airplane and the machine gun were used with deadly effect, and a new invention, the tank, was introduced. To support such an effort, it was necessary for governments and organizations to engage the will of the entire population. The pertinent information that was needed was supplied by traditional means — newspapers and notices — as well as by newer media, like film and posters, which could both persuade and inform. Gaining popularity quickly, by 1914 posters were as well established as press advertising.

שפייז וועט געווינען דיא קריעג!

איהר קומט אהער צו געפינען פרייהייט.
יעצט מוזט איהר העלפען זיא צו בעשיצען
מיר מוזען דיא עלליים פערזארגען מיט ווייץ.

לאזט קיין זאך ניט גיין אין ניוועץ

יונייטעד סטייטס שפייז פערוואלטונג.

Governments exploited this medium. Posters were used to call for recruits, request loans, make national policies acceptable, spur industrial effort, channel emotions, urge conservation of resources, and inform the public. Charitable organizations such as the Red Cross sought financial support through this means.

The majority of the images were aimed at ordinary citizens, reflecting their strength, thriftiness, and common humanity. Food administration notices, for example, made a play on the sacrifices of the troops in Europe to motivate the people at home to contribute.

Since the United States was a country of immigrants, notions of the nation were potentially unstable. The government promoted national unity through labor, service, and the family. Some posters specifically appealed to this audience: for instance, artist C. E. Chambers depicted immigrants arriving on ships, gazing at their new homeland, with the Statue of Liberty in the background and a red, white, and blue rainbow arching over the golden silhouette of Manhattan. The most striking aspect, however, is the accompanying Yiddish text, translated as: "Food will win the war! You came here to find freedom. Now we must help to defend her. We must supply the Allies with wheat. Let nothing go to waste. United States Food Administration."

Certain illustrators played a dominant role in the production of war posters, even though they had not previously been identified with this format. James Montgomery Flagg created a self-portrait for his depiction of Uncle Sam, one of the most widely reproduced images in history, and the collection holds works by Howard Chandler Christy, Adolph Treidler, Edwin Howland Blashfield, Harrison Fisher, Casper Emerson Jr., Henry Patrick Raleigh, and Haskell Coffin.

Although the posters are now seen out of their original context, they were often used as part of a bigger campaign, together with personal appearances by politicians and celebrities, flag days, and the introduction of popular songs. Nevertheless, to look at a group of war posters together is to get an understanding of the immediate response they inspired. The artwork gives a many-sided image of war and its effects: the fatigued soldier, the despair of victims, and apocalyptic scenes of cities as in Joseph Pennell's painting *That Liberty Shall Not Perish From The Earth: Buy Liberty Bonds—Fourth Liberty Loan*. Most important, these posters are historical documents—one's idea of World War I is colored by knowledge of corpse-ridden battlefields and the appalling conditions of trench warfare.

Although the United States entered World War I rather late—April 1917—it produced more propaganda advertising than any other nation. During the interwar period and in World War II, other countries, particularly Germany, were inspired by the American examples. And it is interesting to note that the latter part of the twentieth century produced propaganda posters that were used to protest wars as much as to support them.

Description by Aaron Wirth, M.A. 2009, PH.D. 2014

Sacco and Vanzetti Collections

The case against Nicola Sacco and Bartolomeo Vanzetti is among the most widely known and debated criminal trials in United States history. On April 15, 1920, two paymasters from the Slater-Morrill Shoe Company were shot and killed in an armed robbery on the streets of South Braintree, Massachusetts. Though robberies of this kind were by no means exceptional during the post–World War I period, this particular case garnered worldwide attention as an example of egregious injustice. Sacco and Vanzetti, two Italian anarchists, were tried, convicted, and ultimately executed for the crime, despite what many considered to be flimsy evidence against them. The case created an international outcry on the defendants' behalf and was seen by many as part of a larger movement in this country to crack down on immigrants and radicals during the postwar 1920s.

Sacco and Vanzetti's trial and executions, which took place on August 23, 1927, have inspired a great number of plays, artworks, poems, and books over the years. Brandeis University Archives and Special Collections includes four separate sets of holdings on the subject: the Gardner Jackson Collection, the Mrs. Walter Frank Collection, the Tom O'Connor Collection, and the Francis Russell Collection.

Perhaps among the most interesting objects are the cast-plaster death masks of Sacco and Vanzetti from the Mrs. Walter Frank Collection. These are the original death masks made following the men's executions. According to letters between Gardner Jackson, the director of the Sacco-Vanzetti Memorial Committee, and Margaret S. Huntley, a secretary for the New York Sacco-Vanzetti National League, the masks were placed on display at meetings held by activist groups that had fought for the defendants' release.

Among the other materials relating to Sacco and Vanzetti is a rare videotape of the funeral procession and surrounding demonstrations on Boston Common. Gardner Jackson wrote to Margaret Huntley, "All motion pictures of the case were ordered destroyed . . . by the Department of Justice. Quantities of news films of the events had been taken. They were all destroyed — a fierce piece of censorship. The film in question escaped destruction."

The Gardner Jackson Memorial Room, in Brandeis University's Goldfarb Library, dedicated on April 19, 1970, houses an aluminum cast of a proposed but never erected monument to the men designed by Gutzon de la Mothe Borglum, famed for the sculptures on Mount Rushmore. Gardner Jackson, a journalist by profession, was a member of the committee dedicated to placing the bas-relief

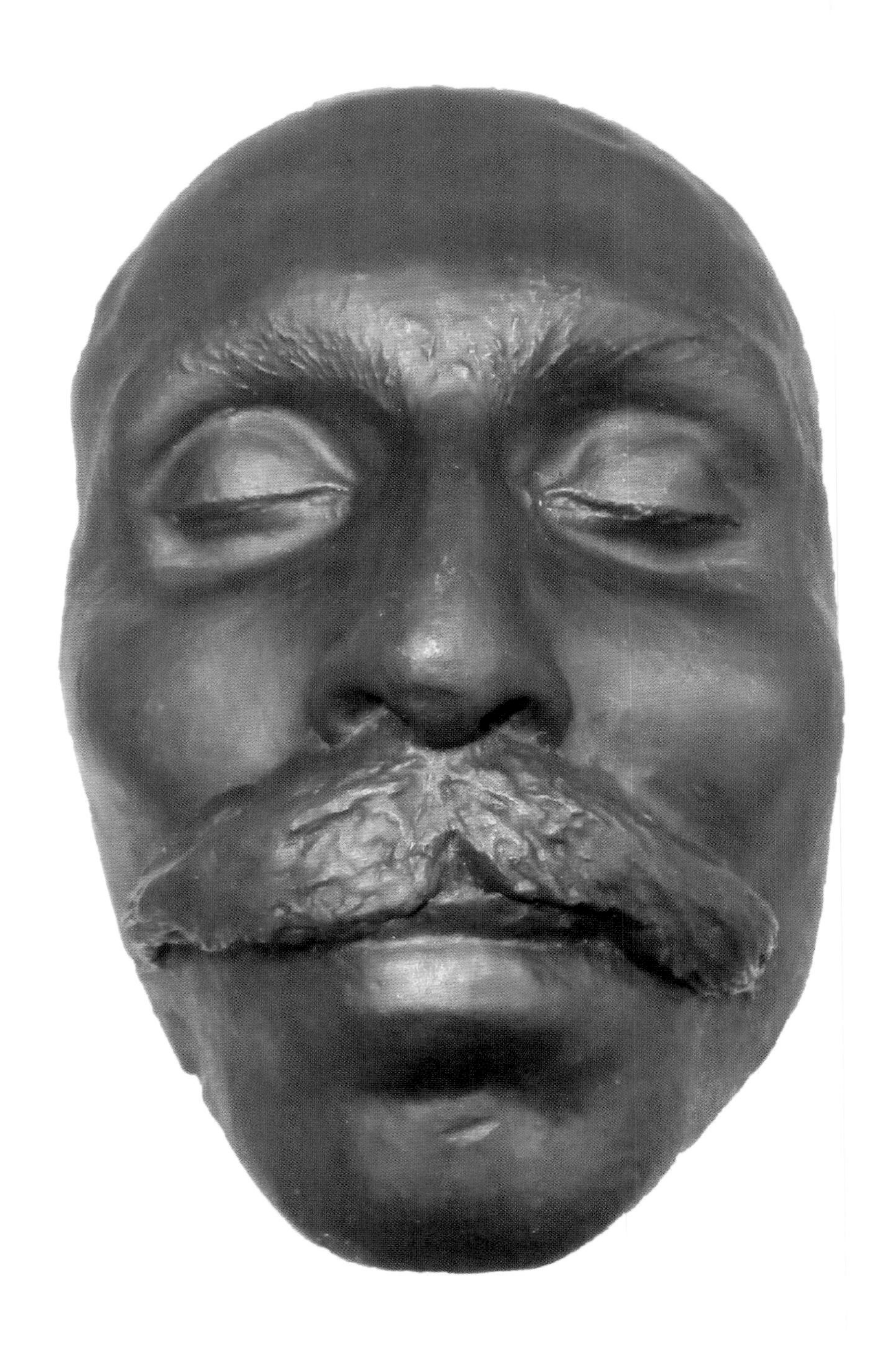

memorial on Boston Common. A quotation by Governor Robert Bradford in the *New York Times* (1947) helps to explain the plan's rejection: "I can see no useful purpose in stirring up the bitter passions and prejudices of twenty years ago, particularly at a time when the whole world is striving for unity, not discord."

Although Sacco and Vanzetti were exonerated by Massachusetts governor Michael Dukakis in 1977, the subject of their guilt or innocence remains contested to this day.

Description by Katie Hargrave, M.A. *2009*

Spanish Civil War Periodicals Collection

In depictions of both trauma and international resonance, the publications of the Spanish Civil War exposed the passions and problematics of this conflict. From 1936 to 1939, Spain was wracked by a brutal civil war sparked by a coup against the elected Second Republic. The rebelling Nationalist forces of General Francisco Franco ultimately overpowered their deeply divided Republican opponents, with the conservative Nationalists benefiting from the military aid of fascist Italy and Nazi Germany, while the Soviet Union gave a lesser degree of support to the leftist, more regional Republicans. The plight of the Republicans became a cause célèbre for the European and North American Left and for minority groups fighting for equality within those same societies. Both camps and their supporters made extensive use of propaganda. The Nationalist victory, however, did not signal the end of publications memorializing, regretting, or continuing the war. The collection holds a notable part of this print legacy—some 394 titles produced both during and after the Spanish Civil War.

A large number of periodicals were created by the fighting forces, many by particular units; they were intended to promote the image of the fighters and to help maintain unit morale and cohesion. The January 23, 1938, edition of *Nuevo Ejercito* (New Army), the newspaper of the Forty-seventh Division of the Republican army, for instance, contained a summary of the division's recent combat activity, a Catalan-language page, and unit news—all interspersed with photographs of the division's soldiers in action.

A similar approach is found in *La Voz de la Sanidad*, the newspaper of the international medical brigade attached to the Fifteenth Division. Befitting the brigade's multinational status, the paper was written in four languages—Spanish, French, English, and German—and presented a mixture of the same articles reproduced in each of the four languages, alongside items, both informative and comic, unique to each.

Other periodicals called for material support for the Republican side. In New York, African Americans combined this need with efforts to combat racism at home. The Negro Committee to Aid Spain, sponsored by such notables as Mary McLeod Bethune, Langston Hughes, A. Philip Randolph, Paul Robeson, and Richard Wright, published a pamphlet titled *A Negro Nurse in Republican Spain*, which recounted the story of Salaria Kee, an African American nurse from Harlem who joined the volunteer American Medical Unit in 1937. Kee's story was juxtaposed with a more general account of African American men who had

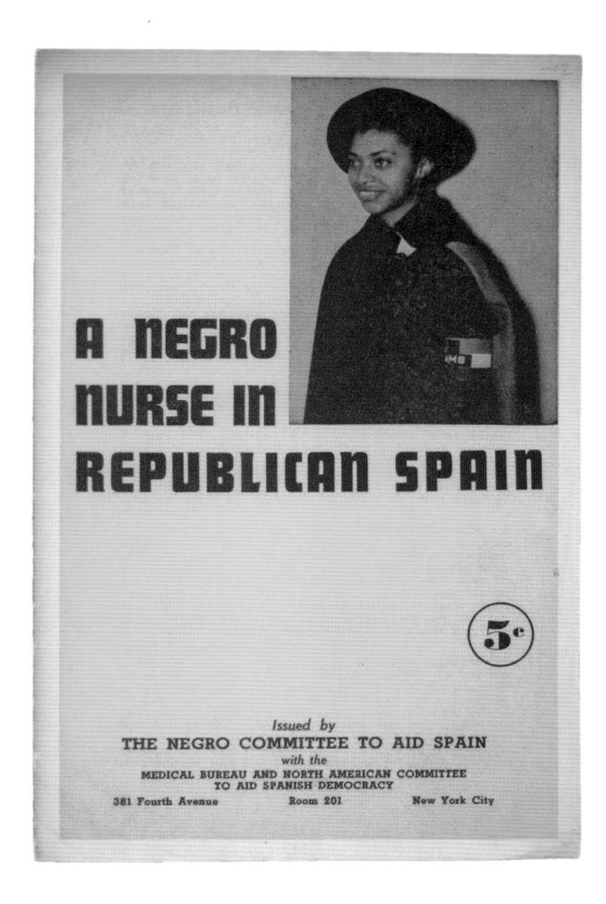

A NEGRO NURSE IN REPUBLICAN SPAIN

5¢

Issued by
THE NEGRO COMMITTEE TO AID SPAIN
with the
MEDICAL BUREAU AND NORTH AMERICAN COMMITTEE TO AID SPANISH DEMOCRACY
381 Fourth Avenue   Room 201   New York City

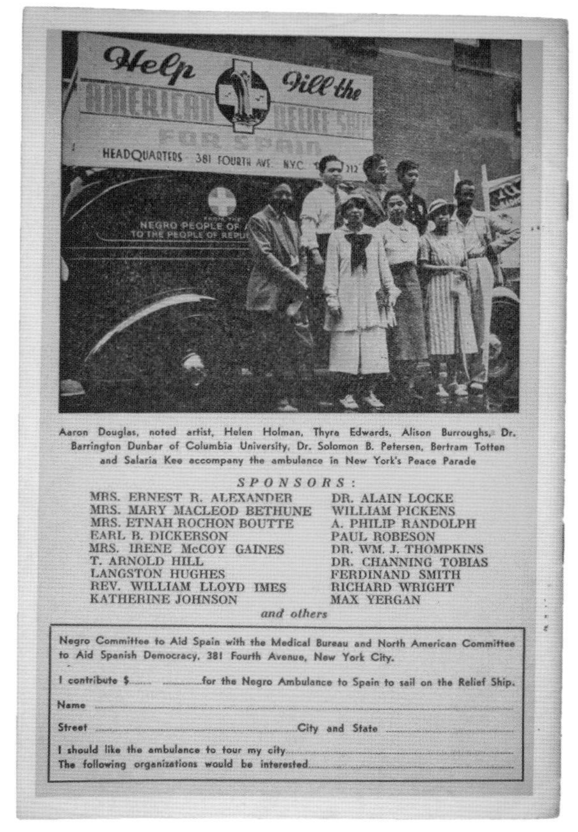

Aaron Douglas, noted artist, Helen Holman, Thyra Edwards, Alison Burroughs, Dr. Barrington Dunbar of Columbia University, Dr. Solomon B. Petersen, Bertram Totten and Salaria Kee accompany the ambulance in New York's Peace Parade

SPONSORS:

MRS. ERNEST R. ALEXANDER
MRS. MARY MACLEOD BETHUNE
MRS. ETNAH ROCHON BOUTTE
EARL B. DICKERSON
MRS. IRENE McCOY GAINES
T. ARNOLD HILL
LANGSTON HUGHES
REV. WILLIAM LLOYD IMES
KATHERINE JOHNSON
DR. ALAIN LOCKE
WILLIAM PICKENS
A. PHILIP RANDOLPH
PAUL ROBESON
DR. WM. J. THOMPKINS
DR. CHANNING TOBIAS
FERDINAND SMITH
RICHARD WRIGHT
MAX YERGAN

and others

Negro Committee to Aid Spain with the Medical Bureau and North American Committee to Aid Spanish Democracy, 381 Fourth Avenue, New York City.

I contribute $............ for the Negro Ambulance to Spain to sail on the Relief Ship.

Name ....

Street .... City and State ....

I should like the ambulance to tour my city............
The following organizations would be interested............

volunteered for the International Brigades, as racism at home "appeared to them as part of the picture of fascism." The pamphlet chronicled Kee's early life and her decision to go to Spain and serve there—in hospitals and directly behind the lines—until a shell wound made her unfit for further service. Kee returned to America and joined the fundraising campaign for which the pamphlet was produced.

Similarly, the German-language pamphlet *Guernica . . . Ein Fanal des Faschismus* (A Beacon of Fascism) was produced after the bombing of that city. The text excoriated the fascist "beast" for the destruction and called for direct material aid to the Basque people in the defense of their "freedom."

Propaganda designed to influence hearts and minds forms an extensive part of the collection. A 1937 edition of the British magazine *Spain Illustrated* features photographs and articles portraying "a year's fight for democracy." The non-interventionist policy of the Western democracies was vilified as an utter failure, with the British Parliament coming in for particular criticism for its "pro-fascist" stance. The April 26, 1939, edition of the German magazine *Die Woche* (The Week), on the other hand, had two celebrations to highlight: Hitler's fiftieth birthday and Franco's triumph in the war.

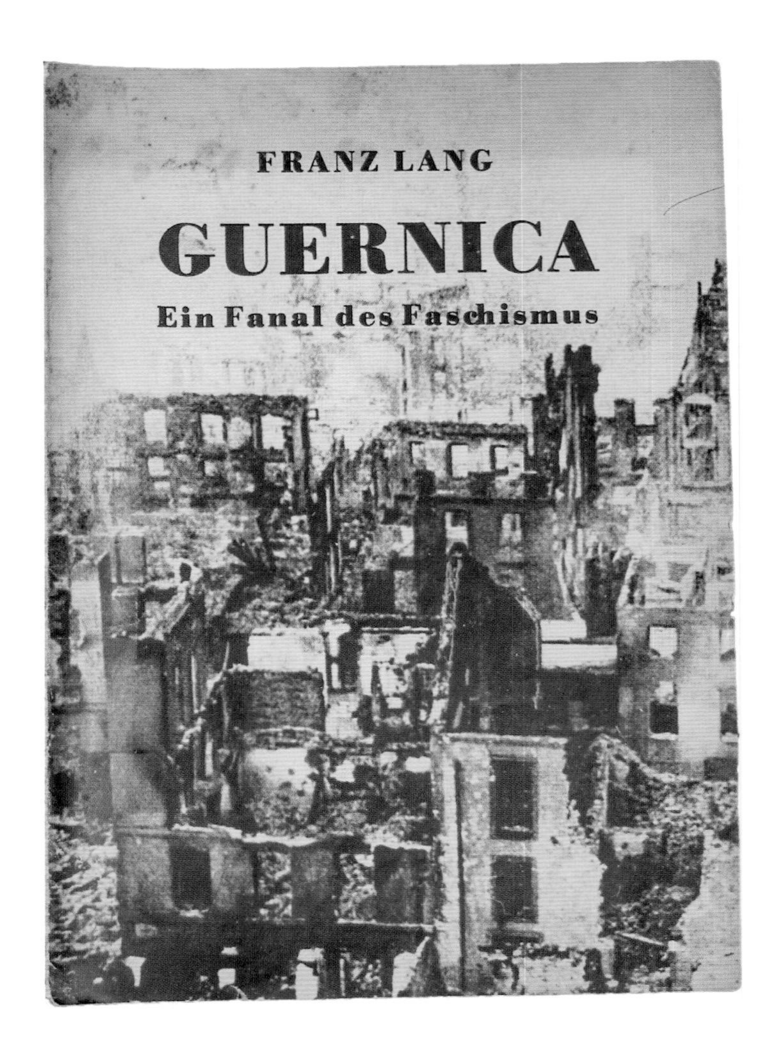

Finally, the example of quasi-neutral international media opens an interesting window onto how the conflict was perceived outside of Spain. In August 1936, the famed French magazine *L'Illustration* published a special edition dedicated to the civil war, depicted as one of utter tragedy. Presented are images of the conflict's devastation—corpses left in public places, defiled churches, cities after bombardments—an almost fatalistic reading of the conflict, in which no action can be taken but to observe the suffering.

Description by Sean Beebe, PH.D. *2020*

L'ILLUSTRATION

ALBUM HORS SÉRIE
PRIX : 5 FRS
AOUT 1936

GUERRE CIVILE EN ESPAGNE

Spanish Civil War Poster Collection

Considered by many historians the prelude to World War II, the Spanish Civil War began in 1936 with the far-right Nationalists' attempted coup of Spain's leftist, duly elected Republican government; it ended in 1939, after much bloodshed, with a Nationalist victory and Spain under the rule of Francisco Franco and an alliance of right-wing political parties.

The posters that were produced during the Spanish Civil War, like all political advertising, are public art with a focused agenda. They were made to serve a broader purpose: to make the viewer feel the importance of a strongly held belief in resisting a fascist takeover of Spain. For thousands, this was a matter of life and death.

While much of the world maintained official neutrality regarding the war, the Nationalists received help from Hitler and Mussolini, which set the stage for the expansion of fascism throughout Europe. The Republicans were aided in their struggle by Stalin and the Soviet forces, as well as by Mexico. Joining the Republicans' cause were members of what were known as the International Brigades, composed of volunteers from other countries, including the United States, who believed that the Spanish Republican government was the legitimate ruling power. During their time in Spain, members of the American Abraham Lincoln Brigade sent or brought home vivid examples of the propaganda posters created for the Republican effort. Preserved in the Brandeis collection are more than 250 visual remembrances of a conflict that resonates to this day.

Created by artists both recognized and anonymous, the artwork is striking in its boldness and style. Many of the posters were produced by members of the Spanish Artists' Union (SPBA), who used graphic, arresting images, sometimes shocking, for greatest effect: gas masks, bandaged soldiers, the symbols of fascism, wounded children, weapons of war. One poster, by José Bardasano, commemorates a year of war with an image of a Republican soldier punching a combatant wearing a uniform emblazoned with a swastika, with barbed wire visible in the background. A Catalonian poster by Pere Catalá Roca features a foot clad in a peasant's sandal stomping on the Nazi emblem. The use of vibrant color and bold lines conveys an urgency and immediacy suited to propaganda posters, which need to be easily seen and visually absorbed from a distance.

The messages, conveyed in both the artwork and the text (in either Spanish or Catalan), were delivered on behalf of government institutions, political parties, the international volunteer brigades, trade unions, youth organizations, and other

EDICIONES
DE LAS
BRIGADAS
INTERNACIONALES
VOLUNTARIOS INTERNACIONALES DE LA LIBERTAD
1936
1937
PARRILLA

LOS INTERNACIONALES

UNIDOS a los ESPAÑOLES, LUCHAMOS CONTRA el INVASOR

LIT. CROMO. MADRID.

SINDICATO DE PROFESIONALES DE LAS BELLAS ARTES. U.G.

AIXAFEM EL FEIXISME
Editat per la Comisaria de Propaganda de la Generalitat de Catalunya.

groups resisting the encroaching fascists. The posters emphasize the need for citizens and volunteers to join in the war effort—to fight fascism, to increase productivity in industry and agriculture, to care for children and the wounded, and to band together. One poster—*La Garra del Invasor Italiano Pretende Esclavizarnos* [The claw of the Italian invader grasps to enslave us]—vividly depicts a huge hand reaching down on Spain, while another, issued by the Aragon Department of Public Order, pictures a man napping: *Un Vago es un Faccioso* [A loafer is a fascist]. The messages changed as the war raged on and as the demise of the Republican effort became more certain.

Despite their haunting imagery, urgent exhortations, and ubiquity, the posters ultimately did not succeed in their aims. To see them today affords us a view not only of an art form put to use for an aim beyond art's sake, but also of a tumultuous and tragic episode of the twentieth century.

Description by Sarah Shoemaker, head of Archives and Special Collections

Hugo Oehler Collection

In the 1930s, activists from around the world flocked to play their part in the Spanish Civil War. Many Americans, including Ernest Hemingway, were drawn to the complex and often dramatic events taking place in Spain. Among those who helped define and shape the struggle was Hugo Oehler, an American communist. His letters, reports, publications, and personal notes help illuminate one of the many camps engaged in the Spanish Civil War while revealing important characteristics of the American communist movement at the time.

The roots of the Spanish Civil War are often difficult to understand, label, and define, even today. When Hugo Oehler, who had found success in organizing trade unions in the American South and in Colorado, traveled to Spain in 1937, he hoped to steer the hostilities toward his ultimate vision: an international proletarian revolution and the advent of worldwide communism. In May 1937, after witnessing the armed conflict between radical left-wing groups and the Barcelona police, Oehler produced a pamphlet titled *Barricades in Barcelona*, along with

Vol. II N.° 2 Barcelona, February 3, 1937 Please reprint

THE SPANISH REVOLUTION

BULLETIN OF THE WORKERS' PARTY OF MARXIST UNIFICATION
P. O. U. M.

AGENTS FOR ENGLAND:
The I. L. P.
The Marxist League
PRICE IN ENGLAND: 2d.

AGENTS FOR U. S. A.:
Y P S. L
The Labor Book Shop
PRICE IN U. S. A.. 05

EDITORIAL OFFICE:
«THE SPANISH REVOLUTION»
10, Rambla de los Estudios
BARCELONA

CONTENTS

STALINISM

The POUM Before the Workers

The official Communist press of Spain and elsewhere has been carrying on the campaign begun by the official Soviet organs, «Pravda» and «Isvestia», and has brought very grave accusations against the P. O. U. M.

We are accused of being agents provocateurs in the pay of the Gestapo and the «Fifth Column». In several organs of the Communist International it has been stated that the P.O.U.M. in collaboration with the Fascists, organised a plot aiming at the assassination of Azaña, Largo Caballero, Dolores Ibarruti (Passionaria) and José Diaz. These are concrete accusations and appeared in the Communist press.

Comrade Victor Serge, in an article sent to «La Batalla», suggests, among other measures, the constitution of an International Comission of Enquiry, composed of well-know persons in the working-class movement. The Executive Committee of the P.O.U.M. has decided to follow the suggestion of Victor Serge. In order that it may command the greatest possible measure of authority, the International Commision of Enquiry should include a representative of each of the following organisations: the Communist International, the Labour and Socialist International, the Fourth International, the International Workingmens' Association and the International Bureau of Revolutionary Socialist Unity. This Commission should investigate independently and freely the concrete accusations levelled against the P.O.U.M. It should begin, in our opinion, by demanding the evidence for these accusations.

We are convinced that the working-class of Spain and of the world will understand and support the P.O.U.M.'s demand, a demand which no one can legitimately oppose.

A new sensational trial has been started in Moscow. This time the prisoners' bench is occupied by Radeck, Piatakov, Muralov, Sokolnikov, Serebriakov and others not so well-known, sixteen in all. Those shot in September were also sixteen. That seems to be the capacity of the executioner's cart of the Stalinite Thermidorians. The accused in this trial as in the one of last summer, are old guard Bolsheviks, revolutionary fighters from the heroic days, old friends and comrades of Lenin.

What has happened is simply that in Russia the most elementary workers democracy has been abolished to make way for the bureaucratic regime of a personal dictator. Of the October Revolution and the Leninist tradition nothing or very little remains. The fighters of October, the old comrades of Lenin have become embarrassing witnesses, in fact real obstacles, to those who are now trying to exterminate them physically after having suppressed them politically. Last time it was Zinoviev, Kamenev, and Smirnov. To-day it is Radeck, Piatakov, Muralov. To-morrow it will be Bukharin. They are already preparing a new cartload. Stalin unquestionably bases his power on terror.

The accused are denied all possibility of defence. In Lenin's time, at the trial of the Socialist Revolutionaries, a foreign workers' delegation was allowed to attend. During the famous «industrial trial» the accused, many of whom occupy bureaucratic posts in Russia to-day, enjoved every sort of means of defence. Why are these denied to-day to the men who, together with Lenin, forged the revolution of 1917?

After the shooting of Zinoviev and Kamenev, the International Bureau for Revolutionary Socialist Unity proposed the formation of an international commission of enquiry to investigate the charges against them and against Trotsky himself. At the time we supported this step, and we continue to do so with the greatest energy to-day. The international proletariat must know the whole truth. The workers cannot be expected to support the soviet cause unless they know what is going on in Russia.

From the resolution of the Executive Committee of the P. O. U. M.

We Demand THE FORMATION OF AN INTERNATIONAL COMMISSION OF ENQUIRY TO EXAMINE THE ACCUSATIONS LEVELLED AGAINST US.

countless letters, reports, and articles centered around this event. The papers in the collection follow Oehler's attempts to communicate the developments in Spain to his American comrades, along with the efforts of a group of Americans to define, shape, and direct a crucial moment in Spanish history.

Many of the documents relay the general upheaval and dire domestic situation in Spain. Oehler's correspondence with Rosalio Negrete (many sources show that this was probably a pseudonym for fellow Revolutionary Workers League member Russell Blackwell) is filled with expressions of frustration that reveal the disorder in Spain. Negrete and Oehler discuss complications with the mail, censorship, and border control. In one letter, dated January 16, 1937, Negrete writes that Oehler's letter faced a "delay due to censorship," and relates: "[I]t has been impossible as yet to organize a satisfactory system for mail." He later warns Oehler of possible complications in entering the country: "You cannot get in here without some political or trade union organization OKing you." Oehler's correspondence reveals a war-torn, distressed country, setting the stage for his own political involvement.

Oehler and his fellow American communists focused their observations on the left wing and their efforts to defeat both the fascist and Republican forces. Periodicals in the collection—including two major publications of the Workers' Party of Marxist Unification (POUM), one in English, *The Spanish Revolution*, and the other in Spanish, *Boletín Interior*—relate, firsthand, the ideas and policies of left-wing Spanish groups.

Although the periodicals directly reflect the voices of the Spanish Left, much of the collection focuses less on Spanish visions of the future and more on an American dream of an international revolution. In countless reports, Oehler's solution to a fractured Spanish Left is a unified Marxist front that will bring about the advent of international communism. While the collection reveals much about the fortunes of the left wing in the Spanish Civil War, it reveals even more about the American communist movement in the 1930s.

Description by Katie Doody, B.A. 2014

ACQUIRED FROM HUGO OEHLER IN 1972

Lewis S. Feuer Papers

A distinguished academic, public intellectual, and polymath, Lewis Samuel Feuer (1912–2002) produced a substantial body of research on the history of science and the sociology of ideas. Aside from his prolific scholarship, Feuer was also known for his lifelong political activism. He advocated on behalf of the political left during the 1920s and 1930s, but by the 1960s and 1970s he had become a prominent neoconservative. The collection documents the history of these important political and intellectual movements in America through Feuer's life and experiences.

Born to Jewish parents in New York City's Lower East Side, Feuer earned his bachelor's degree at City College in 1932 and went on to complete a doctor-

Proceedings of the Hearing of Lewis Feuer
before the Rapp-Coudert Committee, March 20, 1941,
Thursday, 4 P.M., at 165 Broadway.

There was no assemblyman present. The two lawyers offered
to call off the proceedings and arrange a meeting
later. I said I did not wish to have
my class work interfered with so often, and therefore
requested solely that the stenographer note down
my objection. I then asked for a transcript of the
hearing. I was told that that was contrary to
the procedure of legislative committees. I said I
had studied the law of legislative committees at
Columbia Law School, and I knew definitely that
legislative committees had given out transcripts
in the past. I was told that they were a
fact-finding committee and that therefore their
policy was secrecy as to their methods. I said
I could understand a policy of secrecy if this
were a prosecuting committee but I did not
understand why a fact-finding committee should
object to one's possessing a statement of fact.
I was asked whether I wished to halt the
hearing on these grounds. I asked the stenographer
to note my objections to the policy of the committee.

Asked as to my biography:
Through the N.Y. school system, P.S. 64,
De Witt Clinton H.S., College of the City of New York.
Then I accepted a scholarship to continue graduate

ate in philosophy at Harvard University in 1935. He began his academic career with teaching positions at Harvard, City College, Vassar, and the University of Vermont. In 1963, he moved to the University of California, Berkeley, where his encounters with the school's student movement led to his most well-known (and controversial) book, *The Conflict of Generations: The Character and Significance of Student Movements*. Unhappy with the political environment fostered by student radicalism, in 1966 Feuer took a position at the University of Toronto. He returned to the United States in 1976 to teach at the University of Virginia, where he remained until his retirement in 1988.

Feuer's radical ties threatened his early career. His private papers from the 1930s detail conversations with colleagues who refused to renew his contract or write him letters of recommendation because of his connections to the Communist Party. Due to his radical associations, in 1941 New York State's Rapp-Coudert Committee on educational subversion (what historian Ellen Schrecker has dubbed the "direct forerunner to McCarthyism") called on Feuer to testify.

The collection includes Feuer's extensive files of journals and correspondence stretching from his involvement with the radical left in New York and Boston during the 1920s and 1930s, through his antagonistic relationship with the New Left in the 1960s, to his growing conservatism in the 1970s and 1980s. Throughout these years, Feuer kept up a lively correspondence with other influential intellectuals, including Nathan Glazer, Sidney Hook, and Horace Kallen. His papers also contain draft articles, revisions, and book manuscripts, which provide a guide to following the course of this scholar's complex intellectual development.

Description by Julian Nemeth, PH.D. 2014

GIVEN BY THE FAMILY OF LEWIS FEUER

Carl Van Vechten Photographs

Some 1,689 black-and-white portraits showcase the work of Carl Van Vechten (1880–1964), a man fully engaged in the cultural world of the early twentieth century. Beginning his career as an arts critic for the *New York Times*, Van Vechten became acquainted with many of the artistic and intellectual greats of his day. At times, he was a newsworthy subject himself, as his eccentric personal taste and lifestyle garnered notice in the fashion and gossip columns. His connections and influence fostered his role as a patron of the Harlem Renaissance, uniting his interest in the arts with his lifelong regard for Black culture.

Although Van Vechten wrote a number of novels as well as several volumes of literary criticism, it is his photography that has endured. With new portable-camera options, affordable film, and financial independence from an inheritance, Van Vechten took up photography in 1932 without the need to worry about commercial success. Availing himself of these resources, he was able to record a burgeoning era of history as it unfolded, and his work is central to remembering this time and its most prominent cultural figures.

Van Vechten was known for throwing lavish parties that brought his Black artist and powerful white friends together, influencing the careers of many during the Harlem Renaissance. One such encounter orchestrated by Van Vechten was between his close friend Langston Hughes and his friend and editor Alfred A. Knopf. This meeting resulted in the publication of Hughes's first book, *The Weary Blues*, for which Van Vechten wrote the introduction. Later, both men would appear in Van Vechten's photographs.

The portraits reveal the personality of his subjects through a medium in which true intimacy can be shown, and he himself would refer to the art of photography as a way of capturing people. His subjects appear sometimes in costume, sometimes with wild patterned backgrounds, and sometimes in dramatic poses that reflect their professions. Subtler shots also reveal a great deal about their subjects, allowing larger-than-life personas to be translated to static images. One portrait that vividly illuminates the personality of its subjects is that of Salvador Dali and Man Ray. Photographed in front of an exhibit in Paris, the two surrealists present wide-eyed expressions for Van Vechten, reflecting their own work as artists.

Often his subjects were just on the cusp of stardom when Van Vechten photographed them, evidence of his taste as well as his influence. His 1948 portrait of a young Marlon Brando is from the initial stage run of *A Streetcar Named Desire*, for which the actor would first become famous. Conversely, Van Vechten's 1946 portrait of W.E.B. Du Bois was taken well into the activist's long career championing civil rights.

Van Vechten's many portraits illustrate not only the cultural milieu of his time but his influence in its formation. They provide a rare view into a world as seen by the man who seemed to know everyone in it.

Description by Brittany Joyce, B.A. 2015, M.A. 2019

DONATED TO BRANDEIS IN 1966 BY THE
CARL VAN VECHTEN ESTATE

Victor Young Collection

More than one hundred musical scores and LP recordings, awards that include an Oscar and a Golden Globe, and clippings, photographs, and memorabilia document the life and career of Victor Young (1900–1956), an American composer, arranger, conductor, and violinist who wrote and directed music for Hollywood motion pictures from the 1930s to the 1950s.

Born in Chicago, Young spent much of his childhood in Poland, where he studied violin; in 1917 he became a violinist with the Warsaw Philharmonic before returning to the United States and embarking on a career as a music director and composer. Performing in the 1920s as a vaudeville violinist and theater concertmaster and then as assistant musical director for the Chicago-based Balaban and Katz theaters—where he arranged music for silent film accompaniment—Young was displaced temporarily by the coming of sound film into radio and recording work.

In 1935 he was wooed to Hollywood by Paramount Pictures, most likely on the basis of his work at the Balaban and Katz chain, which the studio owned. For the rest of Young's life he wrote and directed music at Paramount, including scores of *For Whom the Bell Tolls* and *Shane*, as well as many films by key Paramount directors such as Cecil B. DeMille and Preston Sturges. Several of the best-remembered movies in Young's filmography, however, were produced for other studios: *Golden Boy* for Columbia, *Johnny Guitar* for Republic, and *The Quiet Man* and *Rio Grande* for director-producer John Ford's independent Argosy Pictures. Along the way, he racked up twenty-two Academy Award nominations—four each in 1940 and 1941—before finally winning a posthumous Oscar for Paramount's *Around the World in Eighty Days* in 1956.

Critics and scholars have long noted that Young's compositions are distinguished by a gift for melody, and his scores often produced hit songs, such as "Stella by Starlight," a theme originally written for *The Uninvited*. But in certain ways, Young's reputation for straightforward tunefulness worked against him; had his scores been less easy on the ears, he might have more readily attracted serious attention in a critical climate that often holds sentimentality under suspicion.

Young's genre-spanning catalog reveals a striking chameleonic skill, as do his impersonations of national and ethnic idioms: Irish in *The Quiet Man*, Spanish in *For Whom the Bell Tolls*, and countless others in *Around the World in Eighty Days*. While versatility of style (along with speed) was one of the basic job quali-

Golden Earrings

8·C
11422
LYDIA HAS A PLAN
(Time 13 3/10 sec.)
("GOLDEN EARRINGS")
VICTOR YOUNG
ARR: GEORGE PARRISH
:00
AFTER SP. "THIS ISN'T YOUR WAR. GO ON."
:03
:13 3/10
FINISH AT END OF SP: "... VICINITY OF FREIBURG"
REIKMAN'S HANDS.

fications for a studio composer, Young seemed to submerge his personality more thoroughly than others. Yet this is part of what made him an exemplary studio-system composer of the classical Hollywood era, and why he remains a crucial figure still for film-music studies: his mastery of the system's demand for effective yet unobtrusive music to give a final polish to its products.

Description by Scott D. Paulin, lecturer in musicology,
Bienen School of Music, Northwestern University

DONATED BY THE FAMILY OF VICTOR YOUNG

Le Témoin

The French journal of political satire *Le Témoin* (The Witness), created by Paul Iribe, was not only a scathing report on French political life, but also a magnificent display of Iribe's artwork in its most mature state. The publication, while short-lived — it was distributed weekly from December 10, 1933, to June 30, 1935, for a total of 69 issues — is noteworthy in its richness and complexity. *Le Témoin* stopped production during its summer hiatus in June 1935, and never appeared again, as Iribe died shortly before the fall issue was to be released.

Today it is exceedingly difficult to find any issues of this journal, let alone the full run, which Brandeis is fortunate to hold. The 1933–1935 series of *Le Témoin* is in fact the second journal of that name by Iribe: he published the first from 1906 to 1910, one of several newspapers and journals Iribe would publish and to which he would contribute. The 1906–1910 sequence prominently featured the work of famous artists in its pages, in contrast to the 1933–1935 run, which appears to be written and illustrated almost entirely by Iribe (there is no masthead, but some of the minor illustrations are signed by other artists).

An intriguing figure, Iribe was known for his early contributions to the art deco movement, his illustrations for the fashion industry, his work in film, and, perhaps most famously, his love affair with Coco Chanel. In addition to the artistic and intellectual achievements of his published work, Iribe created advertising campaigns, worked with clothing designers, including Paul Poiret, and worked briefly as a costume and set designer in Hollywood. The second appearance of *Le Témoin* can rightly be called the capstone to a varied and successful career.

Unlike many other politically oriented papers of the period, *Le Témoin* is witty as well as cutting. Both the art and the text are intelligent, informed, and cleverly designed. While most of each issue is in black and white, all of the major illustrations are enhanced with the blue, white, and red of the French flag (or a subset of the three), with the principal pieces being the front and back covers and the centerfold. The main recurring character is Marianne, the anthropomorphized symbol of France, who was drawn to resemble Coco Chanel in both physical appearance and design aesthetic. The front covers generally depict the main focus of Iribe's political critique and are usually straightforward and topical. Highly stylized and often shockingly stark, the centerfold illustrations focus on the larger issues faced by France and are rendered in a more thought-provoking style. The back covers are devoted to publicity for French industry, whether touting a particular product or promoting French business.

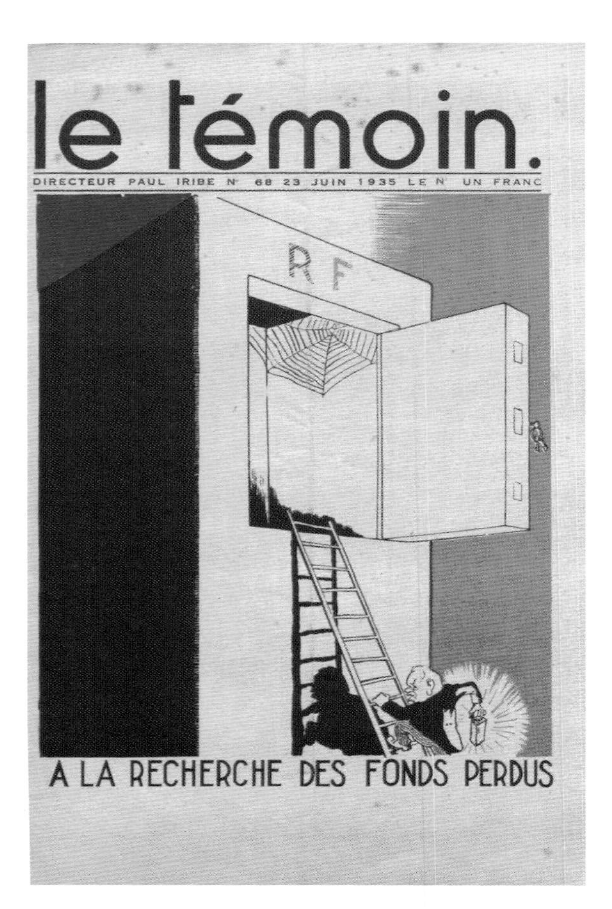
le témoin.
DIRECTEUR PAUL IRIBE N° 68 23 JUIN 1935 LE N° UN FRANC
RF
A LA RECHERCHE DES FONDS PERDUS

VOIX
DALADIER
JO
FROT
DUBARRY
CHAUTEMPS
ROMAGNINO
PRESSARD
DE BOUE LES VIVANTS.

le témoin.

DIRECTEUR PAUL IRIBE N° 5 7 JANVIER 1934 LE N° 1 FRANC 50

Iribe most often depicted Marianne (i.e., France) in relation to the leaders of the major Western powers of that time, particularly the United States (Roosevelt), Great Britain (MacDonald), Germany (Hitler), Russia (Stalin), and Italy (Mussolini). These relationships lay at the core of Iribe's political agenda, which was distinctly and perhaps myopically nationalistic. Iribe's nationalism was less about the superiority of the French nation and more about the importance of its independence and strength in the face of overbearing foreign influence. Iribe mocked the foreign heads of state *qua* leaders, as political players rather than as stand-ins for their nations. And while Iribe was not above satirizing these men, he reserved his sharpest critiques for France's statesmen, whom he saw as capitulating to the hegemony of other nations and leading France into a spiral of weakness and subjugation.

Iribe had much to say on the domestic front—recurring themes included the misery inflicted on French people by the "taxman" and the obsolescence of the rail system. The French government—its ineptitude and weakness in the face of foreign intervention—and the specters of communism, fascism, and Freemasonry were all grist for Iribe's mill; Leon Blum and the conspirators of the Stavisky Affair held a vaunted place throughout *Le Témoin*'s run.

But in a small piece at the end of the third issue, Iribe offered his readers a close look into his political thinking. Here Iribe addressed several letters he received from readers calling for him to denounce the Jewish population of France as outsiders. Iribe responded in a tightly worded, unapologetic note that any man who was willing to take up arms on behalf of France was his "brother," and as such he had no problem with Jews (not that that prevented him from depicting Jews in stereotypical fashion, hook-nose and all—almost as if this were the only way that anyone would know someone was Jewish). This brief note seems a perfect exemplar of the man's stance: an unsentimental and unprejudiced nationalism. Iribe focused his energy and concern on what was good about France rather than on what was wrong with other countries. And while he never seemed to make a sustained case for including some, Iribe certainly seemed to find it a waste of time to bother with excluding others. If you would fight for France, how were you not a Frenchman?

The 1933–1935 issues of *Le Témoin* document a vital moment in the history of France and the West. Its commentary and illustrations are not only stunning and evocative but provide an additional view into an arena in which much of the world was lining up for the major conflict to come.

Description by Surella Evanor Seelig, M.A. 2005,
Outreach and Special Projects archivist

Helmut Hirsch Collection

Correspondence, notebooks, diaries, artwork, poetry, and memorial publications document the life and trials of Helmut "Helle" Hirsch (1916–1937), a young German Jew who opposed the Nazi regime and was executed on June 4, 1937. While the facts surrounding the case remain murky—Hirsch was tried and convicted in secret—what is known is that Helmut Hirsch was involved in a plot to bomb the Nazi headquarters at Nuremberg. This collection is one of a number at Brandeis that focus on antisemitism, Jewish resistance to persecution, and radical social movements in the United States and Europe.

Born and raised in Stuttgart, Germany, Hirsch demonstrated a precocious creativity at a young age and was an excellent artist and draughtsman, leaving behind sketches, paintings, ink drawings, block prints, and art books that he produced as a child and adolescent.

The Nuremberg Laws of 1935 prevented Hirsch from attending university in Germany, so he moved to Prague, Czechoslovakia, to enroll as an architecture student at the Deutsche Technische Hochschule (German Institute of Technology). While there, he became involved in the Black Front, a group of German expatriates and former Nazi party members who actively opposed Hitler.

By the time Hirsch's family joined him in Prague, he was engaged in underground activities, a secret he never shared with them. In December 1936, Hirsch informed his parents that he would be going skiing with a friend, when in fact he was planning on returning to Germany to bomb key Nazi targets. He may have wavered in his commitment to the plot, for rather than traveling directly to

Nuremberg as planned, Hirsch took a detour to Stuttgart to meet a friend. Unbeknownst to him, German agents had likely been infiltrating the Black Front for some time and the Gestapo was waiting.

Hirsch was tried in secret before the Volksgericht (People's Court) in Berlin in March 1937 and sentenced to death. It was only when his family heard his death sentence announced on the radio that they learned of his fate and made appeals for his release.

Compounding the tragedy was the fact that Helmut Hirsch was technically an American citizen—his father had lived in the United States as a young man and been naturalized. But due to a bureaucratic error, Siegfried Hirsch's American citizenship was revoked after he returned to Europe and, by the time Helmut was born, he and his family were considered "stateless persons." It was only when Helmut was imprisoned that his family fought to reinstate their American citizenship, which was formally granted in April 1937. However, neither this action nor the efforts of U.S. Ambassador William E. Dodd secured his freedom. The day before his execution, Hirsch wrote this final letter to his family from his jail cell (excerpted and translated from the German):

> June 3, 1937
> Berlin-Ploetzensee
> Dear Mother, dear Father,
>
> I have just been told that my appeal for clemency was turned down. I must die then.
>
> We need not say anything anymore to each other. You know that in these last months I have really found the way to myself and to life. Real beauty must stand before unswerving honesty. You know that I have lived every moment fervently and that I have remained true to myself until the end. You must live on. There can be no giving up for you. No becoming soft or sentimental. In these days I have learned to say "yes" to life. Not only to endure it but to love life as it is.
>
> The only way I know how to thank you is by showing you until the last moment that I have used all your love and goodness towards becoming a whole being of my time and my heritage. Do not think of the unused possibilities, but take my life as a whole. A great search, a foolish error, but on its path to finding of final truth, final peace.
>
> Yours forever,
> Helmut

Description by Karen Adler Abramson, B.A. 1985, M.A. 1994; university archivist, 2003–2005; head of Archives and Special Collections, 2005–2010

DONATED TO BRANDEIS BY HELMUT HIRSCH'S SISTER, CATHERINE SUGARMAN, NÉE KAETE HIRSCH

Spitzer Family Papers

A small but noteworthy collection, the Spitzer Family Papers provide a rich history of the lives of a Czechoslovak Jewish family before, during, and after World War II. Written mainly in Czech and German (the family spent a great deal of time in Franzensbad, a predominantly German-speaking town in Czechoslovakia), the papers date from the last decades of the nineteenth century through the late 1970s.

The collection was compiled by Bruno Spitzer, the only member of the family to have escaped Czechoslovakia prior to the German invasion. While most of the family perished in the Holocaust, Bruno (an active and well-known political lawyer in Czechoslovakia) and his wife, Draga, came to the United States in 1939. Upon arriving in Massachusetts, Bruno worked as a laborer in a furniture factory, while Draga was employed first by National Research in Cambridge and later as a librarian at Harvard's Peabody Museum. They lived in Lynn for twenty-one years, moved to Austria for a brief time, and returned to the United States to settle in Brookline.

Among the holdings is a portfolio of letters, papers, and books (including a copy of the rare *Menorat ha-Maor* by fourteenth-century scholar Isaac Aboab) dating to the nineteenth century collected by Rabbi David Spitzer, father to Bruno and his siblings, Harry and Gerta. Rabbi Spitzer was born in Vienna and spent much of his life in Prague.

A large and remarkable section comprises hundreds of photographs of the

Boston, Massachusetts
July 3, 1945

Reverend Waitstill Sharp
c/o American Relief for Czechoslovakia
1819 Broadway
New York 23, New York

Dear Sir:

Mrs. J. Philip Lane gave me your new address and told me that you are leaving soon for Czechoslovakia.

I realize that your time is precious, but knowing how you have helped and are still helping so many people, I am taking the liberty of asking your advice and help for my brother.

On June 30th I received the following telegram: "I am well, parents dead, send visum". Indirectly I had heard before that my brother and my parents were deported to Poland and now he has turned up in Praha alone. He was 14 years old at the time of occupation and is now 21 and has no relatives in Europe.

I would like to do everything possible to help him now, and to bring him to this country as soon as circumstances permit. Mrs. Lane suggested that I get in touch with you.

I would be most grateful if you could contact and advise him, and let me know what I could do to help him now and what steps to take to bring him over.

His name is Harry Spitzer and he lives in Praha 5, Meislova 7.

Thanking you very much, I am, Dear Sir,

Respectfully yours,

Dr. Bruno Spitzer

Spitzer family, dating from the 1920s through the 1970s. These images—a great many of which were taken in Franzensbad in the interwar period—draw a stunning and intimate portrait of a happy family just before the sky fell.

The lives of Bruno and Draga (who, though rarely separated, wrote prolifically when apart) in both Europe and America is well documented through their letters to each other as well as with friends and family back in Europe. The papers include correspondence and other documents regarding the T.G. Masaryk Circle, an association of Czechoslovak citizens residing in Boston with whom the Spitzers were involved.

Perhaps the most gripping materials are those documenting Bruno and Draga's herculean efforts to get Harry Spitzer, Bruno's younger brother, out of Czechoslovakia after the war and, later on, Harry's application for restitution from the German government. Bearing witness to these campaigns are several letters and telegrams from Harry, who had been interned with his stepmother, Dora (Schwartz) Spitzerova, and father in Theresienstadt (where his father died) before being transferred to Auschwitz (where his stepmother perished). Included as well is Harry's own harrowing account of his time in the camps and his parents' deaths. In the end, Bruno and Draga were successful in bringing Harry to the United States, and it is in fact Harry's daughter who donated this collection to Brandeis.

Description by Surella Evanor Seelig, M.A. 2005,
Outreach and Special Projects archivist

DONATED BY LINDA POWERS

Theresienstadt Concentration Camp Documents

Among the most complete collections of administrative documents from the Theresienstadt concentration camp still in existence are the two hundred daily bulletins of the "Jewish Self-Administration" dating from 1942 to 1944. Found within these documents are orders relating to issues that range from housing and personnel to lists of Jews to be kept at Theresienstadt or deported to work and death camps.

The collection was donated to Brandeis in 1973 by Emma Goldscheider Fuchs, a Holocaust survivor who was held at the camp along with her first husband and their two children. Fuchs's husband, Alfred Goldscheider, managed to collect and hide the documents while working in a minor position within the Jewish Self-Administration. Alfred and the couple's son, Hanus, died in German custody, and when Emma and her daughter, Nina, were freed by Allied troops, they returned to Czechoslovakia to reclaim their home and business. Finding their factory under the control of the new communist government, they departed for the United States with a single package in tow—the documents from Theresienstadt, although Emma did not realize their full import at the time.

The German-run camp in the ghetto of Theresienstadt, Czechoslovakia, served as a hybrid concentration/transit camp for European Jews from November 1941 to May 1945. While initially a transit stop for Czech Jews, it soon came to have a more specialized role as a holding base for Jews from Germany, Austria, and Czechoslovakia who were either elderly, disabled due to military service, or famous for their cultural and artistic work. From Theresienstadt, most inmates were sent to their deaths elsewhere.

Theresienstadt was unique in its role as a propaganda stage employed by the Nazis to hide the full extent of their crimes against the Jewish population of Europe and other peoples they deemed inferior. The fiction that the state sought to promote was that Jews were being sent to occupied Eastern Europe solely to take part in forced labor. In order to support that version of events, Theresienstadt was maintained as a camp for the elderly and others who could not be expected to perform hard labor. An infamous visit by the International Red Cross in 1942, for example, provided the Nazis with the opportunity to present a fantasy version of camp life, with inmates painting houses, landscaping, and staging cultural events. The records are evidence of the Nazis' willingness to allow for a

continuation of Jewish cultural life within the camp—to show that the Jews were being treated humanely—while at the same time obscuring the extent of state-sponsored mass murder.

Documents detail regulations for inmates and camp staff alike, as well as statistics and reports on events. Although *Tagesbefehl* (Order of the Day) Number 185, of August 1, 1942, consists of just one double-sided page, it is unusually informative, revealing aspects of daily life and providing evidence of the deliberate manner in which misery was forced on the inmates. Reference is made to the Ostentransport—the deportation of Jews to concentration and death camps in the East. Most of those sent east went to their deaths by gas, bullets, overwork, or starvation. Other orders contain lists of those to be deported and those to be retained. Between January and October 1942, some 42,005 people were deported from Theresienstadt, mostly to their deaths. Between October 1942 and October 1944, an additional 46,750 Jews went from the camp to Auschwitz-Birkenau.

Another particularly instructive report is the December 15, 1942, *Rundschreiben* (newsletter) of the building management department. While primarily concerned with issues such as housing, building maintenance, and fire prevention, this account also lists planned leisure activities, including comedy shows, operettas, and readings from the Bible and Jewish literature. The strangeness of these events occurring amid such suffering and in the context of an ongoing genocide points to the unique nature of Theresienstadt and its propaganda function.

The documents are especially illuminating in their revelations about the role of Jewish self-administration in the camp, which could not be truly independent and was, in fact, responsible to the SS. This unit provided a front by which the Nazis could disguise their aims and even shift some of the blame for harsh conditions onto the Jews themselves.

Care should be taken in interpreting the documents in this collection, given the will of the Nazi regime to make Theresienstadt appear humane to outside observers. While they attest to the suffering of the camp inmates, they also bear witness to the resilience of the Jewish community and its desire to maintain a degree of normalcy, collective identity, and hope in the very shadow of death.

Description by Drew Flanagan, M.A. 2011, PH.D. 2018

Eric M. Lipman Collection of Nazi Documents

The Eric M. Lipman Collection of Nazi Documents offers a glimpse into the evolution of the Third Reich's political and military apparatus, in addition to revealing salient aspects of Nazi racial policy in action. The papers disclose how Nazi figures as well as their institutions responded in the face of significant external and internal pressures, particularly the assassination attempt on Hitler on July 20, 1944, and the January 1945 bombing raids over Munich.

A native of Stolzenau an der Weser, Germany, Lipman graduated from the University of Geneva before emigrating to the United States in the late 1930s to escape the Holocaust. During World War II, as an Army master sergeant, he specialized in enemy documents collection and analysis, then stayed on as a field investigator locating and preparing documents that would be submitted to the International Military Tribunal in Nuremberg. Lipman was honorably discharged in 1946 and worked abroad in international trade before relocating to Richmond, Virginia, in 1950.

The collection consists chiefly of correspondence written between 1921 and 1945. Both diverse and fragmented, the documents include government letters and classified internal correspondence to and from Nazi party officials and military figures, personal diaries, and official decrees. Some of this correspondence indicates how early party and military leaders felt about Hitler's reign as Führer during the initial phases of the National Socialist consolidation of power. Notable senders and recipients include Adolf Hitler, Heinrich Himmler, Joseph Goebbels, Martin Bormann, Wilhelm Keitel, Ulrich Greifelt, and Franz von Papen.

A historically significant document in the collection is a July 1942 letter from Heinrich Himmler to Wolfram Sievers, the managing director of the Ahnenerbe (Research and Teaching Community for Ancestral Heritage). This brief and seemingly innocuous letter serves as a clear indictment of the role of the SS in the establishment and financial sanctioning of medical experiments on human subjects at Dachau, and the Ahnenerbe's role in conducting these atrocities.

The letter establishes the Institut für Wehrwissenschaftliche Zweckforschung (Institute for Military Scientific Research). Examples of the scientific "research" include extensive human experimentation to determine safety thresholds for German servicemen in the Luftwaffe; camp inmates were placed in vacuum chambers in order to simulate high-altitude conditions or exposed to freezing water

IM NAMEN
DES DEUTSCHEN VOLKES

entbinde ich
den Reichsminister
Dr. Wilhelm Frick

von seinem Amt als Reichs- und Preußischer Minister des Innern. Dr. Frick bleibt weiterhin Reichsminister.

Führer-Hauptquartier, den 20. August 1943

Der Führer

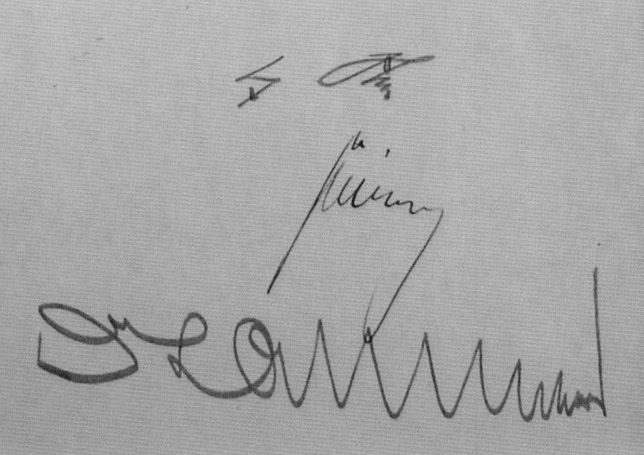

for hours while naked to determine how long pilots could survive after being shot down over open water. Many subjects perished in the process.

Official documents represent one of the most complete and compelling investigations into the local impact of the assassination attempt upon Hitler of July 20, 1944. Chief among these are a July and August 1944 internal report and correspondence between Herbert Wiktorin, Wehrmacht general of the infantry, and Himmler and Hitler. An August 1944 letter addressed to Wiktorin indicates that he was summoned for interrogation by the chief of the SD (Sicherheitsdienst, the covert intelligence branch of the SS), and informed that the Gestapo and the SD suspected him of involvement in the plot. A terse birthday letter from Hitler to Wiktorin sent later that month appears to indicate that the Gestapo eventually cleared him of suspicion. A more "official" counterpoint intended for public consumption is a speech delivered on July 25, 1944, by Deputy Party Leader Karl Holz to the local Franconian population. This is the officially sanctioned version of the assassination attempt and its aftermath in which Holz implores the local German population to keep their faith and loyalty to Hitler.

A crown jewel of the collection is one of only four surviving original copies of a seventy-page top-secret speech delivered by Hitler to high-ranking generals in Platterhof in June 1944. Wrought in oversized typescript, ostensibly so that Hitler did not have to don glasses in public, the speech took almost two hours to deliver. The general tenor is that the Third Reich is in no real danger of losing the war effort, and that victory is inevitable "because we are the best organized state." Hitler notes that Germany lost World War I because of "the traitors within—the Jews," and that no such threat exists in 1944 since "I removed the Jews."

A valuable cache of documents originally from archival holdings of the SD consists primarily of local reports detailing the wide impact of the January 1945 British strategic bombing on the civilian populace of Munich. These record in painstaking statistical detail the tremendous loss of human life as well as the destruction of material resources and essential public services. Of particular importance, the reports identify the severely flagging public morale as a direct result of the "terror raids" and note that the low morale is the most pressing threat to the Reich's survival. This file also contains secret reports by Gestapo informers and SD plainclothes officers who measured the pulse of civilian morale. Collectively, these documents indicate that the SS was extremely concerned with both quantifying as well as influencing the contours of popular opinion. The cumulative tenor of these reports indicates that the Allied strategic bombing of Munich proved devastating to civilian morale while inflicting staggering human casualties and widespread destruction of property.

Interestingly, these documents are interspersed with Allied propaganda leaflets presumably dropped over Munich or the surrounding areas. An undated red leaflet boldly proclaims: "East Prussia cut off! The Red Army deep in Silesia! The 'Ruhr of the East' paralyzed! Zukov's army in Brandenburg! Evacuation of state and party officials in Berlin in progress!" The back of the leaflet features two sections titled "Roosevelt" and "Churchill" along with their national flags, extolling the social and political virtues of each nation's system while simultaneously denigrating the dictatorial nature of the Third Reich.

Description and all translations from German by Clinton Walding, M.A. 2007

GIFT OF ERIC LIPMAN

Jewish Resistance Collection

The Jewish Resistance Collection contains propaganda material, individual testimonies, newsletters, and other documents in several languages pertaining to Jewish resistance movements in Europe during World War II. The collection's holdings regarding the 1943 Warsaw Ghetto Uprising, for example, reveal differing interpretations of one of the central events of Jewish resistance under Nazi domination. These documents shed light on the varied experiences of Europe's Jews, as well as on the ideological divergences within the Jewish resistance.

Communist groups involved in the resistance emphasized the role of (or fabricated one for) the Soviet Union. The April 1944 issue of *Notre Voix*, a Jewish communist resistance newspaper, contains an account of how "inspired by the glorious example of their Soviet brothers, 35,000 Jews of Warsaw raised themselves, weapons in hand, against the ferocious enemy." But factual inaccuracies subvert this narrative—most likely, 600 to 800 Jewish fighters engaged in the uprising, causing relatively minor damage to the German army. In this telling, however, "some thousands of Jews" also managed to flee with their lives and join the Polish partisans. While a number of ghetto residents and fighters did escape into the forest, this newsletter implies that acts of hopeless armed resistance had positive strategic value. In addition to converting a small and futile rebellion into a major battle, communist propaganda transformed a ghetto population that might otherwise have appeared passive into a community of heroes.

Another account found in a July 1944 document from the Comité d'unité et de défense juive (Jewish Committee of Unity and Defense) places the uprising within a broader context. This portrayal of the same event reflects the tension between images of the Jew as resister and as victim. Here, the heroic Red Army is nowhere in sight, while the Polish underground and the armed forces of the Western allies take its place.

Of particular interest in the reporting is the handling of a controversial individual: the head of Warsaw's Jewish Council, Adam Czerniakow. In this account, no attempt is made to deal with the implications of Jewish collaboration, and instead, Czerniakow is treated as a victim. As the document relates: "two functionaries of the German police visited again with Czerniakoff, who committed suicide a few moments after their departure. No one knew what had happened, but it seems from the notes found after his death . . . that he had decided to give his life. . . . It is thus that the heroic mayor of the ghetto of Warsaw demonstrated

ארבעטער צייטונג.

"הפועל-הצעיר" אורגאַן פאַר די ייִדישע אַרבעטער און פאָלקס-שיכטן.
פראַנקרײַך, סעפּטעמבער, 1944. לייענט און גיבט איבער צו לייענען.

דאָס בלוטיקע געזעגענען
פון ה. ביגרער.

אין דעם שרעקלעכן גרויסן גערעגנעל, וואָס דאָס נאַצי דײַטשלאַנד האָט איצט דורך. אין די לעצטע קאָנוואַלסיעס פון דער צע-שמעטערטער היטלערס קריגס מאַשין, איז אים געבליבן נאָך אײן "מאַכט" מיט וועלכן ער ראַט די פעלקער וואָס וועלן אויף די חורבנות פון "דריטן רײַך" ווידער אויפבויען זייער נאַציאָנאַל לעבן און זעלבסט-שטענדיקייט. דאָס זענען די מיליאָנען קריגס געפאַנגענע און אויסלענדישע אַרבעטער וועל-כע זענען געשלעפּט [illegible] אין די דײַטשע פאַבריקן און גרובנס.

דער קרומער גע[illegible] וועגן דער"טאָטאַלער מאָביליזאַ-ציע" איז: ניט ב[illegible] אַרבעט מענער, פרויען און קינדער וואָס געפינען זי[illegible]אַמליזירט, צו אַלע אויפגאַבן וואָס די ווײַטער[illegible]ן. ווען מען באַטראַכט דעם אַר-שטאַנד פון די ד[illegible]לטיקן איבערגעגעבנקייט פון דער אַ-לײַרטער אָרגאַניזאַצי[illegible]ײַטשלאַנד, כדי צו דורכפירן די קריגס אינדוסטרי[illegible] גלויבן אַז די וועלט מערדער מײַ-נען ניט אויסצו[illegible]גענע פאַר פּראָדוקציע צוועקן, נאָר בפירוש פאַר מלחמה[illegible]

צווישן די מיל[illegible]ער טויזנטער ייִד. סאָלדאַטן פון די פּוילישע, טשעכישע[illegible] אַנדערע אַרמייען. זיי געפינען זיך אין די הענט[illegible]ן דער גרעסטער סכנה. ייִדן מאַג וואָס די מלחמה ט[illegible]רם זייער לאַגע...

אין די שטיט[illegible]סטע געביטן אין: פּוילן. טשעכן. אונגאַרן. רומעני[illegible]טער ייִשובים, פאַרשפּאַרטע ייִדן; די נאַצי באַרבאַרן[illegible]כורן טויט. פון די מיליאָנען ייִדן וואָס די רוצחים[illegible]שו געבליבן קליינע טיילן, פון וועמען די באַנדיטן צאַפּן[illegible]רוחות. דאָס-זענען די שארית החורבן פון אונזערע שיינע[illegible] קאָן מען, מוז מען נאָך ראַטעווען.

די נאַצים זענען גאַר[illegible] דערפילן וועם קעגן כח, דאָס האָבן מיר אַלעמאָל געזען ווען די [illegible]ענע קאָנקרעטע אַקציעס קעגן די ווילדע טאַטן פון די ברוינע הענקער. קאָן מען די זעלבע אַקציע ניט אָנווענדן ווען עס האַנדלט זיך וועגן הונדערטער טויזנטער גאָך ביים לעבן געבליבענע ייִדן? מוזן אַלע פאַרשפּאַרטע און דעפּאָרטירטע ייִדן- ווײַל זיי זענען ייִדן- אומקומען אונטער דעם בלוטיקן היטלער רעזשים?... דאָס היטלער דײַטשלאַנד האַלט ביים פאַלן, אָבער ביז דעם טאָג ווען דאָס וועט געשען, זענען די ס.ס. און געשטאַפּאָ באַנדיטן די הערשער און באַלעבאַטים איבער די הונדערטער טויזנטער לעבנס. נאָר אַ דירעקטע דראָהונג קאָן זיי אָפּהאַלטן פון די מערדערישע הענט.

פאַרבינדעטע מלוכות. אייער כח איז אומבאַגרענעצט. אײַערע מעגלעכקייטן אומבאַגרע-נעצט. גרויס בריטאַניע. פאַראייניקטע שטאַטן. ראַטן פאַרבאַנד. פראַנקרײַך און דער אַרבעטס-קלאַס פון די אַלע לענדער, וועמענס אַנזען וואָרט אַלץ שטאַרקער און ווירקזאַמער. איר האָט דאָס וואָרט. ראַטעוועט אונזערע ברידער. איר קאָנט עס נאָך טאָן. ס איז נאָך צײַט...

די ערשטע זיצונג פון צענטראַל קאָמיטעט פון דער ייִד. אַרב. פּאַרטיי. "פּועלי – ציון" אין באַפרײַטן פראַנקרײַך. שיקט איבער די הײַליקסטע גרוסן דעם פאַרבאַנד בירא און אַלע "פּ-צ" פאַרטייען. באַזונדער די חברים אין פּוילן וואָס האָבן הערואיש געקעמפט קעגן די פאַשיסטי-שע מערדער, און זענען ווײַטער פאַר אונזער אַלע אויסשטענדן דעם קאַמף פאַר פרײַהייט און רעכט. דער צ.ק. שיקט איבער זײַנע הײַסטע גרוסן די "פּועלי ציון" חברים אין בעלגיע צו זייער באַפרײַונג פון נאַצישן יאָך, און דריקט אויס זײַן אָנערקענונג פאַר זייער מוטיקע און קעמפערישער האַלטונג פאַר דער גאַנצער צײַט פון דער באַרבאַרישער מערדערישער אָקופּאַציע

...

AVRIL 1944 **Notre Voix** N° 7I

L'ARMEE ROUGE POURSUIT LES NAZIS EN FUITE EN ROUMANIE!

DANS SON IRRESISTIBLE MARCHE EN AVANT, ELLE PORTE LA

LIBERTE A TOUS LES PEUPLES OPPRIMES!

8 MILLE JUIFS DE PARIS DEPORTES A L'EST SONT SAUVES PAR LES SOLDATS DE L'ARMEE ROUGE!

François BILLOUX et Fernand GRENIER membres du C.C. du Parti Communiste entrent dans le C.F.L.N.

En réponse à la campagne xénophobe et anti-juive, renforçons notre participation à la lutte libératrice de la France!

COMMEMORONS LE Ier ANNIVERSAIRE DU SOULEVEMENT HEROIQUE DU GHETTO DE VARSOVIE PAR UNE JOURNEE NATIONALE DE DEUIL ET DE COMBAT!

Le désastre de l'armée allemande sur le front sud s'accroît d'heure en heure. La glorieuse Armée Rouge a franchi le Prouth et poursuit les bandits fascistes en fuite sur le territoire roumain. Comme l'a déclaré le Commissaire aux Affaires Etrangères, Molotov, l'Union Soviétique ne touchera pas à l'intégrité territoriale de la Roumanie, l'Armée Rouge n'a qu'une seule tâche: poursuivre et battre l'ennemi par tout où il se sauve; jusqu'à ce qu'il dépose les armes et capitule.

Une des leçons les plus importantes des évènements du front de l'est, c'est que l'Allemagne n'est plus capable de tenir tête sur plusieurs fronts, ce qui prouve qu'une attaque massive des alliés sur la forteresse européenne aura comme résultat la défaite complète des bandits nazis. Déjà l'Allemagne nazie se bat toute seule et ce n'est que par la terreur qu'elle empêche certains de ses satellites de se détacher d'elle. Partout les positions allemandes sont menacées par la lutte des partisans et les peuples, encouragés par les grandioses victoires de l'Armée Rouge, se lèvent pour la bataille décisive

(suite page 2)

MERCI !

Une nouvelle qui réjouira tous les Juifs de France nous parvient par les ondes de Radio-Moscou. Qui d'entre nous n'a pas un frère, une soeur, un époux, un parent parmi les déportés de Paris? Et qui ne ressentira pas une joie intense à la pensée que huit mille Juifs de Paris viennent d'être sauvés de la mort par la glorieuse Armée ROuge.

C'EST UN D'EUX QUI RACONTA A LA RADIO-MOSCOU COMMENT IL AVAIT ETE SAUVE DE LA MORT, EN MEME TEMPS QUE HUIT MILLE AUTRES JUIFS PARISIENS. ILS SE TROUVAIENT TOUS EN UKRAINE AU MOMENT DE LA DERNIERE OFFENSIVE SOVIETIQUE ET LES BANDITS S.S. DEVAIENT LES FUSILLER AVANT DE QUITTER LE PAYS.

Connaissant le sort qui leur était réservé et ayant appris que les troupes soviétiques n'étaient pas loin, les Juifs déportés décidèrent de s'enfuir. Ils ont été bientôt recueillis par l'Armée Rouge, et sont maintenant tous en Union Soviétique. L'héroïque Armée Rouge aura ainsi mérité, une fois de plus, la profonde reconnaissance de la communaute juive de France.

VIVE L'ARMEE ROUGE-LA LIBERATRICE!

. . . the horror and the indignation that he felt before the mass deportation of his people."

In addition to the characterization of Czerniakow as a "heroic mayor" rather than a complex, tragic figure, and a collaborator, the recounting serves as a preface to the description of the fighting in the ghetto. After depicting the battle rather vaguely, the document concludes: "thus the Jewish population of Warsaw paid even more dearly than the Poles for its resistance to the Germans . . . but resistance was achieved in the silent protest of death with the extermination of the last Jew and the complete destruction of the ghetto itself." This note of despair contrasts sharply with the nearly fanatical dynamism of the communist account. The piece finds a nuanced synthesis between the very real victimization of the Jews and their equally real and courageous resistance. What appears to be a story of fruitless sacrifice is here revalorized as evidence of the "virility" and quality of Polish Jewry, and an example to French Jews.

In these retellings of the Warsaw Ghetto Uprising one year after it occurred, the two accounts offer different interpretations of the Jewish role in the resistance. The communist perspective presents a view that reconciles the Jew as both victim and resister—a small, symbolic uprising is presented as a mass revolt in which every resident died fighting, although many of the ghetto's Jews did not or could not fight. The version told by the Jewish Committee of Unity and Defense is more factually accurate and provides a more positive impression of the moral strength of the Jewish people.

Over time, French Jewish resistance began to turn to retrospective visions that were politically useful and emotionally acceptable—visions that could take into account both the worst humiliations of the Holocaust and the greatest acts of heroism.

Description by Drew Flanagan, M.A. 2011, PH.D. 2018

World War II Guernsey Scrapbook

The Channel Islands northwest of the French coast are the oldest possessions of the British Crown, though they are not part of the United Kingdom. Guernsey is one of the two autonomous island groupings; the other is Jersey.

Brandeis is home to an unusual scrapbook of the Channel Islands—the only British soil occupied by Germany during World War II. Created by "W.T. Oliver, 8 Rouge-Val Road, St Johns, Guernsey" and dating from November 16, 1943, to August 21, 1944, the book is titled "Volume 2" (the location of Volume 1 is unknown). It includes handwritten records of BBC war broadcasts juxtaposed with newspaper clippings of German wartime reports from local commandeered newspapers.

To understand the import of the scrapbook, it is necessary to understand Guernsey's status and role in the war. Realizing that they could not properly defend the Channel Islands, and seeing only minimal strategic importance, the British demilitarized the region in 1940 to prevent military targeting and bloodshed. The British also offered to pay for the evacuation of all Channel Island resi-

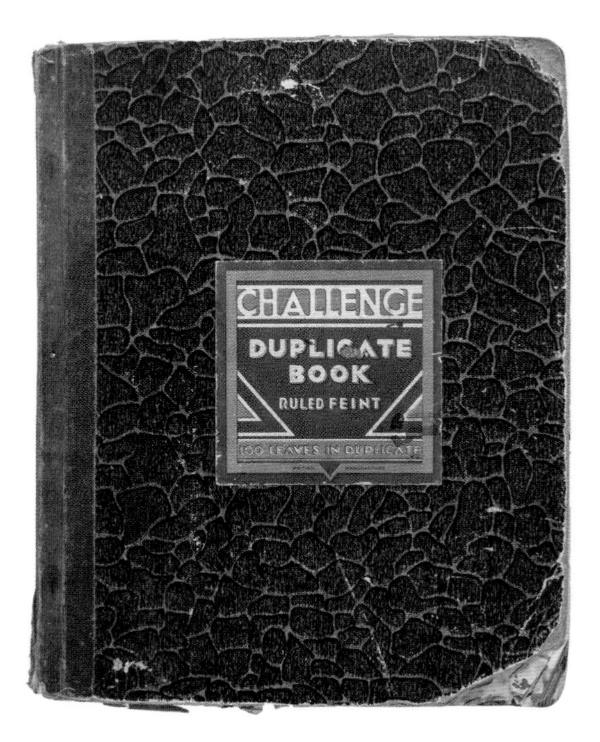

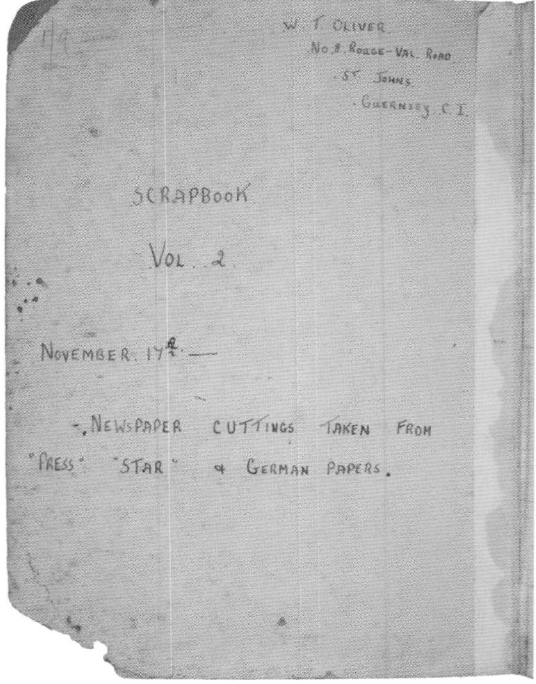

Press. Nov. 19th

Marines of the German Forces stand by the flag-draped coffin of naval men.

Bailiff of Guernsey, Mr. Victor G. Carey, places a wreath on behalf of the people of the Island.

"Star" of Nov. 20th also contained photos & account of funeral, so I have again kept the full paper.

Press. Nov. 24th

£10 REWARD

Will be paid for information leading to the conviction and imprisonment of the persons who raided La Colombelle grounds in the evening of 24th November, and stole Vegetables and Poultry.

Press. Nov. 24th. B.B.C. News Nov. 24th

The ~~R~~. R.A.F. bombed Berlin again last night. Over 2,000 tons of bombs were dropped, mostly 4,000 lb bombs.

Reports from Sweden state that Hitler's, Ribbentrop's & Goerring's mansions were destroyed during the raid.

The town the Russians evacuated last Saturday was Zhitomir.

Reinforcements have arrived in Italy for the Canadians.

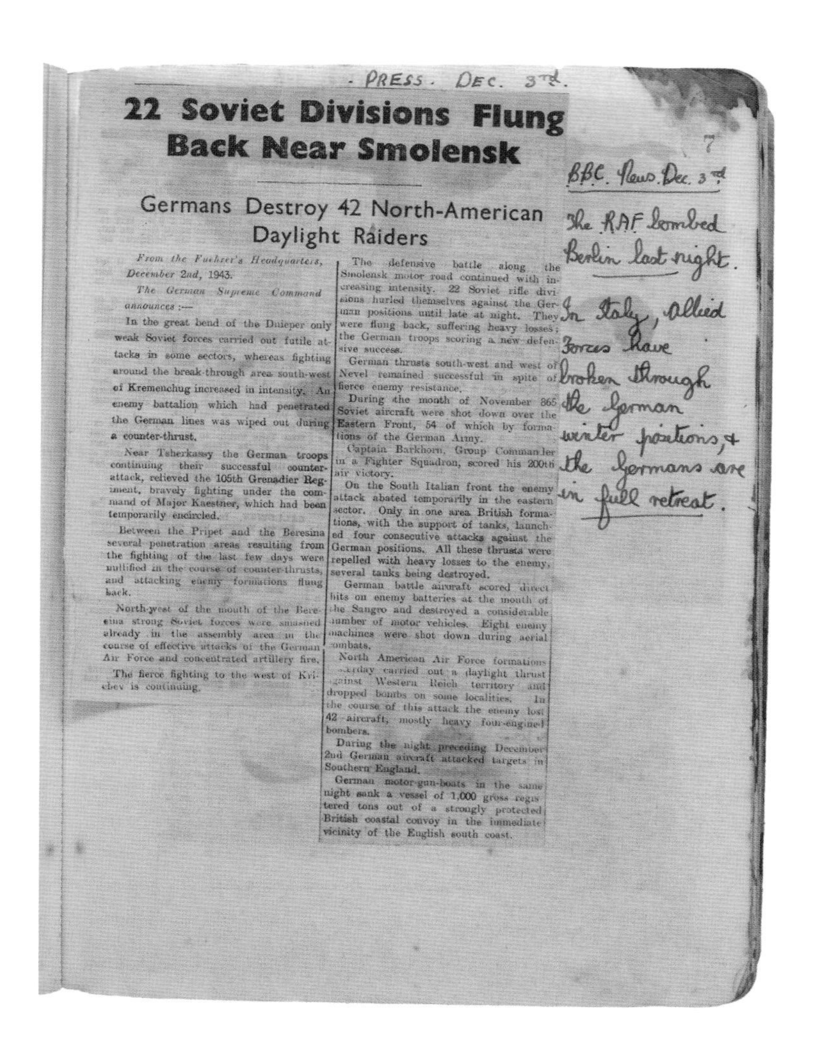

· PRESS. DEC. 3rd.

22 Soviet Divisions Flung Back Near Smolensk

Germans Destroy 42 North-American Daylight Raiders

From the Fuehrer's Headquarters, December 2nd, 1943.

The German Supreme Command announces :—

In the great bend of the Dnieper only weak Soviet forces carried out futile attacks in some sectors, whereas fighting around the break-through area south-west of Kremenchug increased in intensity. An enemy battalion which had penetrated the German lines was wiped out during a counter-thrust.

Near Tsherkassy the German troops continuing their successful counter-attack, relieved the 105th Grenadier Regiment, bravely fighting under the command of Major Kaestner, which had been temporarily encircled.

Between the Pripet and the Beresina several penetration areas resulting from the fighting of the last few days were nullified in the course of counter-thrusts, and attacking enemy formations flung back.

North-west of the mouth of the Beresina strong Soviet forces were smashed already in the assembly area in the course of effective attacks of the German Air Force and concentrated artillery fire.

The fierce fighting to the west of Krichev is continuing.

The defensive battle along the Smolensk motor road continued with increasing intensity. 22 Soviet rifle divisions hurled themselves against the German positions until late at night. They were flung back, suffering heavy losses; the German troops scoring a new defensive success.

German thrusts south-west and west of Nevel remained successful in spite of fierce enemy resistance.

During the month of November 865 Soviet aircraft were shot down over the Eastern Front, 54 of which by formations of the German Army.

Captain Barkhorn, Group Commander in a Fighter Squadron, scored his 200th air victory.

On the South Italian front the enemy attack abated temporarily in the eastern sector. Only in one area British formations, with the support of tanks, launched four consecutive attacks against the German positions. All these thrusts were repelled with heavy losses to the enemy, several tanks being destroyed.

German battle aircraft scored direct hits on enemy batteries at the mouth of the Sangro and destroyed a considerable number of motor vehicles. Eight enemy machines were shot down during aerial combats.

North American Air Force formations yesterday carried out a daylight thrust against Western Reich territory and dropped bombs on some localities. In the course of this attack the enemy lost 42 aircraft, mostly heavy four-engined bombers.

During the night preceding December 2nd German aircraft attacked targets in Southern England.

German motor-gun-boats in the same night sank a vessel of 1,000 gross registered tons out of a strongly protected British coastal convoy in the immediate vicinity of the English south coast.

7

BBC. News. Dec. 3rd

The RAF bombed Berlin last night.

In Italy, allied forces have broken through the German winter positions, & the Germans are in full retreat.

dents to England, but only half of the residents had left when Germany—which had not learned of the British demilitarization—bombed Guernsey's main harbor on June 28, 1940, killing or critically injuring more than sixty residents. Two days later, the Germans quickly and quietly occupied the Channel Islands.

Until liberation on May 9, 1945, the residents lived uneasily under German occupying forces. The two local newspapers—the *Star* and the *Evening Press*—continued publication but remained heavily censored and replete with propaganda. A few citizens collaborated with the Germans, but the majority neither abetted nor resisted the invading army.

Outnumbered by a large and well-armed German force—and with little chance of leaving the island—residents knew that large-scale resistance would lead to equivalent retaliation. Even so, some residents regularly committed small acts of sabotage, such as cutting cable lines and defusing mines. When the Germans imported Jews and other political prisoners from Europe to slave labor camps on the islands (the only instance of Nazi concentration camps on British soil), some residents objected to the harsh treatment and offered food, shelter, and hiding places for escape.

By far the most common act of resistance involved owning and listening to a radio. The Germans banned radio ownership in June 1942. If found in possession of a radio, residents could be punished with fines, imprisonment, hard labor, or even death. In response, some turned in their radios, then built their own crystal radio receivers; others hid theirs in "prams, manure heaps, beds, even . . . a washtub full of soapsuds." Still others organized news services and secretly recorded BBC reports in shorthand and then distributed the information via word of mouth or printed news briefs.

The Guernsey scrapbook is one such illegal record, detailing reports of the Allies' successes and bombing raids. The scrapbook also gives insight into the day-to-day wartime experiences of the residents. It is perhaps most valuable for its record of comparative wartime propaganda. While BBC reports describe Allied bombing raids in terms of factories or military camps destroyed, Nazi-influenced *Star* and *Evening Press* news clippings of the same events detail the "terror attacks" of the "British air gangsters" and the "yankee monster."

The scrapbook's combination of BBC broadcasts and Nazi war reports creates a particularly chilling reflection of the war in the days surrounding June 6, 1944, later known as D-Day, the Allied invasion of Normandy. While scrapbook entries suggest that BBC broadcasts were silent on the topic prior to June 6, rumors of the invasion were evident in Nazi-controlled Guernsey papers in late May. On June 6, the *Star* published an ominous report from the German Supreme Command: "this morning early, 5:30 A.M., our enemies in the west have, upon orders from Moscow, started their bloody sacrifice . . . . We will give them a very warm welcome. Germany is conscious of the meaning of the hour. She will fight with her whole might and passionate resolution in order to protect Europe, her culture, and the life of her people from barbarism."

Items similar to this Guernsey scrapbook caused numerous residents to be imprisoned and some sent to their deaths in Nazi camps. In all, over 2,000 Channel Islanders were deported to prison camps for "crimes" that included radio listening, minor sabotage, and prisoner aid.

An uncommon combination of material, the scrapbook documents the wartime views and propaganda of opposing sides in World War II. Considering the risks involved in its creation, the Guernsey scrapbook is a testament to the determination of the residents to maintain their hope in and patriotic connection with England in the years of German occupation.

Description by Anne Marie Reardon, M.A. 2007, PH.D. 2014

Hall-Hoag Collection of Extremist Literature in the United States

"What I do is essentially engage them eyeball to eyeball. Confrontation on a daily basis. No one else does it," remarked independent collector, archivist, and researcher Gordon Hall in a *Boston Globe* article from May 7, 1967. Hall was speaking of his interactions with the extreme left- and right-wing groups whose materials he painstakingly collected for the better part of his life.

Gordon Hall was an American soldier stationed in the Pacific theater in World War II. During his time in the service, he was introduced to many left-wing political ideas while he was fighting the fascist ideology whose ideas would later be reflected in the writings of right-wing groups in America. Though Hall never finished high school, his studious nature made him curious about both ends of the political and religious spectrum and led to his investigations into the history and aims of political organizations. In the same *Boston Globe* article, he observed: "Communism is bad, but this [antisemitism and racism] are just as bad. As far as I can see, there are two extremes worth fighting and I guess that's what I really want to do." The materials Hall preserved date from the late 1940s through the early 1980s. Together, they act as a barometer of the political climate during the postwar period.

The documents tell us as much about their time as they do about our own moment. Such materials as the Manion Forum Organization brochure demonstrate the importance of the media and street organizing in creating a movement. The tools of the Manion Forum Organization, a conservative club "concerned about liberals, socialists, and communists," included radio and television advertisements, distribution of printed materials, and door-to-door volunteers. The brochure's graphics of numerous modest homes are paired with the caption: "The Manion Forum Penetrates Millions of American Homes Every Week." The map on the opposite side shows the potential reach of radio, television, conservative clubs, and campus radio networks across the country.

Similarly, the *Student Voice* newspaper of February 25, 1964, discusses an effort by the Student Nonviolent Coordinating Committee (SNCC) that resulted in "at least 100" attempts to register African American voters throughout southwest Georgia. On the facing page, a photograph shows two white businessmen standing with the Atlanta NAACP president with signs touting economic frugality,

THE STUDENT VOICE

VOL. 4 NO. 7 The Student Voice, Inc. 6 Raymond Street, N.W., Atlanta 14, Ga. FEBRUARY 25, 1964

Ga. Judge Gives Coed 18 Months

ATLANTA, GA. - An 18-year-old white girl, a student at Connecticut College for Women, was sentenced here Feb. 20 to six months in the common jail and 12 months on the public works.

She was fined $1,000. Her appeal bond was set at $15,000.

The girl, Mardon Walker, formerly an exchange student at Spelman College here, was arrested during a Jan. 13 sit-in attempt at a segregated restaurant.

She was charged with violation of Georgia's trespass law, passed in 1960 after student anti-segregation demonstrations began.

The judge, Fulton County Superior Court Judge Durwood T. Pye, requires that appeal bonds be posted with unencumbered-property located in Fulton County.

Georgia's Supreme Court reversed an earlier bail of $20,000 Judge Pye set for an elderly white man, the Reverend Ashton Jones, 67, jailed during a church

CONTINUED ON PAGE 4

IN PINE BLUFF

LEADERS CALL 72 HOUR TRUCE

ARKANSAS DEMONSTRATORS protest segregation at Ray's Barbecue, where comedian Dick Gregory and SNCC worker William Hansen were jailed Feb. 18.

Dick Gregory Released From Jail

PINE BLUFF, ARK. - Anti-segregation demonstrations have have halted here for 72 hours while mediators attempt to negotiate a settlement between Ray's Barbecue and members of the Pine Bluff Movement.

Dick Gregory, jailed with SNCC Arkansas Project Director William Hansen on Feb. 17, left the Phillips County jail to make contact with Federal officials and to complain about jail conditions.

"Its like somebody's secret torture chamber," Gregory said.

Demonstrations began here on Feb. 17, when Hansen and Gregory were jailed.

On Feb. 18, 15 people were jailed, and crowds of whites - some identified by newsmen as "professional segregationists" - began to gather at the segregated eating place.

SNCC worker James Jones was punched by a state trooper..

On Feb. 19, 39 others were jailed.

Reverend Benjamin Grinnage, chairman of the Pine Bluff Movement, was fired at during a demonstration on the evening of Feb. 20.

A group of protesters were met by two white men, one - who identified himself as the owner - carrying a 12 gauge shotgun and one carrying a .38 caliber pistol.

The owner told the group "I am the owner. This is private property. Why do you want to integrate me? If you come up on the sidewalk, I'll shoot you. I'm a mental patient, I've killed 1,000 Japs. God didn't mean for it to be like this."

CONTINUED ON PAGE 2

100 REGISTER IN SOUTHWEST GEORGIA FREEDOM DAY

Albany citizens attempt to register at courthouse

SOUTHWEST GEORGIA - A four - county "Freedom Day" Feb. 22 has resulted in "at least 100" attempts to register to vote here.

Vote attempts were made in Terrell, Sumter and Dougherty Counties. In Lee County, where registration books were closed, 150 Negroes gathered at New Piney Grove Baptist Church for a vote rally.

Like Hattiesburg, Mississippi's Jan. 22 Freedom Day, Southwest Georgia's was a victory.

"We have never picketed and leafleted downtown without having arrests before today" SNCC's Southwest Georgia project head Charles Sherrod said in Albany.

Here's a breakdown on activity

CONTINUED ON PAGE 4

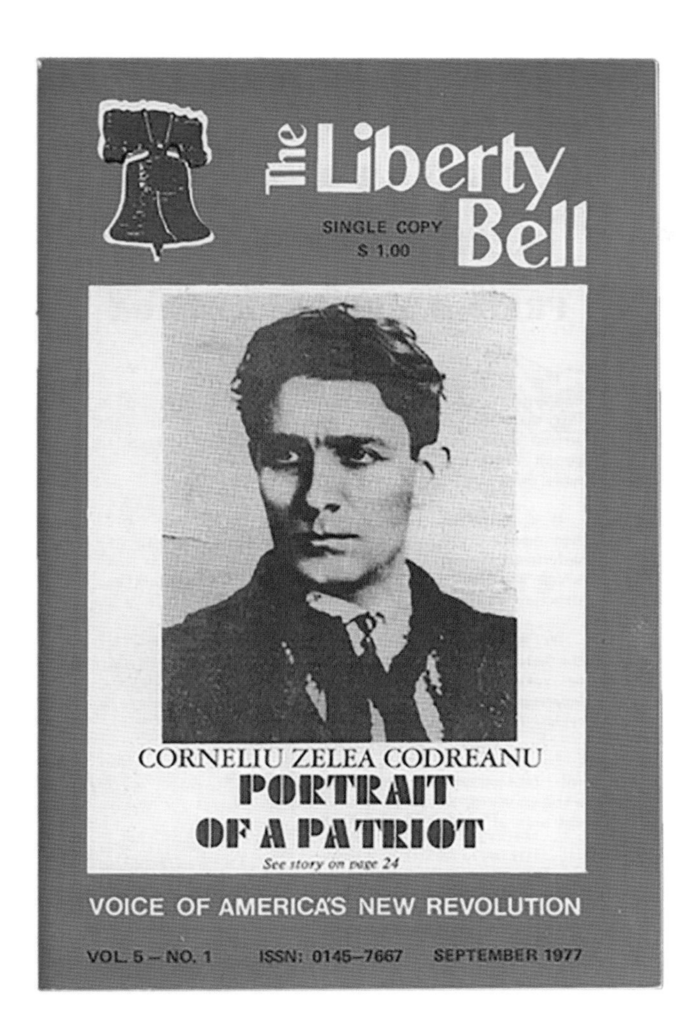

admonishing "wear old clothes *this* Easter" and "Easter frills *or* Freedom. You cannot have both now."

The striking graphics employed by various organizations are of special interest. Throughout the collection, several right-wing groups employ the well-worn Liberty Bell motif: a few of these include the Liberty Bell Press from Missouri, which investigated communist activity within the United States; the publication *Through To Victory*, from a Christian anticommunist organization; the Liberty Belles, a women-only organization interested in reining in government power and spending as well as eradicating communism, socialism, and anarchism; and *The Liberty Bell*, an antisemitic publication.

Though some of the documents are independently well-known, like the Weather Underground's *Prairie Fire*, this collection is an invaluable gathering of materials relating to extremist movements within the United States. Several are shocking, and all are sectarian.

Description by Katie Hargrave, M.A. 2009

Lenny Bruce Collection

Comedian, satirist, social commentator, and rule breaker, Lenny Bruce wrote and performed brilliant, disturbing, and divisive comedy routines. His bold use of language; his fearlessness in naming social, legal, and political hypocrisies; and his fight for his First Amendment rights paved the way for important changes in this country, not only to its comedic landscape but also to the rights of its citizens to speak freely and without fear.

The collection of photographs, writings, show transcripts, correspondence, audio recordings, and trial papers documents Bruce's professional career as well as his personal life. News clippings and articles provide insight into the public response to Bruce's humor and performance style, his legal battles, and the state of free speech in mid-twentieth-century America, including materials that were gathered by Bruce's close friend, Ralph J. Gleason, a journalist for the *San Francisco Chronicle* who later became the founding editor of *Rolling Stone* magazine.

Leonard Alfred Schneider was born on October 13, 1925, in Mineola, New York, to Myron Schneider and Sally Marr. Bruce's parents divorced when he was young, and Bruce's early relationship with his father was strained, although it improved later in his life and some of their correspondence can be found in this collection. Bruce was always very close with his mother. Marr, a stand-up comic, was one of the first female comedians; in fact, one of Bruce's earliest public performances was as part of a Sally Marr show. Bruce joined the Navy at age sixteen, serving in both Africa and Italy during World War II. He performed his first comedy routine for his shipmates.

Best known for his stand-up comedy, much of which was improvised, Bruce often took a rather free-form, jazz-style approach to his performances, rarely writing his routines down in advance (though he transcribed many of them). As his legal battles began to heat up, Bruce's routines often dealt with his multiple arrests and court cases. He made several albums of original material and was also a prolific writer, authoring plays, sketch-comedy routines, screenplays, magazine articles, and an autobiography titled *How to Talk Dirty and Influence People*, first published in 1965 and rereleased in 2016.

In his stand-up routines, Bruce regularly discussed issues of race, gender, sexuality, sex, politics, and religion. At the time, the language he used was often classified as "vulgar," "obscene," or "sick." Branded the "sick comedian," he was arrested and tried several times on charges of obscenity. His first such arrest, at the Jazz Workshop in San Francisco on October 4, 1961, resulted in an acquittal,

Introducing ...

LENNY BRUCE

AN EXHIBITION OF THE LENNY BRUCE COLLECTION

Robert D. Farber University Archives &
Special Collections Department
Goldfarb Library, Level 2
Monday-Friday, 9:00 a.m.-5:00 p.m.

"Satire is tragedy plus time. You give it enough time, the public, the reviewers will allow you to satirize it. Which is rather ridiculous, when you think about it."

Brandeis University

Office of Communications ©2018 Brandeis University H011e
Image courtesy of Robert D. Farber University Archives & Special Collections Department. All rights reserved. Kitty Bruce

but it was not his last brush with the law. Eventually he was found guilty of obscenity on November 4, 1964, for charges that stemmed from his performances at Greenwich Village's Café au Go Go in April of that year; he was sentenced to serve time in a workhouse, but died during the appeals process. By the end of his life, Bruce had been blacklisted from most clubs in America and barred from entering England. His court cases were highly publicized and continue to be considered important moments in the fight for freedom of speech.

When Lenny Bruce died of an accidental heroin overdose on August 3, 1966, he left behind a legacy of groundbreaking comedy and commentary and an enduring mark on generations of comedians—many of whom cite him as a major influence on their work. His unwavering struggle with the American legal system in a years-long battle to speak freely while performing his art likewise left a lasting impression. In 2003, thirty-seven years after his death, Bruce was granted a pardon for his 1964 obscenity conviction by New York governor George Pataki.

Description by Surella Evanor Seelig, M.A. 2005,
Outreach and Special Projects archivist

ACQUIRED FROM LENNY BRUCE'S DAUGHTER,
KITTY BRUCE, IN 2014 WITH A GENEROUS GIFT FROM
THE HUGH M. HEFNER FOUNDATION

Leo Rosten Papers

In 1908, the man who would become known professionally as Leo Calvin Rosten was born in Łódź, Poland. Rosten was raised in Chicago, having moved to the United States with his parents in 1911. He earned his bachelor's and doctoral degrees in political science from the University of Chicago before conducting postgraduate work at the London School of Economics.

While best known as a humorist and for his books *The Education of H*Y*M*A*N K*A*P*L*A*N* (1937) and *The Joys of Yiddish* (1968), Rosten produced work that crossed a number of genres. A scholar, novelist, lexicographer, scriptwriter, journalist, playwright, biographer, and essayist, he was a hugely prolific public intellectual. Many of his pieces for *Look* magazine dealt with major contemporary political and social issues, and he is generally considered to have brought an understanding of Yiddish and its reflection of Jewish culture to American consciousness. In Rosten's *New York Times* obituary of 1997, *The Joys of Yiddish* was described as "the de facto standard reference work on the language, serving as a bridge between the world of Mr. Rosten's forebears and that

Sept. 1, 1936 — Austerlitz — Anytime) ~~2000 words~~ set slug

use stars

for style

Mr. K*A*P*L*A*N's Hobo

#6

#3239

3=line indent + caps

11pt / 13½ picas

Perhaps Mr. Parkhill should have known better. Perhaps he should have known Mr. Kaplan better. And yet, in Mr. Parkhill's conscientious concern for every student in the Beginners' Grade of the American Night Preparatory School for Adults ("English — Americanization — Civics — Preparation for Naturalization") there could be no discrimination. Despite Mr. Kaplan's distressing class record, despite his amazing rendition of the English language, Mr. Parkhill insisted on treating him as any other student. Just because Mr. Kaplan referred to rubber heels as "robber hills", or called a pencil-sharpener a "pantsil-chopner", or gave the opposite of "new" as "second-hand" was no reason why he should not participate in the regular exercises of the class on an equal footing. And so Mr. Kaplan stood at the front of the room before the forty-odd adults in the class, ready to speak for ten minutes during the Recitation and Speech period.

"Speak slowly, Mr. Kaplan," said Mr. Parkhill. "Watch your pronunciation. Remember it isn't how fast you talk, or how much you say. Try to be accurate and speak distinctly."

Mr. Kaplan nodded confidently with his great, broad smile.

"And watch your e's and a's. You always confuse them in your speech."

roman

Mr. Kaplan nodded again, smiling. "I'll be so careful, Mr. Pockheel, you'll be soprize," he said.

"And the class will feel free to interrupt with corrections at any time," finished Mr. Parkhill with an encouraging nod to the class. Allowing them to interrupt with corrections had proved very successful. It kept them alert, and it made the student reciting particularly careful, since there was a certain of the more assimilated readers of our own age." That his writing was widely read and influential is evident from the many fan letters he received, particularly those from famous political, literary, and artistic names of the period, including Allan Bloom, Ray Bradbury, William F. Buckley, Jr., Norman Cousins, John Kenneth Galbraith, Cary Grant, J. Edgar Hoover, Henry Kissinger, Groucho Marx, Bill Moyers, Richard Nixon, Gregory Peck, Arthur Schlesinger, Jr., and Thornton Wilder.

In addition to literary accomplishments, Rosten's long career included a variety of professional experiences, many of which informed his writing. First published in *The New Yorker* under the name Leonard Q. Ross, the Hyman Kaplan stories were inspired by the people Rosten had met while teaching English to speakers of other languages during the Great Depression. He also served at the Office of War Information during World War II, worked for the RAND Corporation, edited *Look* magazine (from 1949 to 1971), and taught political science at a number of universities.

Created and donated by Rosten himself, the collection provides a meticulous catalog of his long and fascinating career. It includes boxes of notecards of research material, drafts and final manuscripts, galleys and printers' copies, texts of interviews and speeches, tapes of his readings, publicity materials, correspondence, book reviews, fan mail, dictionaries, reference books, and files from his time at the Office of War Information. Items such as his academic hood, writing utensils, passport, and appointment books offer a more intimate view into Rosten's personal life.

The university also holds an annotated typescript of "Mr. Kaplan's Hobo," a Rosten short story published in *The New Yorker*. Signed by the author, with editor's notes, the typescript provides significant and rare insight into the thinking and methods of this extraordinary man and the era in which he lived.

Description by Surella Evanor Seelig, M.A. 2005,
Outreach and Special Projects archivist

Arthur Laurents Collection

Any Shakespeare student or fan of musicals is aware that the tale behind *West Side Story* is *Romeo and Juliet*. But there is another story behind the award-winning musical, one that stars its creators—Arthur Laurents, Leonard Bernstein, Stephen Sondheim, and Jerome Robbins—who did not always agree about the direction of the show. The Laurents correspondence brings to light the frequent back-and-forth between the principal creative agents, offering insight into their disagreements over particular characters and scenes as well as larger issues of creative control.

While perhaps best known for his book for *West Side Story*, Arthur Laurents (1917–2011) was a playwright, novelist, and director, celebrated for many successful projects for stage and film. The correspondence relates mainly to the development of *West Side Story* and *I Can Get it for You Wholesale*, and features letters from Irving Berlin, Jerome Robbins, and Harold Rome, among others involved with the two shows.

Included are communications from Cheryl Crawford, who had been the producer for *West Side Story* until she dropped it shortly before rehearsals began for its Broadway debut in September 1957. She voices doubts about the production in a letter to Laurents in April of that year: "I think we are in trouble. Although I want so much to be constructive and not destructive, it does no good to shut my mind and trust to blind luck." She outlines problems with the plans for the show, including the critique that "the story at present has no real depth or urgency." In a reply, Laurents addresses Crawford's concerns: "I apologize for my vehemence on the subject of naturalism but it is something I am sick to death of in the theatre and is one reason why I wanted to do a musical." He continues, "the biggest problem in the book has always been to me the second act. Because it is based completely on a gimmick in Shakespeare, it must be replaced by a gimmick in ours. It is where we really depart from the original and our replacement had better be as good or better or we fall."

Not all of the letters show displeasure. Some of the richest observations come from Jerome Robbins, the show's director and choreographer, who writes in a postscript to his letter of November 7, 1955: "Just read balcony scene—Bravo—it's so good."

About a week later, Robbins points out what he finds to be the strongest parts of the work-in-progress, and his theory as to why: "I like best the sections in which you have gone on your own path, writing in your own style with your own

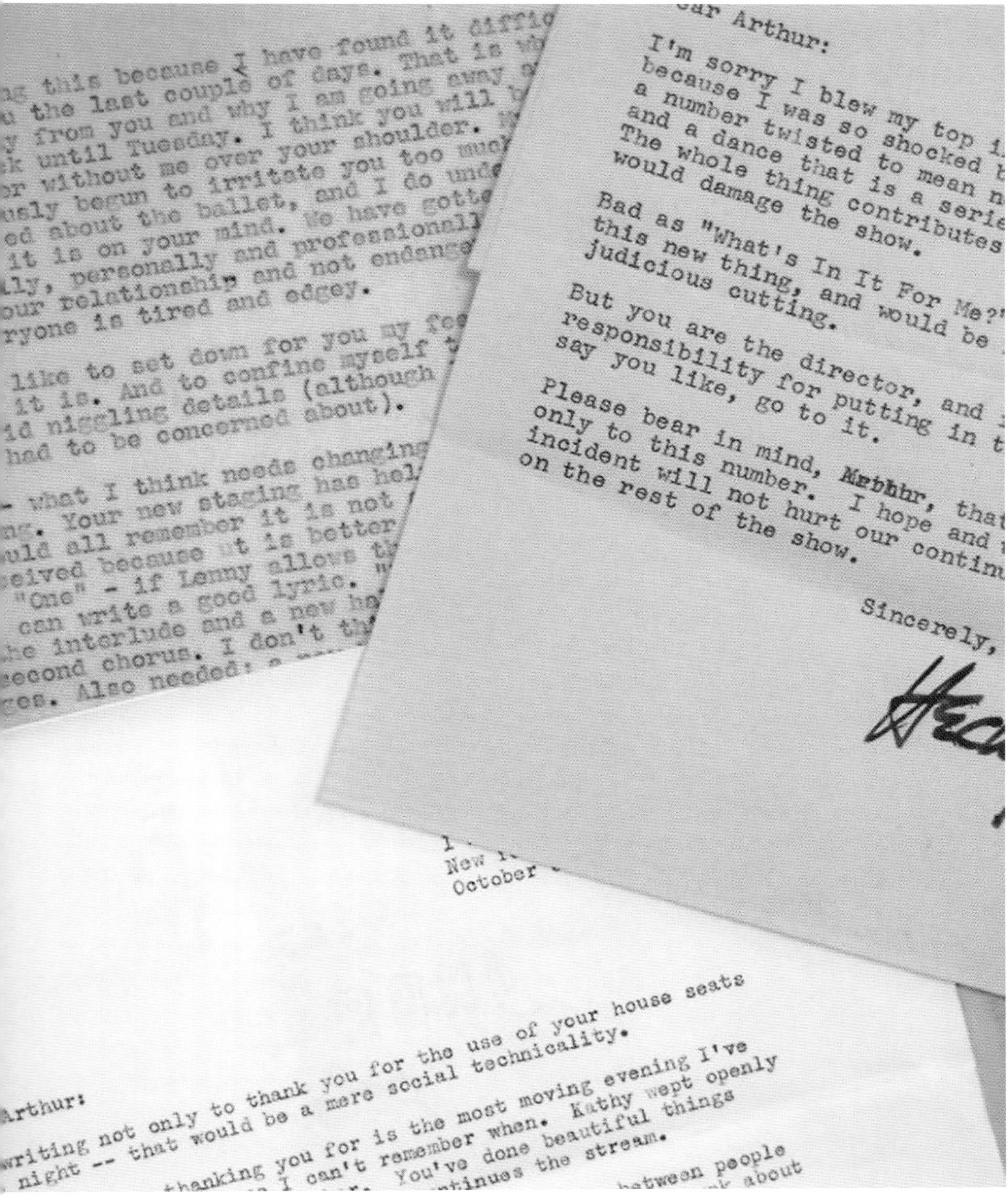

ng this because I have found it diffic
u the last couple of days. That is wh
y from you and why I am going away a
k until Tuesday. I think you will b
or without me over your shoulder. M
usly begun to irritate you too much
ed about the ballet, and I do und
it is on your mind. We have gotte
lly, personally and professionall
our relationship and not endange
ryone is tired and edgey.

like to set down for you my fe
it is. And to confine myself t
id niggling details (although
had to be concerned about).

- what I think needs changin
ng. Your new staging has hel
uld all remember it is not
eived because ut is better
"One" - if Lenny allows th
can write a good lyric. "
he interlude and a new h
second chorus. I don't th
ges. Also needed: a ne

Dear Arthur:

I'm sorry I blew my top i
because I was so shocked b
a number twisted to mean n
and a dance that is a serie
The whole thing contributes
would damage the show.

Bad as "What's In It For Me?"
this new thing, and would be
judicious cutting.

But you are the director, and
responsibility for putting in t
say you like, go to it.

Please bear in mind, Arthur, that
only to this number. I hope and
incident will not hurt our contin
on the rest of the show.

Sincerely,

Hea

I
New Y
October

Arthur:

writing not only to thank you for the use of your house seats
night -- that would be a mere social technicality.

thanking you for is the most moving evening I've
I can't remember when. Kathy wept openly
You've done beautiful things
ntinues the stream.

between people
k about

characters and imagination. Least successful are the sections in which I sense the intimidation of Shakespeare standing behind you."

Similar themes appear in letters related to the 1962 musical *I Can Get It for You Wholesale*, with music and lyrics by Harold Rome and direction by Laurents (with a cast that included a young Barbra Streisand in her Broadway debut), revealing the nature of their collaboration. Rome wrote to Laurents on March 5, 1962, a couple of weeks before the opening, "I'm sorry I blew my top in the theatre. I lost control because I was so shocked by what I saw on the stage—a number twisted to mean nothing—that goes nowhere and a dance that is a series of meaningless gymnastics." But Rome then strikes a conciliatory tone ("you are the director") and expresses hope that they can continue to cooperate.

The Laurents correspondence exposes professional relationships in which artistic personalities clash, reconcile, and attempt to navigate a way to work together, opening a remarkable window into the sometimes messy process behind the creation of iconic Broadway productions.

Description by Sarah Shoemaker, head of Archives and Special Collections

DONATED BY ARTHUR LAURENTS

Joseph Heller's *Catch-22* Manuscript and Correspondence

A year after his first novel appeared, Joseph Heller got a query from his Finnish translator, who needed to solve the following riddle: "Would you please explain me one thing: What means Catch-22? I didn't find it in any vocabulary." By 1974 the translator could have consulted *Webster's New World Dictionary of the American Language* (Second College Edition), which classifies "catch-22" as a common noun. Yet only an uncommon author could coin so indispensable a term, and indeed much about his book is unusual. It was the first novel Heller tried writing, and though the first chapter had been published in a journal in 1955, six more years were needed to finish the book. Had he known how long it would take, Heller later remarked, he might not have started writing it.

Catch-22 never came close to making the *New York Times* bestseller list, and at first lived precariously as a word-of-mouth "cult" novel. But as the military intervention in Vietnam gained momentum, as that disaster helped to spawn a counterculture, the novel became a phenomenal popular success, guaranteeing that Heller would never need to dig for quarters out of car seats. A decade later, *Catch-22* was *more* popular than it was immediately after publication, and dwarfed the later, growing success of other serious novels that had appeared around the same time—like Ken Kesey's *One Flew Over the Cuckoo's Nest* (1962) and Kurt Vonnegut's *Cat's Cradle* (1963). In fact, *Catch-22* has become one of the most popular novels ever written. Such phenomenal success makes Heller's manuscripts and correspondence archived at Brandeis of unusual value and interest, including the original manuscript of *Catch-22*, written on yellow legal pads, with its myriad corrections and editorial changes.

Catch-22 is populated with "characters whose antics were far loonier than anything ever seen before in war fiction—or, for that matter, in any fiction," literary scholar John Aldridge observed. From Ernest Hemingway and John Dos Passos down to Norman Mailer, war novels were supposed to be written in the vein of spare, austere "documentary realism." But what was Heller getting at? Was he joking about the most horrifying of all themes, turning on laughing gas to get rid of the stench of death? The characters he had invented were mostly cartoons, and some were grotesque. The situations were outlandish. Lip-readers might well have inferred that the men who defeated the Axis in the most awful of wars were uncomprehending buffoons whose commanding officers were either

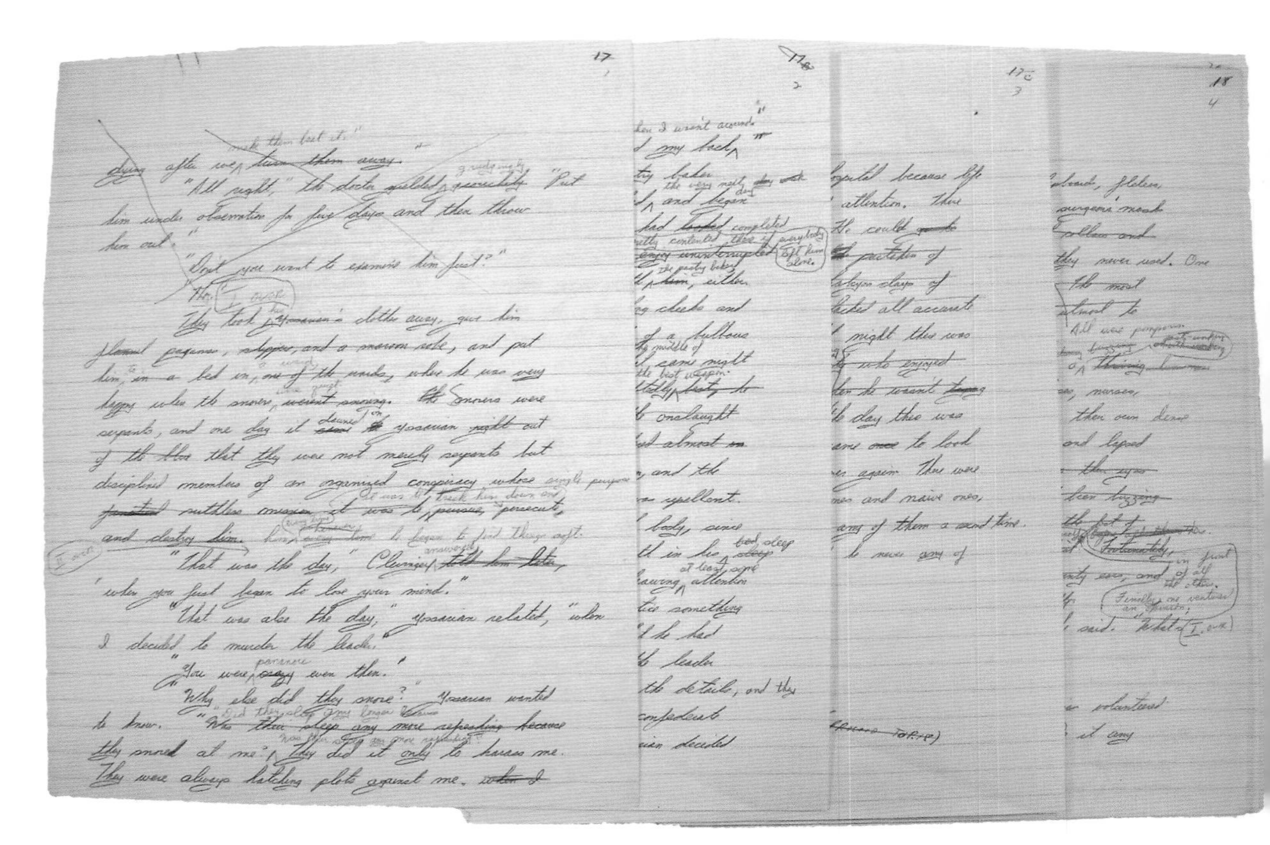

mad or moronic. Infantry platoons were often celebrated as rainbow coalitions, yet why would the protagonist of Heller's novel be an Assyrian and the chaplain an Anabaptist? No wonder then that Aldridge claimed that critics and other readers had to learn to become more sophisticated to fathom the striking originality of Heller's novel.

Yet private correspondence with Heller, available in this collection, cannot be perfectly squared with Aldridge's argument. Many of Heller's fellow writers were quick to understand and to welcome what he accomplished. Two years after the novel was published, Dos Passos, then a conservative and a Republican, spoke highly of so subversive a text. The legacy of John Steinbeck includes *The Moon Is Down* (1942), set in World War II; no American novelist did more for social realism. Yet the Nobel laureate realized that *Catch-22* merited rereading, that "a good book" the first time around proved to be "loaded with things that must be come at slowly. . . . My wife says she knows when I am reading *Catch-22* because she can hear me laughing in the next room and it is a different kind of laugh."

Old-fashioned sorts of writers were thus quick to pick up the radically disorienting portrayal that this first novel was presenting. This essay would be incomplete, however, if it did not mention the impact that *Catch-22* exerted on a twenty-three-year-old unknown whom Heller's agent claimed was "the only other genius" she had the privilege of representing. From the future author of another novel set in World War II, *Gravity's Rainbow* (1973), Candida Donadio received the following letter: "You thought I'd LIKE it. Jesus. I love it. I won't tell you how much, or why," Thomas Pynchon wrote, "because I always sound phony whenever I start running off at the mouth like a literary critic. But it's close to the finest novel I've ever read. . . . Who is this guy Heller[?]"

This guy also received unsolicited fan mail from Nelson Algren ("the laughter is hard-won. . . . Thanks for writing *Catch-22*"); from novelist and political activist Jeremy Larner '58 ("I read every word of *Catch-22* with great delight and ended up scared and moved and happy"); and from Stephen Ambrose, who would become a prolific military historian. "For sixteen years I have been waiting for the great anti-war book which I knew World War II must produce," Ambrose wrote. "I rather doubted, however, that it would come out of America; I would have guessed Germany. I am happy to have been wrong."

Such responses are even more striking when the structure of his novel is considered. If reduced to plot summarization, *Catch-22* is rather thin. It recounts the conflict between a bombardier and a superior officer over how many missions should be flown. Rearranged in chronological order, *Catch-22* seems rather uneventful: three missions to Avignon, to Bologna, and to Ferrara have all occurred before the time of the first chapter, and M&M Enterprises has been formed. As characterizations, Heller's three dozen servicemen do not exactly bulge with the three-dimensionality that is often credited to the finest fiction. Most—but not all—are caricatures, and even what protagonist John Yossarian looks like is sketchy. For all of its scale, this novel lacks lyrical descriptions, or precise evocations of the natural world, or metaphysical depth.

Yet, by this book, we as well as our posterity are likely to know Heller the way we also know Cervantes and Swift and Voltaire—which is by one book, and only one book. The cauterizing humor and pungent politics that Heller stirred together have been enduring enough to catch the reader's attention—and that's some catch, that *Catch-22*.

Description by Stephen J. Whitfield, Max Richter
Professor of American Civilization, emeritus

DONATED BY JOSEPH HELLER

Sophie Tucker Scrapbooks

Nicknamed "The Last of the Red Hot Mamas," entertainer Sophie Tucker was famous for her risqué performances in which she challenged accepted ideas about race, ethnicity, and gender. The scrapbooks that Tucker (and, later, her assistants) meticulously collected and arranged for more than fifty years throughout her performing career as a singer and comedian reveal both her professional and personal life from 1906 until her death in 1966 at the age of eighty. She accumulated more than four hundred volumes over her lifetime, with Brandeis housing those from 1957 to 1965.

Born Sonya Kalish in Russia in 1886, Sophie Tucker and her family immigrated to the United States with Italian papers soon after her birth, changing the family name to Abuza. At seventeen, she married Louis Tuck. The marriage failed (the first of three to end in divorce) soon after the birth of her only child, Albert; she left her son with her family and went to New York City to find work as an entertainer. Adding "er" to her married name, she began performing as a singer, sometimes in blackface. As the story goes, her makeup box disappeared before

THE DEAUVILLE presents
LAST 2 NIGHTS
PHIL SILVERS
and his SGT. BILKO REVUE
WITH THE MELLO-LARKS
AND WALTER DARE WAHL
PLUS THE CASANOVA MILITARY DANCERS
OPENING THURSDAY — FEB. 11
SOPHIE TUCKER
ACCOMPANIED BY TED SHAPIRO
JAN MURRAY
PLUS THE CASANOVA CONTINENTAL DANCERS
2 SHOWS NIGHTLY 9 and 12 PM
Reservations MARCEL, UNion 5-8511
DANCING TO HENRY LEVINE and his Orchestra
IN THE MAGNIFICENT Casanova Room

DALLAS, TEX. NEWS
JAN 15 1960

Ole Olsen and Chic Johnson, celebrating their fortieth year in show business, laugh it up for the first-

Dallas After Dark

By TONY ZOPPI

'60 'Hellzapoppin' At Century Room

Olsen & Johnson blew the lid off the 1960 version of "Hellzapoppin'" at Hotel Adolphus Thursday night to the delight of the young-at-heart who attended the laugh-packed premiere.

The all-star cast features Marty May, June Johnson, Eileen O'Dare, Rudy Tronto, the Laurie Sisters and Bobby May.

Chic and Ole, one of the most suffessful duos in the history of show business, are about as subtle as the 7-year itch. They depend on the broadest of comedy to draw laughs, but the end justifies the means. Their audience was left limp with laughter by such shennigans as a pistol being fired out of the southern end of a north-bound horse, and the suave Mr. May stepping out of his trousers.

The crowd was entertained less boisterously by the Laurie girls —a singing group who last appeared at the Mural Room five years ago.

LONG-STEMMED hoofer Eileen O'Dare and Rudy Tronto, who had the dance lead in "Guys and Dolls," presented excellent dance routines.

Miss Johnson, who is Chic's [...] action, the reason for their [...]cess seemed obvious. The [...]dience is there to be entertai[ned] so bring on the laughs.

Bill Tieber and the Joe Re[...]man band lend superb support [to] the revue. Their dance rhyth[ms] kept the floor packed with d[anc]ers, and who could ask for [any]thing more.

AROUND THE TOWN: Orle[ans] Room will offer "Disco[very] Nights" every Friday and Sa[tur]day. Any talent seeking a sh[ow]case is invited to appear. Co[n]tracts will be offered those a[cts] which click with the audie[nce]. Area agents and bookers are [in]vited to attend . . . Phil Gord[on] is up next at the Upstairs Dow[n]stairs Club. He has had a sol[id] TV background in such shows a[s] Alfred Hitchcock Presents, P[ete] Kelly's Blues and "The Untouch[ables]." He'll do standup comedy and play piano. . . . King's Cl[ub] has signed Helen Boice for tw[o] weeks starting Monday. She [is a] ringer for Sophie Tucker. . . Barney Weinstein, who is r[e]decorating the Theater Loung[e] prior to the Marquis Chimp[s] opening Monday, found a glass eye under one of the ringside tables! . . . Breck Wall's new revue, "In The Meantime," open[s] Jan. 27. He will debut as director [...]

Thinking of you

HARTFORD, CONN. TIMES
JAN 21 1960

Coast-to-Coast

with

Allen M. Widem

Times Theater Editor

Continental Distributing's "Pretty Boy Floyd," opening a saturation New England premiere next week (Jan. 28 at Loew's Poli, Hartford, and within day or two at other Loew's Poli-New England Theaters Inc. situations in Bridgeport, New Haven, Waterbury, Meriden in Connecticut, and Springfield and Worcester in Massachusetts), marks screen debut for a New England trained thespian.

* * *

BARRY NEWMAN, AT 28 already a veteran of a decade of varied stage and television portrayals, is a Yonkers, N. Y., native, and member of the first graduating class at Brandeis University, Waltham, Mass., we're informed by his brother, Edmund, Boston-based sales representative for a New York concern.

The latter joined Lou Cohen, Loew's Poli-New England Theaters Inc. Hartford city manager, and representatives of law enforcement agencies and the press at an afternoon screening of "Pretty Boy Floyd" at the Palace Theater here.

"Barry's wanted to be an actor as long as anybody in the family can remember," Edmund continued. "When he was a kid, he used to 'act out' or improvise, I guess the trade term would be, a number of intended dramatic roles. After getting out of Brandeis, where he had majored in both drama and sociology, incidentally, he decided to concentrate on a career in the theater in New York.

John Kriyna — Herman Wouk — Sophie Tucker — Valerian Yaversky

Sophie Tucker in St. Louis:

Hartfordite Sophie Tucker observed her 72nd birthday while performing at the Chase Hotel, St. Louis, the other night, Beulah Schacht reports in The Globe-Democrat.

"In a day when many entertainers hang on to a microphone simply because they don't know what else to do with their hands, it's a thrill to watch a gal like Sophie work!" adds Miss Schacht.

"During her 56 years in show business, the last of the red-hot-mamas has always concentrated on fresh material, dramatic, glittering gowns and the latest hair-dos. For 38 of those years, Ted Shapiro has been her musical director and accompanist. Their timing is so perfect, the show skips along with the meter of a witty poem.

"Her birthday party was no sobby down-memory-lane affair. She didn't once slip in a reference to the good old days which most people consider far better than the present days.

"'Retire?' Sophie bellowed when the subject was tossed in her ample lap. 'I'm working on next year's material right now!'"

Jack Kofoed Says

History Erred, Kraut Isn't German Dish

BECAUSE NATIONAL Kraut Week slipped by without notice from this pillar of wisdom and infallibility, the infallibility sign will have to be taken down. Kraut is popular, and statisticians estimated no less than a billion servings will be forked over American tables during 1960.

It has long been accepted that this is a German dish. So deep was the conviction that, in World War I we called the Kaiser's soldiers "kraut," and in a spirit of misguided patriotism, renamed the dish "liberty cabbage."

Now, we are informed that history erred. Sauerkraut was invented during the reign of Emperor Shih Hwang, when the Great Wall of China was being built. Cabbage was cured with rice wine, and it wasn't until centuries later that a German discovered salt was a much better curing agent than wine. Then, the kraut we know today came into being.

This vital information may add nothing to your success and happiness, but here it is for what it is worth. Besides, it may forestall another "first" claim by the Russians. They invented everything else, so why not sauerkraut?

* * *

HE WAS AN important man in the small Canadian town of Thedford, chief of police, street inspector, in charge of garbage collection, and dog catching. After years of hard work and long hours, the official decided that, since he seemed almost, irreplaceable to the community, he deserved more pay.

Dolling up in his uniform, cleanly shaved and smart, he appeared before the town council to argue the point. There was no argument. The councilmen said their budget wouldn't permit extravagance such as salary raises, and fired him. Maybe they were right. The police chief, etc., etc. was getting \$87 a month! Any complaint about your income?

* * *

MAURICE CHEVALIER, who's 71, won the critics' ap[...]

WHO KNOWS?

Who knows what dreams lie, hidden,
Behind the blushing rose,
Where they may creep, forbidden,
To stretch themselves? Who knows?

Who knows the secrets trampled
Beneath the winter snows,
Where hearts in June had sampled
The wine of love? Who knows?

Who knows what tears, unbridled
Flow, as the river flows,
Where lovers met and idled
Too long — Too late —? Who knows?

Who knows why Fate, unfeeling,
Beckons, and smiles on those
With hungry hearts appealing—
Then locks the door? Who knows?

MAURINE C. DUPUY

* * *

plause in an hour long one-man show on television. Jimmy Durante, who's 69, is a top hand in night clubs and TV. Now Sophie Tucker, who's older than either, though it may be unkind to mention a lady's age, comes to our town again.

creeping up, give a thought to Chevalier, Durante and Tucker. They prove a person is no older than he thinks he is.

* * *

NOTES ON a shabby cuff: Milton Berle, who played in the most popular movie serial of all time, "The Perils of Pauline," when he was a little fellow, probably knows more about the history of ancient silent flickers than anyone else . . . How far the fight game has fallen is shown by attendance at the Wilf Greaves-Tiger Jones bout. Both good middleweights, who always put on a slugging battle, they attracted 308 customers and a gate of \$1,007. Even "Diamond Lou" Bailey's "Bucket of Blood" in Philadelphia 50 years ago would have considered that disgraceful.

As mother told me there would be, there are days when you fumble even the easiest grounder. I plead guilty to boots. Joe E. Lewis my "post time" pal, will be at the Eden Roc for another week, and the dinner Paul Caspers is giving 92-year-old Fred Gates is at that hotel.

Dear Aunt Soph –
As always I'm saying thank you for being you and loving me and talking to me from the heart & many wise years experience.
This year Ryan joins me in this small token as a way of saying we [...]

SOPHIE TUCKER — At Deauville.

Last Of Red Hot Mamas To Open At Deauville

There's just one performer who tops Sophie Tucker year after year, and that's "The Last of the Red Hot Mama's" herself!

La belle Tucker, "The First Lady of Show Business," is the greatest cafe star of all times, and getting greater year by year.

For her engagement in the Deauville's Casanova Room beginning tomorrow, Sophie has worked up the most terrific show of all. She has sensational new numbers, hilarious new comedy material, out-of-this world costumes and coiffure — and Sophie herself is more bombastic than ever!

There's never been anyone like Sophie — and probably never will be. She's the first and the last of the Red Hot Mamas — she evokes an avalanche of spontaneous applause, the applause of anticipation, the instant she steps out on stage.

"There is nothing mysterious about my staying on top all these years," says Sophie. "I have simply kept abreast of the times. I'm a vaudeville trouper, you know. Early in the game I learned that you can't rest on yesterday's laurels. Your audience always expects something new, something better. And I always try to deliver! That means a constant hunt for new songs, new material, new methods. Nightclubbers want highly concentrated entertainment: action, speed, smartness, color, music, laughter."

When Sophie steps out on the floor, she represents a personal production outlay of anywhere from \$15,000 to \$25,000! She is a showman to her fingertips. Every detail of dress and material are carefully planned.

Sophie's career is a thrilling saga of show business. She is one of the most popular and best-loved entertainers in the world, and one of the most charitable women in the profession. Her heart and purse are always open to anyone in need.

For a Dear and Special Friend

Thinking of You

Thinking of you

one performance, compelling her to appear onstage without her blackened face. She was a hit and never performed in blackface again.

Tucker's music and style were influenced by the blues and jazz, music styles dominated by African Americans at the time. She worked with a number of African American composers and artists, which was unusual for white performers in the early twentieth century.

In Tucker's 1945 autobiography, *Some of These Days* (named after one of her hit songs), she wrote of her early career in burlesque: "Folks wanted a belly laugh every so often. They wanted to let down their hair and unbutton their vests and be natural. They wanted to laugh at sex. Sex was funny, not necessarily intense and tragic the way the playwrights such as [Henrik] Ibsen made it out to be. Why, weren't the best jokes in the world the ones that played on sex?" Although Tucker did not stay on the burlesque circuit for long, her goal of entertaining audiences through comedic, risqué performances remained part of her act.

Tucker deliberately cultivated an aura of intrigue. Discrepancies in her stories appear frequently as she told and retold them. She never seems to have revealed her original name or the year of her birth to the press, for example. In the scrapbooks, her public persona emerges as she envisioned it. The thorough organization of the materials suggests that she created her public image just as carefully as she arranged her scrapbooks.

Newspaper clippings include articles mentioning Tucker and her performances as well as interviews in theater and entertainment columns. The articles are trimmed to fit as many on the page as possible. In the headlines from newspapers published across the United States, Tucker's name appears with those of popular figures such as Jackie Kennedy and Frank Sinatra. The scrapbooks include correspondence with U.S. presidents, fellow entertainers, personal friends, family members, and fans. She kept greeting cards commemorating her birthday, holidays, and other celebrations in addition to telegrams and letters. To maximize space, the telegrams were pasted to the page one atop the other.

Tucker spent much time and money in support of charitable causes and contributed to a wide range of charities. A practicing Jew, Tucker supported Jewish-affiliated organizations and universities, including Brandeis. She also spread her wealth to Christian institutions, American soldiers overseas, and organizations dedicated to preventing and curing diseases. Her scrapbooks include correspondence and thanks from those who benefited from her generosity, and among the notes she saved were those acknowledging her donation to the Brandeis National Women's Committee in support of the campus library and her endowment of a chair at Brandeis in 1955, the Sophie Tucker Chair in the Theatre Arts.

Description by Allison Lange, M.A. 2009, PH.D. 2014

DONATED BY SOPHIE TUCKER

Radical Pamphlet Collection

During the late 1960s and early 1970s, a new generation of American radicals protested the Vietnam War, proclaimed Black power, and demanded women's liberation. Partly in response to the era's political ferment, Brandeis began to collect radical literature from the twentieth century, with over four thousand documents that help illuminate the history of trans-Atlantic radicalism, especially Anglo-American labor radicalism. Not limited to national politics, the collection includes a large number of publications produced at the state and municipal levels.

With a primary emphasis on radicalism in the first half of the twentieth century, especially between 1930 and 1950, the wide array of printed materials—including pamphlets, magazines, journals, books, and campaign advertisements—

AMERICA'S "THOUGHT" POLICE

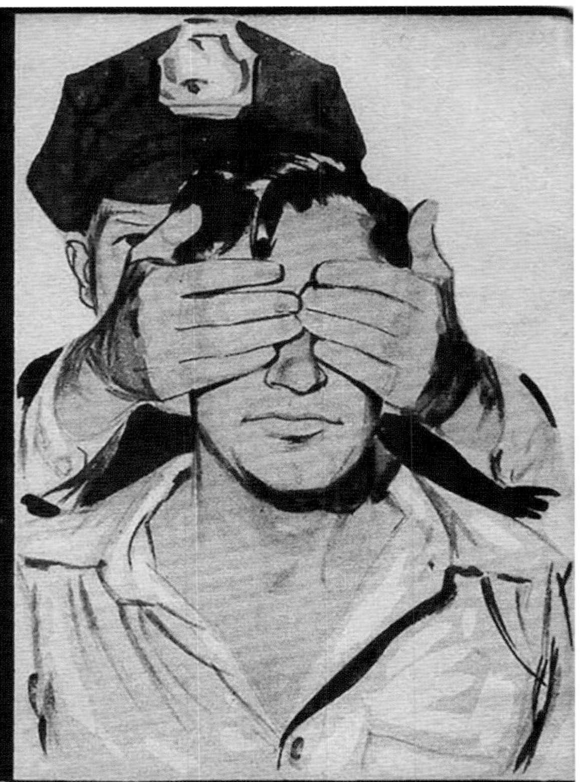

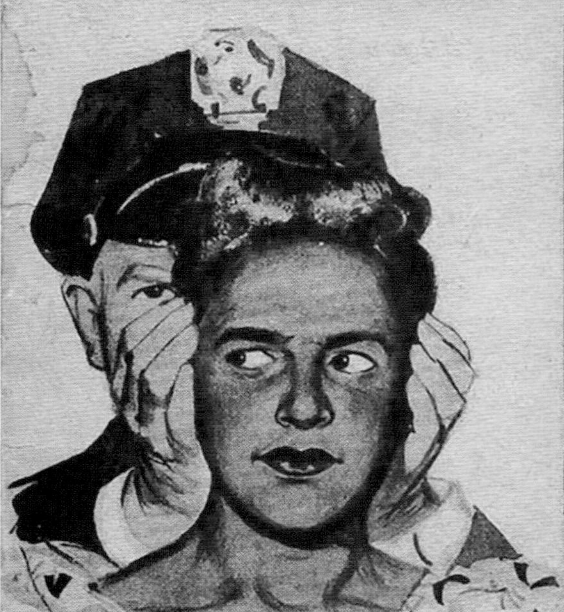

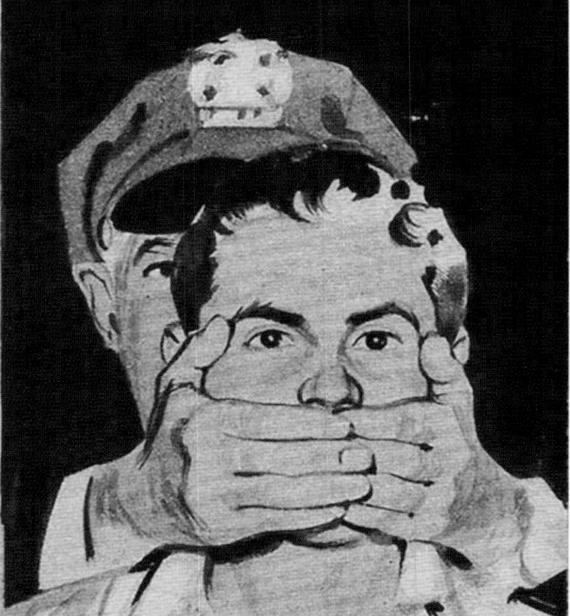

RECORD OF THE UN-AMERICAN ACTIVITIES COMMITTEE — 15c

with a foreword by HENRY A. WALLACE

constitutes an extensive catalog of British and American Communist Party literature that highlights the parties' responses to the Great Depression, World War II, and the war's aftermath. The materials produced by American communists show the ways the party tried to attract African Americans and women by emphasizing (what were then considered) its radical positions on gender and racial equality. At the same time, the documents reveal how the party attacked its socialist enemies and vigorously defended Stalinism and the Soviet occupation of Eastern and Central Europe.

In addition to pamphlets and political tracts are a number of radical and artistically inventive magazines and journals from the first half of the century, including *Mother Earth*, *Americana*, *The Masses*, *The New Masses*, *Class Struggle*, and *Labor Defender*.

Also well represented are the views of civil libertarians, who defended the rights of communists and radicals as they faced repression from both state and federal authorities. A number of booklets defending civil liberties during the McCarthy era, as well as many publications produced by the American Civil Liberties Union from the 1920s through the 1950s, are part of the holdings.

Complementing the focus on left-wing radicalism are documents related to right-wing anticommunism. These include published reports from the House Un-American Activities Committee and pamphlets such as the staunchly anticommunist *The Truth About Communism*.

The breadth of the collection provides an overview of the trajectory of American radicalism during the twentieth century—from its height during the Popular Front of the 1930s, to its relative decline during the McCarthy era, to its rejuvenation with the movements of the New Left in the late 1950s and 1960s.

Description by Julian Nemeth, PH.D. *2014*

Havurat Shalom Records

Committed to the mission of serving as "a still, small voice," Havurat Shalom Community Seminary, a center for new forms of Jewish worship and religious study, was established in Cambridge, Massachusetts, in the fall of 1968 to bring new energy to Jewish spiritual and communal life. The records of Havurat Shalom, created between 1968 and 1976, document the founding and early years of this groundbreaking institution.

While Havurat Shalom provided intensive courses in Jewish theology and Judaic studies, the Havurah also fostered a social community, merging intellectual and communal life. The belief was that such a fusion would nurture a deeper kind of spirituality not possible in other Jewish religious settings.

The archives shed light on the articulation of the Havurah's founding values. Included are drafts of Havurat Shalom's founding covenant, minutes of planning discussions, and promotional brochures. These documents underscore the extent to which the founding members believed in the Havurah's extraordinary potential to revitalize Jewish life, to connect the traditions of Judaism and the needs of the present.

Out of this rich community came the bestselling and influential *Jewish Catalog*. Authored by members of Havurat Shalom and Brandeis alumni, this do-it-yourself manual for Judaism was modeled on the counterculture bible, *The Whole Earth Catalog*, and dedicated "to an old rambling yellow house in Somerville, MA . . . to Havurat Shalom."

Although Havurat Shalom was intended to be more than an educational institution, the collection includes materials that demonstrate its functions as a center of religious education. Course lists highlight the founders' desire to ensure a diverse curriculum; class topics ranged from scripture and theology to Jewish culture and philosophy. Courses were offered not only to official students of the seminary but to members of the wider community as well, through Havurat Shalom's House of Study for Adults.

Brandeis University and Havurat Shalom were linked from the very beginning. The Havurah's primary founder, Rabbi Art Green, earned his B.A. ('61) and PH.D. ('75) from Brandeis. In addition, Rabbi Albert Axelrad—a longtime director of Brandeis Hillel—was intensely involved in the early efforts. He communicated plans for Havurat Shalom to other Jewish institutions, helped seek the participation of scholars and theologians for its advisory committee, took part in fundraising efforts, and corresponded with potential students. With Brandeis

I. PURPOSE. We, the members of Havurat Shalom Community Seminary, define ourselves first as a religious community, as a group of Jews whose lives are guided by spiritual search, and who see in a religious community the possibility for a kind of study and worship ~~and communion~~ not available to one man alone.

We are a Seminary, in the sense that we are a place for the study of the traditions and texts which make up our heritage as Jews. We do not view the Havurat Shalom experience as primarily one of professional preparation, but we are committed to a deep involvement in the life of the larger religious community, whatever our livelihoods. Our aim, rather than the training of religious professionals, is the education of religious personalities on the basis of a personal encounter with the sources of Judaism.

II. CLASSES. Members of the Havurah meet regularly for textual study ~~and sys-tematic discussion of matters of con-temporary~~. Our teachers are members of our community who have distinguished

alumni among the Havurah's first members, Brandeis students spread the word, telling their friends at other universities of its impending creation and helping to expand interest in the project.

The collection sheds light on an important moment in American Jewish life, a time of experimentation with new forms of worship and spirituality. The documents offer insight into the energy and enthusiasm that accompanied this experiment, as a younger generation of Jews strove to rethink religiosity in the context of the late 1960s.

Description by Sean Beebe, PH.D. *2020*

DONATED BY HAVURAT SHALOM

Marcia Freedman Papers

An interesting addition to the growing body of collections on Jewish feminism are the papers pertaining to the life and work of Marcia Freedman, an American-Israeli activist and feminist. While the materials date from 1968 to 2016, the majority relate to Freedman's time in Israel during the 1970s, as well as her return there in the late 1990s.

Born in Newark, New Jersey, in 1938, Freedman earned a bachelor's degree from Bennington College and a master's from the City College of New York. In 1967, while pursuing a doctorate in philosophy, she moved with her family to Israel, just after the Six-Day War. In the early 1970s, Freedman taught philosophy at Haifa University and a course on women in Western philosophy at Oranim College. After a brief return to the United States in 1971, she went back to Israel with her burgeoning interest in and experience with American feminism.

As one of the leaders of the feminist movement in Israel, and the first openly gay person elected to the Knesset (Israel's national legislature), Freedman fought many uphill battles advocating for women's rights at a time when men in the Knesset did not take women or women's issues seriously. During her tenure from 1973 to 1977, Freedman worked tirelessly to bring feminist consciousness to the

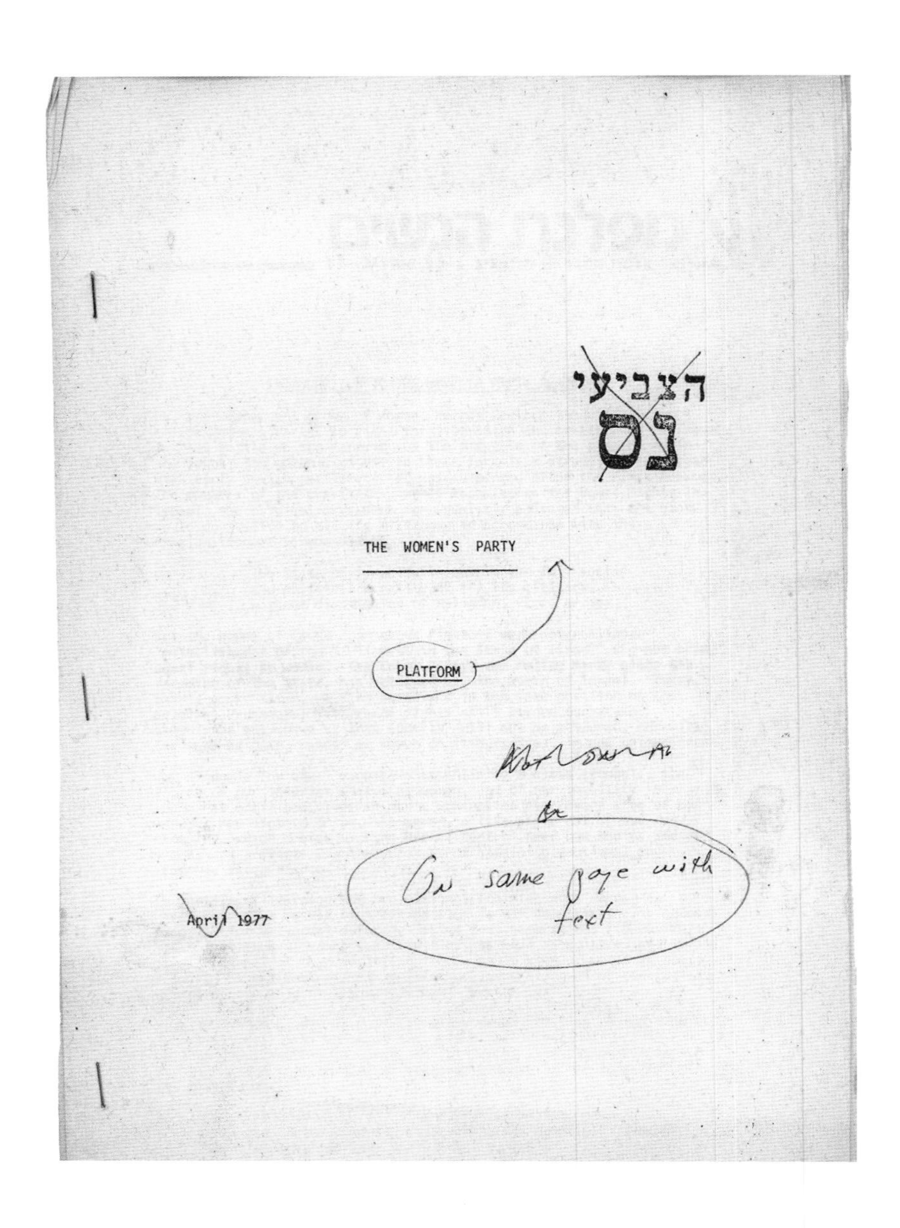

הצביעי
נס

THE WOMEN'S PARTY

PLATFORM

On same page with text

April 1977

forefront of Israel's parliament. Her many accomplishments include working to reform Israel's restrictive abortion laws, opening the first battered-women's shelter in Israel, and co-founding the Women's Party. In 1981, Freedman returned to the United States, where she continued to raise awareness of Israel and feminist issues. Between 1997 and 2002, she embarked on another series of extended stays in Israel, after which she became the founding president of Brit Tzedek v'Shalom, the American Jewish Alliance for Justice and Peace.

Freedman's papers include newspaper clippings, lecture notes, research files, correspondence, writings (personal, scholarly, and activist in nature), and several incomplete manuscripts and typescripts. Among the many highlights of this collection are the numerous notes, letters, and telegrams Freedman received upon

Israel: What's a Radical Feminist Doing in a Place Like This?

Marcia Freedman

Member of Knesset
Jerusalem, Israel

These are Marcia Freedman's personal observations of the fate of feminism in Israel. Her observations reveal that the current emphasis on "machismo" could spell the decline of feminist gains, and she concludes by showing the country's need for a strengthened feminism and a realistic cooperation between men and women. Freedman was a member of the Knesset in Jerusalem at the time she made these observations.

Purim, March 1977: Out on the streets are hundreds of little Queen Esthers dressed in long white gowns, flowing trains, veils, and little gold crowns. If you didn't know where you were or what day it was, you would think the streets were full of child brides. Which, of course, is exactly what they are. Queen Esther, the unparalleled heroine of Israeli littlegirlhood? Not Devora? Not Naomi? Not Yael? Not Miriam? Certainly not Vashti. Instead, Queen Esther, the obedient, the lovely, the sneaky, she who replaces Vashti, the rebel, and becomes a warning to all womanhood that it is dangerous to rise up against one's husband. The message of Esther is that female heroism is but the unstinting, uncomplaining giving of one's virgin body. And who are the grooms of all these little child brides? They are, at the moment, dressed up as cowboys, pirates, soldiers, Indian chiefs—warriors, one and all.

As I wander the streets on Purim morning observing all those children's secret dreams on parade, I can't help asking myself that one question that I have always preferred not to ask: What is a nice Jewish radical feminist doing in a place like this?

Requests for reprints should be sent to Ms. Freedman at 66 Derech Hayam, Haifa, Israel.

There was a time among Jews when the idealized male was no warrior; he was the very opposite—a saint, a scholar, a *tzaddik*, devoted to studying the holy literature and fulfilling the prescriptions of Jewish law for the conduct of his daily and religious life. He did no physical labor, he was no businessperson, he did not provide a living for his family, he certainly was not a soldier—he didn't even argue. His pride was his humility before God; his strength was his faith. The things of this earth mattered little to him. His protection was his God—and his wife. She, as all wives, took care of his physical needs, was his comforter, his consultant, his psychological support. But she was more—she was also his husband, his provider, his merchant, wheeler-dealer, his "woman of valor":

> Like a ship laden with merchandise,
> she brings home food from far off.
> She rises while it is still night
> and sets meat before her household.
> After careful thought she buys a field
> and plants a vineyard out of her earnings.
>
> She weaves linen and sells it
> and supplies merchants with their sashes.
> She is clothed in dignity and power
> and can afford to laugh at tommorrow.
> (Proverbs 31: 14–6, 24–5)

No queen Esther that one. In that world, sex roles as we know them today were unclear; the ideal male was "feminine," the ideal female "masculine."

Machismo, it seems, is characteristic of the Jewish male only when he is on his own territory. (Machismo, of course, is not to be confused with sexism, male supremacy. Judaism, the archetype of patriarchal religion, has always been sexist. It is not for nothing that the Jewish male is directed to say each morning, "Thank Thee O Lord for not having made me a woman.") It runs all through the Old Testament and reappears in recent Jewish history as an explicit element of Zionist thinking. The return to the homeland required two major changes in the Jewish male's character and lifestyle: The first was *kibush avoda*, learning how to do physical labor. *Tzaddikim*, as a rule, worked only with their heads and hearts, but no state could be built without a laboring class. One of the ironies of the early days of the settlement in Palestine is that those people most suited by diaspora history for "the conquest of physical labor"—women—were

her election to the Knesset in 1973 as a member of the nascent Citizens' Rights Movement—words of praise and congratulations for her breaking of the gender barrier in Israel's historically patriarchal government body. There is also a series of newspaper clippings related to Freedman's involvement in the founding of the Jewish feminist movement in Israel, her work as a member of the Knesset, and her role as a co-founder of the Women's Party (1977), as well as a number of reviews of her memoir, *Exile in the Promised Land*.

In addition, the collection contains Freedman's typewritten email correspondence about the political climate and women's peace movement in Israel from 1997 to 2002; her personal journal with commentaries on the Israeli-Palestinian conflict and Jewish feminism; and more than twenty years of transcribed conversations with her support/discussion group for aging women, the Wandering Menstruals.

This collection is but a small testament to the trailblazing life and career of an American-Israeli Jewish feminist and activist and her place in the history of Jewish feminism.

Description by Jeff Hayes, Archives and Special Collections intern, 2017

DONATED BY MARCIA FREEDMAN

ACKNOWLEDGMENTS

Thank you to Stephen Friedberg, unwavering supporter of the Brandeis National Committee, the Brandeis Library, and the Honoring Our History campaign, for his gift to underwrite the production of this book.

The Brandeis National Committee would also like to thank Merle Carrus, Carol Kern, and Judith Levine, chairs of the Honoring Our History campaign.

We would also like to acknowledge the support, contributions, and cooperation of the following:

Karen Adler Abramson, B.A. 1985, M.A. 1994
Victor A. Berch, M.A. 1966
Beth Bernstein, M.A. 1990
The Brandeis Bibliophiles
Brandeis University Press
Kitty Bruce
Colonel Edward H. McCrahon family
Lillian Dunaj
The Estate of Carl Van Vechten
The Estate of Joseph Heller
Arlan Ettinger
Chloe Gerson
Family of Helmut Hirsch
Family of Leo Rosten
Family of Pauline Trigère
Marcia Freedman
Friends of the Howe Library
Frank and Ann Gilbert
Alex Glomset, B.A. 2014
Guido Goldman
Art Green
Hollie Harder
The Hugh M. Hefner Foundation
Tom Hutchings
Dania Khandaker
Sarah Mead
Robin Feuer Miller
Susan Pasternack
John Plotz
Sue Ramin
Ken Schoen
Surella Seelig
Matthew Sheehy
Spitzer family
Stephen J. Whitfield
Anne Woodrum

And the many donors, students, interns, researchers, and others who make the Archives and Special Collections Department at the Brandeis Library a vibrant and vital part of the noble work of the university.

Karen Adler Abramson, B.A. 1985, M.A. 1994; university archivist, 2003–2005; head of Archives and Special Collections, 2005–2010
Zachary Fine Albert, M.A. 2012
Sean Beebe, PH.D. 2020
Winston Bowman, M.A. 2011, PH.D. 2015
Max Close, B.A. 2016
Katie Doody, B.A. 2014
Rochelle Fayngor, B.S. 2017
Drew Flanagan, M.A. 2011, PH.D. 2018
Max Goldberg, Archives and Special Collections reference assistant, 2014
Adam Gurfinkel, B.A. 2017
Hollie Harder, professor of French and Francophone studies and director of the French and Italian language programs
Katie Hargrave, M.A. 2009
Jeff Hayes, Archives and Special Collections intern, 2017
Brittany Joyce, B.A. 2015, M.A. 2019
Margo Kolenda-Mason, B.A. 2014
Allison Lange, M.A. 2009, PH.D. 2014
Emily Lapworth, B.A. 2012
Hansol Lee, former undergraduate
Leah Lefkowitz, B.A. 2011
Alexandra Wagner Lough, PH.D. 2013
Sarah Mead, professor of the practice of music and director of the Brandeis Early Music Ensemble
Julian Nemeth, PH.D. 2014
Scott D. Paulin, lecturer in musicology, Bienen School of Music, Northwestern University
John Plotz, professor of English and Barbara Mandel Professor of the Humanities
Anne Marie Reardon, M.A. 2007, PH.D. 2014
Jim Rosenbloom, Judaica Library, 1976–2019
Adam Rutledge, PH.D. 2017
Surella Evanor Seelig, M.A. 2005, Outreach and Special Projects archivist
Sarah Shoemaker, head of Archives and Special Collections
Craig Bruce Smith, M.A. 2009, PH.D. 2014
Clinton Walding, M.A. 2007
Stephen J. Whitfield, Max Richter Professor of American Civilization, emeritus
Aaron Wirth, M.A. 2009, PH.D. 2014

About the Editor

SARAH SHOEMAKER is the Associate University Librarian for Archives and Special Collections at Brandeis University. She holds an M.S. in library and information science with a concentration in archives from Simmons University, as well as an M.Phil in medieval history from Trinity College Dublin and a B.A. in comparative literature from the University of Massachusetts at Amherst.